D0216266

Design for Micro-Utopias

Design for Social Responsibility Series

Series Editor: Rachel Cooper

Social responsibility, in various disguises, has been a recurring theme in design for many years. Since the 1960s several more or less commercial approaches have evolved. In the 1970s designers were encouraged to abandon 'design for profit' in favour of a more compassionate approach inspired by Papanek.

In the 1980s and 1990s profit and ethical issues were no longer considered mutually exclusive and more market-oriented concepts emerged, such as the 'green consumer' and ethical investment. The purchase of socially responsible, 'ethical' products and services has been stimulated by the dissemination of research into sustainability issues in consumer publications. Accessibility and inclusivity have also attracted a great deal of design interest and recently designers have turned to solving social and crime-related problems.

Organisations supporting and funding such projects have recently included the NHS (research into design for patient safety); the Home Office has (design against crime); Engineering and Physical Sciences Research Council (design decision-making for urban sustainability). Businesses are encouraged (and increasingly forced by legislation) to set their own socially responsible agendas that depend on design to be realised.

Design decisions all have environmental, social and ethical impacts, so there is a pressing need to provide guidelines for designers and design students within an overarching framework that takes a holistic approach to socially responsible design.

This edited series of guides is aimed at students of design, product development, architecture and marketing, and design and management professionals working in the sectors covered by each title. Each volume includes:

- The background and history of the topic, its significance in social and commercial contexts and trends in the field.

- Exemplar design case studies.

- Guidelines for the designer and advice on tools, techniques and resources available.

Design for Micro-Utopias

Making the Unthinkable Possible

JOHN WOOD

GOWER

Published by
Gower Publishing Limited
Gower House
Croft Road
Aldershot
Hampshire GU11 3HR
England

Ashgate Publishing Company
Suite 420
101 Cherry Street
Burlington, VT 05401-4405
USA

British Library Cataloguing in Publication Data
Wood, John, 1945–
    Design for micro-utopias : making the unthinkable possible.
    – (Design for social responsibility)
    1. Utopias 2. Social planning 3. Social participation
    I. Title
    301
    ISBN-13: 9780754646082

Library of Congress Control Number: 2007929149

Printed and bound in Great Britain by TJ International Ltd, Padstow, Cornwall.

Contents

List of Figures   *vii*
List of Tables   *ix*
Preface   *xi*

Introduction   1

Chapter 1   Our Dysfunctional World   17

Chapter 2   The Rise of Solipsism   33

Chapter 3   Bureaucracy   51

Chapter 4   Academic Rigour   67

Chapter 5   Writing the Design   91

Chapter 6   Clocks Beyond Number   109

Chapter 7   Thinking Beyond the Possible   129

Chapter 8   Synergy   143

Chapter 9   Metadesign   167

Chapter 10   Towards an Ethics of Flow   187

Index   *205*

List of Figures

Figure I.1   A rudimentary map of utopias   12

Figure 2.1   A tool for self-inquiry that uses only two dimensions   47

Figure 4.1   Differences in monastic and crafts-guilds modes of
              knowledge   69

Figure 4.2   Academic writing techniques evolved from the monastic
              tradition   75

Figure 5.1   The four nodes of a tetrahedron   101

Figure 8.1   The rise in relations relative to the number of active agents 151

Figure 8.2   The rise in 'viewpoints' relative to the number of players   154

Figure 8.3   Possible relationship between consciousness and complexity 154

Figure 8.4   Relonics used to map the relations among blood chemicals   157

Figure 8.5   'Chains' (minimum involvement of two parameters and
              one relation)   160

Figure 8.6   'Fans' (minimum involvement of four parameters and
              three relations)   161

Figure 8.7   'Loops' (minimum involvement of three parameters and three
              relations)   161

Figure 8.8   Additional possible configurations   162

Figure 8.9   Simplified (four-fold) model of the challenges in housing
              innovation   163

Figure 8.10   The 28 possible relationships in an 8-player map of vested
              interest   163

Figure 9.1   A tetrahedron depicting a minimum grammar of ethical
              relations   170

Figure 9.2   A tetrahedral set of 'winners'   181

Figure 9.3   A single 'win–win' axis   182

List of Tables

Table 5.1   A comparison of two approaches to writing and researching   94

Table 5.2   Four inward-facing and four outward-facing consequences
             of learning   103

Table 5.3   The 4 grammatical elements   104

Table 5.4   The six relations formed by the four grammatical elements   105

Table 6.1   Levels of temporal 'openness'   123

Table 8.1   Four orders of synergy   151

Table 8.2   Line and node system for mapping relational criteria and
             structures   158

Table 8.3   Examples of player-relations, mapped using Euler's notation 159

Table 9.1   The four groups and their roles   183

Preface

Concern for society has often been a theme amongst designers and craftsworkers. Indeed in the UK, Ruskin and Morris at the turn of the 20th century actively pursued design and production in the material world in a manner consistent with moral and ethical values for the benefit of the wider society. During that century the design profession grew, becoming divorced from both art and crafts and production, first with the commercial designer, then the product designer, interior designer and so on, whilst architecture continued to remain an independent profession outside the broader domains of design. During that period too, the economies of the West, consumption and the use of the world's resources continued to grow at an alarming rate, contributing to the ongoing fragility of society and planet earth.

By the 1960s designers began to actively consider the wider implications of design for society. Several approaches emerged, including green design and consumerism; responsible design and ethical consuming; ecodesign and sustainability; and feminist design. In the 1970s Papanek, amongst others, encouraged designers to abandon 'design for profit' in favour of a more compassionate approach. In the 1980s and 1990s profit and ethical issues were no longer considered mutually exclusive and more market-oriented approaches emerged, such as the 'green consumer' and ethical investment. The purchase of socially responsible, 'ethical' products and services was facilitated by the dissemination of research into sustainability in consumer publications and the emergence of retail entrepreneurs such as the late Anita Roddick of The Body Shop. Accessibility and inclusivity also saw a great deal of design interest and activity and, more recently, designers have turned to resolving issues related to crime.

At the same time governments, businesses and individuals have become increasingly aware of what we are doing, not only to the world, but also to each other. Human rights, sustainability and ethics are all issues of concern, whilst the relationship between national economies and poverty struggles to be resolved. Global businesses have recognized the changing environment and are setting their own corporate social responsibility (CSR) agendas. The World Business Council for Sustainable Development proposes that 'CSR is the continuing commitment by business to behave ethically and contribute to economic development while improving the quality of life of the workforce and their families as well as of the local community and society at large' (Moir, 2001). If businesses and organizations are to turn these ideas into reality, 'design' is an essential ingredient.

Designers make daily decisions with regard to the use of resources, and to the lifestyle and use of products, places and communications. In order to achieve the needs of businesses, the desires of the consumer and improvement of the world, the designer in making decisions must embrace dimensions of social responsibility. However, there is now a need to shift from focusing on a single issue towards taking a more holistic approach to socially responsible design. This book is part of a series that brings together the leading authors and researchers to provide texts on each of the major socially responsible dimensions. Each book in the series provides a background to the history and emergence of the topic, provides case study exemplars and indicates where the reader can access further information and help.

This book in the series turns much of our traditional thinking in design upside down and inside out. It challenges designers and society to look at things in a different and holistic way. It addresses philosophy, politics, the economy and society and looks for a new way of imagining the world. It challenges designers to embrace the unattainable and to turn the unthinkable into the thinkable, to take dreams as micro-utopias and to translate them into global synergies. An ambitious text, this provides a context in which other books in the series can be used to push forward ideas on any of the socially responsible themes, to achieve more than the sum of the parts and to create a healthier, happy existence through using design skills and thinking.

The book contributes to a series and although it can be read in isolation, the sum of designers' responsibility to society can only be entirely understood by considering all the dimensions that this series covers. However, we are only too acutely aware that the domain changes and evolves, and that the major responsibilities of the designers will be to continue to redefine their role in society and the influence they can have in creating a better world. This book takes us in that direction.

Professor Rachel Cooper
Lancaster University, UK

Introduction

'In Utopia, where every man has a right to everything, they all know that if care is taken to keep the public stores full, no private man can want anything; for among them there is no unequal distribution, so that no man is poor, none in necessity; and though no man has anything, yet they are all rich; for what can make a man so rich as to lead a serene and cheerful life, free from anxieties.'

Thomas More, *Utopia*

Books come and go. Indeed, one of the problems of writing about contemporary issues is that the world changes rapidly. It is good to remind oneself that, to a humble mayfly, a lifetime lasts a day. For a politician, a week can seem like a lifetime. At the time of writing (2007) society is pondering its own extinction, and it is comforting to know that some people have been paying attention. Species are disappearing at between 100 and 1,000 times the 'background' levels found in fossils. The earth's atmosphere has the largest hole in the ozone layer ever recorded, and a carbon dioxide level that has not been so high for 650,000 years or more. It is possible, although not certain, that humans have caused most of the problem. The good news is that the sun should last for up to 5 billion years. One would hope, therefore, that very long-term thinking would be the main priority for governments and educators. Until now, this has been far from the case. Governments have remained more reactive than visionary. Despite the recent fashion for solar panels and bicycles, politics remains stubbornly humanistic, individual-centred, competitive, growth-orientated, and out of touch with the eco-system that supports our existence. Many of our most noble endeavours are therefore doomed by ignorance, short-sightedness, and a woeful lack of imagination. Every so often we have a moment of brilliant collective insight, but this seldom lasts long. The current panic over environmental issues is reminiscent of the oil crisis of 1973. In the UK, with political uncertainty caused by rising fuel prices we suddenly became acutely aware of our environmental predicament. This was an unusual moment that soon ended with a new agreement with the main oil producing countries, and it was 'business as usual'. Recently, the UK government agreed to create a bill on climate change. Many well-informed citizens feel that this decision is seriously overdue. After all, meteorologists and ecologists have long been warning us that we cannot continue to live in the way we do. The change is welcome, but why has it taken so long to arrive? One recent factor was the government-sponsored *Stern Report*, (31st October, 2006), which had more effect than many previous recommendations by scientists. How did Mr Stern succeed where the experts failed? The short answer is that he is an economist, and therefore speaks in a restricted language that makes sense to governments. In short, political discourse seems to have no grasp of events beyond the short-term logic of economic forces. This is why our leaders find it so difficult to be honest with voters.

The received political discourse has implied that every voter (that is 'consumer') has a natural born right to consume, to waste and to travel. Politics is not wholly to blame. Indeed, those of us who discuss human wellbeing largely in terms of income, rather than land use, climate, or species diversity must share the responsibility. What is needed is a shared understanding of the relationship between ecology and economy. How can we 'make poverty history' if the process of wealth creation causes such ecological disruption that it will undo all our economic efforts? This book does not underestimate the importance of money but it tends to see it as a particular dialect or language, rather than as a resource. This is a design issue. Just as certain concepts encourage certain outcomes, so particular currencies will encourage certain behavioural tendencies. The book asks how we might design a better world. In this respect, although it speaks to everyone it outlines a larger framework for design, or what it will describe as 'metadesign' (Chapter 9). At present, money needs re-designing. This is an important issue that is discussed further in Chapter 5. Perhaps inevitably, much of the book is more philosophical than practical. This is a means to an end. Questions are sometimes more useful than answers, especially if they invite practical outcomes. But if this is the case, why does its title sound so fanciful and unrealistic? This is a good question. The idea of utopias not only courts criticism of being 'unrealistic' or 'idealised', it also has a whiff of revolutionary fervour. In the 21st century, revolutions are seen as being both risky and passé. Unfortunately, this aversion to risk has shortened our depth of field. Rather than adopting a long-term vision, mainstream politics tends to favour a rugged and impatient mode of pragmatism. This is why many prominent leaders claim to be 'realists' rather than dreamers.

The book invites 'realists' to relax their grip. Dreaming is not as scary or unhelpful as we are led to believe. Utopia, *Sir Thomas More*'s famous novel of

1516, describes an ideal or perfect place. However, whether he was sketching out a serious design for society or whether he was being ironic is still in doubt. Nevertheless, most people would agree that the idea of utopia still awakens a sense of fascination and longing within each of us. Plato's Republic is a famous description of an ideal society. After the death of his mentor Socrates (circa 470– 399 BC), he also wrote of a lost civilisation called *Atlantis*. Although his text still inspires explorers, dreamers, artists and inventors it is not clear whether the island of *Atlantis* really existed. Some see it as a template for urban and social planning. Others suggest that it was merely a satirical critique or idealised description of the prevailing culture in Athens. It is possible that stories of 'utopia' stir up *dim* memories of a golden age before the invention of large-scale cities, agriculture, weapons and industry. The idea of 'paradise' – for example – is derived from an ancient Iranian word for 'garden'. This may remind us of stories of Shangri-Lah, the Fields of Elysium, The Garden of Eden, Hanging Gardens of Babylon, and so on. Although these names probably depict places that really existed, today they have become images that are no longer seen as attainable. Our culture has appropriated them to stand for a kind of non-reality. Our rather 'hard-hat' world has tended to declare words such as 'love', 'wisdom' or 'miracle' as no-go areas.

Utopia is therefore a particularly provocative idea. It is usually assumed to mean a permanent state of perfection. In a fast-moving, cynical world of plenty it sounds naïve and over-optimistic. This may remind us that naivety and idealism have come, for many, to be synonymous with one another. In today's increasingly pragmatic culture, the idea of a 'perfect space' or a 'perfect time' is dangerously 'new age'. Also, we distrust perfection because it has become tarnished by the false claims of the less scrupulous advertising agencies, travel agents or property developers. In the current climate we might just as well say 'miraculous', and that is just the kind of language that has fallen from favour. One reason that visionary, optimistic projects are out of fashion is that they are associated with a Marxist utopia that was discredited decades ago. Few would be bold enough to claim that they have tried 'dreaming' and found that it does not work, but that is the implication. Nonetheless, at a time when we face so many dangers – both natural and self-imposed – it is vital to dream of alternative futures, even if they seem unrealisable or impossible. This is why this book is proud to promote utopianism, even if what we mean by utopia is a more tentative, temporary, pluralised or truncated version than the ones we may find in the picture books. In short, the book will discuss 'micro-utopias' rather than 'Utopia'.

There are many ways in which we might attain realistic 'micro-utopias'. One of them is by developing a new kind of democratic system that depends less on representation and more on a distributed mode of actions and responses. Our 'democratic' society has become so accustomed to monarchies and hierarchies that the word 'holarchy' (c.f Koestler, 1969) – a network of equal parts, each responsible for the whole – is seldom used in everyday conversation. One of the problems of mainstream democracy is that it depends heavily on choice and delegation, rather than on shared imagination, local involvement, and emerging consensus. This is not to say that mainstream politics is impervious to new inflections or directions, but that bureaucrats and politicians are risk-averse. Many decisions taken by political leaders are top-down, rather than bottom-up. This has led to a situation in which citizens get discouraged from visualising new possibilities that are outside the political cannon. Admittedly, if an average voter is passionate about a given issue, but finds that all of the major parties ignore this issue, he or she has the chance to start a new political movement, and to compete with the other political parties. Of course, if the idea in question is always dismissed as eccentric, misguided or unimportant it is more likely that he or she will lose interest. In a world of political spin, voters become apathetic when the truth is massaged for ballot box success. When this happens, only interests with a strong chance of success are adopted. Similarly, when events are presented in a way that maintains the rhetorical momentum of the party line, dreams get crushed or ignored.

In order to explore a more genuinely bottom-up approach, we need to acknowledge the role of positive feedback within a given trend. The idea of positive feedback came out of systems science, or cybernetics. It describes the process by which a given tendency appears to reinforce itself by virtue of its own impetus. For example, within an epidemic the rise in the number of infected patients works on this principle. The more individuals who are infected, the greater the chances you have of contracting it. When you catch the disease, you make it even more likely that others around you will also catch it. In such a situation, positive feedback may lead to saturation or pandemic, but only when the process reaches a critical level. There is often an uncertain boundary between an outbreak that will fail, and a full-blown epidemic. This boundary is what we may call the 'tipping point' (see Gladwell, 2002). In seeking a more creative, heterarchical society, the transition between competing ideas will become crucially important. This may even mean that the sharing and development of these ideas will therefore take over some of the present duties of our professional politicians. How can we know the difference between a good idea that will 'catch on' and one that will fail? Chapter 7 will argue that a transformation of society can take place once we can create visions, ideals and proven methods that are desirable, attainable, reproducible and maintainable.

What would be required to introduce such a system for change? Answers to this question are already beginning to emerge. For the first time in history, 'Open Source' design and reciprocal pledge-based actions (for example, The BBC's Action Network and the Pledgebank website) make it possible to move from the representation-based politics of Utilitarian compromise (that is, voting) to one in which decisions can be based on a more local, positive, spontaneous, co-creative and emergent process. Now that anyone with access to the Internet can quickly and easily set up alliances with like-minded individuals, the horizon of the 'thinkable' has broadened immensely. Ideas that once may have seemed incomprehensible, ridiculous, or eccentric can now be shared with a sufficient number of 'virtual neighbours' to make them, at least, thinkable. Once they are thinkable, they can be quickly developed into opportunities for beneficial change. This means that citizens can now dare to dream what, hitherto, was deemed either impossible or unthinkable. In order to understand what is possible we need to consider the way human beings think. An aspect of this question relates to the way we perceive the relationship between probabilities and likelihoods. Most of us can accept that, while some diseases are exceptionally rare, we might eventually contract one. We are also accustomed to hearing about an individual who wins the Lottery against almost astronomical odds.

In a probabilistic sense, both of the above events may be seen as miracles, even though we tend to put unpleasant experiences into a different category from the happier variety. Hence we may speak of a patient's 'miracle recovery' but are less likely to use the word to describe the good fortune of a serial killer who evades justice by a series of 'flukes'. Sometimes, events we put into the miracle category can become displaced and redefined. This is often true where miracles are the outcome of design. This is what happens to technological miracles. What are the chances of getting a rocket to land safely on Mars? The answer depends on when and where you ask the question. A thousand years ago the question would have made little sense. In Sir Isaac Newton's day it would have seemed miraculous, or, in practical terms, impossible. Today, with digital systems of self-steering, stellar navigation, and a thousand other clever tricks, we can now accomplish this task as a matter of routine. What is the difference between the first aircraft passenger flight and the most recent? One important difference is the sense of awe, delight, and disbelief that attended the first, but not the latest. The retrieval of wonderment is therefore an important issue within our quest for micro-utopias. However, the book's aim is to not find fault with actual people or actualities, but to probe below the surface. In seeking to design micro-utopias that are desirable and attainable, it looks for positive insight at a deeper intellectual level. In this sense, it takes both a holistic and a homespun approach.

In the pragmatic world of political 'reality', utopia is a 'once upon a time' land that is non-existent. At best, it subsists, rather than exists. This is because political pragmatism evolved as a process of management that deals with events on a week-by-week basis.

Within this belief system it may seem too risky or self-indulgent to dream of utopia. It invokes the dark, superstitious side of our histories and how we choose to remember them. One danger of remembering is that it might become a precedent for the future. In so doing it conceals the path to a way of living that is better than we have ever imagined. There is an old saying that 'history only repeats itself because nobody was listening the first time'. In our Once-upon-a-Time memory, adversity and struggle are almost always present. In fairy tales, life was often cruel, and 'real' people lived in palaces. Before we had glass cities and industrialised deserts, Utopian dreamers lived in non-descript 'lands'. Almost invariably, these were feudal territories ruled by godlike emperors, kings and queens with sacrosanct rights and privileges. And it was they who owned and controlled the lands, and it was they who set the boundaries between rich and poor. Designers were commissioned to make coins bearing an image of the monarch, and the common people had no choice but to pay their taxes by long hours of hard work. *Times* were dangerous. Many lived in fear for their safety. Some of the wiser citizens had tales of better times when people lived in beautiful gardens rather than in noisy, dirty streets.

Children still listen to stories like these. We may have been fearful of the mighty and powerful, but these tales usually carry a residual feeling that ethical values were based less on rules and punishments and more on a sense of wholeness, shared pleasure and good feelings. After the end of the story would come the 'happily-ever-after' epoch, in which crime or misery was over. Perhaps this was because the garden villages were just the right size for optimising danger and security. Everyone felt loved and needed. Life was hard, but it was free of wars, agriculture, and automation. Children's stories reminisce about a 'golden age', but historians and archaeologists have a different version. Pre-agricultural life was probably hazardous for the majority, and life was hard. We may surmise that, when you lived this way, your primary duty would only have extended to those on whom you had to trust. In such an unstable world, ethical relations were therefore confined to your tribe. 'Rights' were something for which you would have had to fight, and 'responsibilities' were the conditions that others forced upon you. This led to a refined sense of the citizen's responsibility to the monarch. Now we may rationalise this by saying that it was a symbolic allegiance to society and to the land.

Around 1705 the Dutchman Bernard de Mandeville wrote a playful satire that, in English, was called *The Fable of the Bees*. His book explored the provocative argument that individual greed and selfishness might lead to benefits for all. This made a deep impression on Adam Smith (1723–90), who was initially troubled by the idea. However, after some pondering, he began to take the joke more seriously. In short, it inspired his famous theories of self-help and the Invisible Hand. These emerged in a now far more famous book, *The Wealth of Nations*, that was published in 1776, the same year that Jefferson drafted the American Declaration of Independence. It also influenced Darwin's theory of evolution a hundred years later (1859), and laid the foundations for many subsequent generations of laissez-faire economists, laissez-faire being a French word that (roughly) means 'letting things take care of themselves'. In part, the book addresses the political problem of government without monarchy. We may remember how this logic evolved during the French Revolution in 1789. It seemed, at the time, that if everyone is equal, they should have the same rights and powers as those of a sovereign ruler. Although the principle was simple and appealing it had important limitations. Those of us who live in 'developed' countries can see what they are.

A hundred years before the French Revolution, Thomas Hobbes (1588-1679) foresaw that a competitive society of equals might turn into a 'war of all against all'. Perhaps this is what is emerging in the global workplace. In order to avoid this we may need to re-balance the relations between rights and responsibilities. The heady rhetoric of the Revolution had, perhaps understandably, tended to focus on citizen rights. This was not surprising; revolutions usually tend to enforce major changes first and leave the details until later. The idea of 'individual freedom' was a new and thrilling invective for change. Today it remains one of the cornerstones of Western pride. To understand how it works we may choose to watch a few Hollywood westerns or 'maverick cop' movies. In a world of truly individual freedom there should be no rulers to tell us how to live, or how to spend our money. Hard-line supporters of Smithsonian freedom and sovereignty suggest that governments are merely parasites on the hard-earned wealth of individuals. It is why we have an economic order that is smart enough to organise itself. This view has created an implicit agenda for very many governments. It is what enables some politicians to take pride in a 'hands-off' approach to leadership. Their implicit claim is that 'the King is dead, long live the Free Market'.

Our era is therefore one of unprecedented affluence and strident 'consumer rights'. Fortunately, we are beginning to notice that material wellbeing is not always a guarantee of utopian bliss. Thorsten Veblen (1902) was one of the first researchers to explore the effect of disposable income on the nouveau riche. It was he who coined the term 'conspicuous consumption' at the end of the 19th century. George Bataille offers a more extreme view of the psychology of consumption. In what he called the 'accursed share' he depicts consumption as a competitive display to see who can afford to waste, or destroy the most. This may be one reason why few people feel ashamed of owning things without ever using them, or using things up without needing to. Indeed, images of profligate waste have proved indispensable to advertisers, because they can elicit patterns of behaviour that lead to higher sales figures. Up to now, orthodox economists tacitly approved of this system, because they assumed that economic growth leads to greater happiness. Yet, at the start of the 21st century, despite an enormous rise in the actual income levels, turnover of goods, and GDP it is clear that we are no happier now than we were in the middle of the 20th century. An increase in disposable income has created new markets and a greater freedom for many individuals, yet this has caused further problems.

Today, a growing number of people in the developed nations are acutely aware of their rights but have little or no awareness of any corresponding responsibilities. We therefore need a new model of citizenship that is more realistic than the one developed since the French Revolution. This must happen soon. In the last 5 years or so we have seen a massive global increase in car ownership. At the time of writing, we have virtually reached the Hubbert Peak (or 'halfway mark') for cheaply accessible global oil reserves. Broadly speaking, prices can only get higher. The biological diversity of species is threatened, and climatic changes are now accepted as a more or less imminent threat to our safety. While in some countries, people are becoming poorer, global consumption is accelerating. We are happy to discuss these events as 'problems', and unable to envision them as opportunities. Why are we so reluctant to discuss how we would like to live when fossil fuels have gone? More surprisingly, why do we seem unable to imagine how we would like to live? OK, at the level of cliché this is easy: castles in Spain, a private tropical island, country cottage in Shropshire, or a world cruise. But, in a world created by smart advertisers and clever spin doctors it is hard to be original. How can we decide what we want, when there are so many stock answers and off-the-shelf visions to fall back on? How can we avoid thinking like passive consumers when this is what we have been trained to become?

One of the binding tales of free-market capitalism is the concept of people-owned consensus. We can see part of its origins in the French Revolution at the end of 18th century. This took place when the privilege and power that had been extended to monarchs were abused, and taken for granted. As is well known, the people became angry and took the law into their own hands. Actually, they took much more than this. In a sense, ordinary people reclaimed the spiritual and material rights that had seemed the natural prerogative of rulers. Many still celebrate this moment as a threshold to new utopias in which freedom, equality and brotherhood are prized above everything else. In some ways this was a disastrous moment in world history, because it was another decisive step towards humanism. We needed to share environmental responsibilities more evenly but we forgot to include this in the constitution. It must have been hard to imagine an ecological form of governance when the prevailing values, expectations and beliefs were couched in the language of a selfish and monopolistic state. But the idea of 'private sovereignty' or 'individual human rights' was not without precedent. Indeed, several thousand years earlier, Socrates suggested that everyone is entitled to an opinion that may differ from those of society as a whole. This idea has grown into an obstinate brand of individualism that is still made in US and Europe, and eagerly imported by developing nations around the world. One reason for this is that it is a catalyst for economic growth.

Like individualism, economic growth was not something we really designed or planned. For this reason, the indicators of its success are seriously deficient, if not downright foolish. For example, they are not designed to regulate shared wellbeing. Loosely speaking, economic growth is measured by the increase in the total flow of money, over a given period of time. We achieve economic growth by encouraging more transactions at greater speed between an increasing number of producers and consumers. At present, virtually all of the major currencies in the world are debt-based (Douthwaite, 1992). As consumers, our desire for products and services creates the need for financial credit. The supply of credit induces the need for us to work harder. Working harder causes more goods to be produced. Finally, we assume that if we make enough things we will create wellbeing. This is the implicit argument for having debt-based economies. Ultimately it is to maintain economic growth. Sadly, it will not work. Although more and more experts are warning that it is a dangerous and ineffective recipe for wellbeing, we behave as though this were not the case.

As I have implied, conventional economic thinking makes only partial sense in ecological terms. For example, one person makes money with a new product but, in so doing, may cause a serious environmental problem because the processes used are highly poisonous, or wasteful. Another person makes money by trying to clean up the mess, or by retrieving the wasted resources. Within the current economic logic this is seen as a welcome process because it makes for higher employment figures and a greater GDP. Where a thoughtful designer might see this as this as a foolish way to do things, many orthodox economists approve of it because it appears to distribute resources more widely. Hence many people are hailing a carbon credit system as the right path to take. While it has some short-term merit, this approach is patently a compromise because it discourages waste rather than inviting transformation. The more creatively we design the money system the better chance we will have of re-designing the way we live. As it stands, global capitalism is devoted to increasing the rate and quantity of transactions, rather than satisfying our deeper needs. Technology facilitates and exaggerates its effects, thereby making the ultimate outcomes easier to attain. For example, modern digital technology makes consumption easier by facilitating instant auditing and payment over large distances. This is what Microsoft entrepreneur Bill Gates calls 'capitalism without friction' (Gates, 1999). However, in the long term our economy only works when its ecological basis is able to flourish. The eradication of transactional 'friction' is really a promotional illusion that is created to make individual consumers feel better. It is an inducement to make consumers buy more products without noticing the damage and waste that each transaction causes.

Despite the long reach of corporate strategy and the surreptitious fiscal regulation by Governments, World Bank and others, the global economy is presented as an autonomous system in its own right. As such it resembles a living creature. We call it 'capital'. It is like a pet that we must look after. When 'capital' grows strong and healthy, politicians and economists are happy. When it stops growing or shrinks we fear that it may die. Politicians may blame 'capital' for poverty or environmental damage, but they are the ones who feed it and watch over it. Although governments do not organise the system directly, they create incentives and subsidies such as trade tariffs and taxes. For example, they allow tax-free aviation fuel in order to make friends with big business, and to stimulate trade across great distances. This sometimes results in the transportation and exchange of virtually identical products between partner nations. Most mainstream politicians assure us that this is the most efficient way to organise the world. This is very hard to swallow. If we make an exceptionally generous reading of economic growth within global capitalism we might say that it ensures the self-regulation of collective wellbeing. This is a big claim. Competitive capitalism creates and shares wealth by mobilising individual ingenuity and labour. Although it may not be solely responsible for environmental damage, design nevertheless can be understood as a form of rhetoric (Buchanan, 1989) that persuades others to sustain, or to increase, the transactional flow of goods and services (Papanek, 1985). In this regard, designers are but one 'cog in the machine'. Charlie Chaplin used this mechanistic image in his film *Modern Times* (1936), a parody of the centralised factory system.

Marx believed that the idea of production-line manufacture was inspired by the invention of mechanical clocks. Computers embody the mechanical principle of the clock and combine it with the programmatic capabilities of alphabetical writing. The digital computer is therefore a hybrid of the book, the clock, and a self-steering governor, such as the thermostat (Wood, 1998). Where clocks offer a temporality that is regimented and arbitrary, alphabetical codes can disseminate rules that must be followed, as it were, blindly (Wittgenstein, 1921). In many sweatshop industries, employees have to work at the speed and efficiency of a machine. Today, in order to sustain this clock-inspired system we also need complementary processes that are equally mechanical. These processes also reflect the system's vanity, and its deeply bureaucratic and materialistic values. The film *Brazil* (Gilliam, 1985) depicts the savage nature of these processes by satirising the mindless pursuit of corporate power and personal extravagance. Perhaps the most chilling aspect of this film is the fact that, after two decades, it looks less like an insane parody and more like everyday life in the early 21st century. Why do we choose to live like this? Metaphorically speaking, where in Revolutionary France the citizen was king, today, the individual consumer is God. This is the belief system that propels the economy. It is as true in Dubai or Shanghai or as it is in Sydney or New York. Consumption drives industrial effort, and we are slaves to this effort. The pain of production is deemed acceptable, because it leads to the comfort of consumption. This trade-off is reminiscent of that which resulted from the early adopters of monocultural farming methods, in Iran 11,000 years ago. Its underlying principle is what many, from Aristotle to Henry Ford, have called the 'economies of scale'. More recently, Toyota evolved the process to include the transportation of products on a 'just-in-time' and a '24-7' basis. In essence, it is the same. In a technologically driven, consumer-centred society, all citizens are tacitly expected to crave, and to experience, 'convenience', 'comfort' and 'mobility' wherever, or whenever they find themselves (Wood, 2000).

It is always easy to be negative about things we do dislike. It is much more difficult to come up with better approaches or more viable solutions. Here, viability means offering solutions that are practicable and operable for all the active parties. This is a huge creative challenge that will require new methods and approaches. We are not used to a 'joined-up' society in which common sense is used to design the way things work. Despite the best endeavours of far-sighted economists, healthcare professionals, educators and planners we are used to an economic system that sees monetary profits and economic growth as adequate indicators of success. Fortunately, many people are now beginning to notice how fragmented, dysfunctional, alienated, and disconnected our society has become. The book will seek to show how citizens can initiate the kind of reforms that can make our societies more healthy and happy. In 2001, I coined the term 'Attainable Utopias' in order to challenge the pragmatism of mainstream politics, bureaucracy and commerce. It is also the name of our virtual '*Think Tank*' (The Au Net) that I co-founded with Andrew Carmichael (Director of the Creative Lewisham Agency). A year into the new millennium we wondered why humanity had failed to create a new 'vision'. Why, despite unparalleled and increasing access to resources, knowledge, and technology, had we become so pessimistic and cynical? Our conclusion was that while, as voters and consumers, we have become experts at choosing and complaining, we have forgotten how to envisage what we really want. Without new dreams humanity will become extinct.

As Carey (1999) has shown, a universal state of Utopia would probably resemble some form of fascism, because it would require a great deal of conformity to one model of wellbeing. However, while utopia may be neither attainable nor desirable, a more interdependent network of 'micro-utopias' (that is, brief, or local utopias) might be both helpful and feasible. But what might this look like? One way to describe 'micro-utopias' is to imagine different

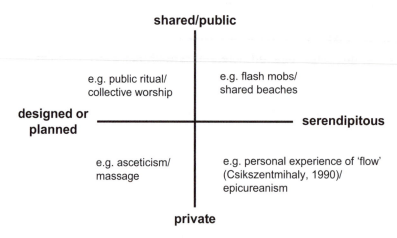

Figure I.1   A rudimentary map of utopias

types of wisdom that are joined together. Hence, we might transcend the idea of an 'information society' or 'knowledge economy', and make it into a 'wisdom economy'. This idea is what the book seeks to explore. Ultimately, it sets out to make a rough map of this new domain. A better aim would be to create a 'wisdom ecology' (Philogene and Wood, 2002). One way to approach this quest is to map existing visions of utopia. Figure 1 shows a very broad starting point with only two axes. Where the vertical axis displays the range that straddles private and shared utopias, the horizontal axis differentiates between serendipitous and designed utopias. Within the private realm there are many examples from attempts to find religious, or personal enlightenment. These might range from asceticism, through to meditative bliss, and personal feelings of love or goodwill. It may even require the voluntary initiation of something akin to 'contagious optimism' within society, and the right balance of 'luck-attracting' approaches will lead to a global pandemic of positive thinking. For many readers, this kind of claim may sound like 'new-age' hogwash. I will try to demonstrate, therefore, that what we have assumed to be unrealistic may, in practice, be attainable.

The first barrier to 'micro-utopias' is neither technological nor political; it is psychological. Ultimately, if we are to be ambitious there is no logical reason why we should not be able to design miracles, assuming we apply a probabilistic definition of miracles. If you search for a miracle you will reduce your chances of success by believing it to be impossible or unreachable. In this way, it is possible to undermine Hume's claim that miracles do not exist (Hume, 1748). Chapter 7 will argue that most of us may find ourselves in close proximity to an extremely low probability event about once or twice a month. However, this kind of event is so trivial or marginal that we might easily overlook it. Mapping the boundaries between the 'thinkable' and the 'unthinkable' will be an important task for 'micro-utopians'. Generally speaking, for human beings, the 'unthinkable' is synonymous with the 'unattainable'. This suggests that, merely by moving some issues from the category of 'unthinkable' to 'thinkable' we could achieve what was hitherto seen as 'impossible'. All of these terms are, to some extent, subject to change, adaptation, and innovation. It is wise to dream beyond what we currently believe to be attainable. Once we have done so, the next step is to co-imagine the dream in a more shareable form. This means exchanging dreams and seeing how they can be conjoined to enhance one another. The third step is to check that we really want what we have dreamed. The fourth step is to see how much of the dream is attainable. The fifth step is to share the task of producing and sharing the dream. If enough people try to connect their 'micro-utopias' together it may be possible to achieve a global 'synergy of synergies' (Fuller, 1975). I will expand this idea in Chapter 8. First I shall briefly outline some of the dystopian aspects of the world that need to be addressed if the quest for micro-utopias is to be successful.

References

Buchanan, R. (1989), 'Declaration by design: rhetoric, argument, and demonstration in design practice' in *Design Discourse: History, Theory and Criticism*, Margolin, V. (ed.), pp. 91-109 (Chicago: University of Chicago Press).

Carey, J. (1999), *The Faber Book of Utopias* (London: Faber & Faber).

Darwin, C. R. (1982), *The Origin of Species by Means of Natural Selection* (London: Penguin Classics).

Douthwaite, R. (1992), *The Growth Illusion* (Hartland: Green Books in association with Lilliput Press, Totnes).

Fuller, R. (1975), *Synergetics: Explorations in the Geometry of Thinking*, in collaboration with Applewhite, E. J. (New York: Macmillan Publishing, Inc.).

Gates, W. with Hemingway, C. (1999), *Business @ the Speed of Thought: Using a Digital Nervous System* (New York: Warner Books).

Gladwell, M. (2002), *The Tipping Point: How Little Things Can Make a Big Difference* (Boston: Little Brown and Company).

Hume, D. (1748), 'Of miracles' in *An Enquiry Concerning Human Understanding*, Selby-Bigge, L. A. (ed.) (1902), pp. 114–16 (Oxford: Clarendon Press).

Koestler, A. (1969), *The Act of Creation* (London: Hutchinson).

More, T. (1966), *Utopia, Vol. 1516* (Leeds: Scolar Press).

Papanek, V. (1985), *Design for the Real World: Human Ecology and Social Change* (London: Thames and Hudson)

Philogene, A. and Wood, J. (2002), *Wisdom Ecology Workshop* (London: British Design Council).

Smith, A. (1776), *An Inquiry into the Nature and Causes of the Wealth of Nations*, 5th edition, Cannan, E. (ed.) (1904) (London: Methuen and Co. Ltd.).

Stern Report (2006), 'Stern review on the economics of climate change'. Available at: www.hm-treasury.gov.uk/independent_reviews/stern_review_ economics_climate_change/stern_review_report.cfm

The Attainable Utopias Network, www.attainable-utopias.org

The BBC Action Network, www.bbc.co.uk/dna/actionnetwork/

The Pledgebank, www.pledgebank.com

Veblen, T. (ed.) (1902), *The Theory of the Leisure Class: An Economic Study of Institutions* (New York: Macmillan).

Wittgenstein, L. (1921), *Tractatus Logico Philosophicus* (London: Routledge and Kegan Paul).

Wood, J. (1998), *The Virtual Embodied* (London and New York: Routledge).

Wood, J. (2000), 'Towards an ethics of flow: design as an anticipatory system' in *International Journal of Computing Anticipatory Systems*, Dubois, D. M. (ed.), 10, pp. 87–102, ISSN 1373–541. (Belgium: Centre for Hyperincursive Anticipation in Ordered Systems).

Our Dysfunctional World

'We live in a culture centred in domination and submission, mistrust and control, dishonesty, commerce and greediness, appropriation and mutual manipulation… and unless our emotioning changes all that will change in our lives will be the way in which we continue in wars, greediness, mistrust, dishonesty, and abuse of others and of nature. Indeed, we shall remain the same.'

(Maturana, 1997)

Writing this chapter was both agreeable and useful, as it helped me to put together many of my pet hates, and it provided a context upon which all of the other, more positive chapters would build; but I feel that I should apologise to the reader for its uncharacteristically negative tone. I sincerely hope it does not sour the rest of the book, which is intended to offer an optimistic approach. For example, Chapter 8 will argue that, for the first time in its history, humanity has the potential to cultivate planet Earth as a 'synergy of synergies'. In advocating a more joined up, inclusive and holistic approach to design and ecology (Chapter 9) the book will outline a new form of imaginative organisation to be called 'metadesign'. In achieving both aims we have a long way to go. Unfortunately, many well-intentioned projects fail because they are conducted against a backdrop of disconnection, alienation, and confusion about politics and money. This sense of contradiction is clear from the way newspapers juxtapose stories about the environment and the economy. On the business page, a headline will dramatise our anguish at falling share prices, job losses and a given corporation's failure to meet its sales targets. On the following page an environment story will lament the pollution of rivers, loss of ancient woodlands, or the extinction of another few hundred species. We have grown accustomed to state-sanctioned surprises of all types, from illegal wars, the unleashing of untested bio-technologies into the eco-system, global systems of mutual self-destruction, the profligate use of non-renewables, pesticides, and dangerous pharmaceutical products in all regions of our daily lives. Ultimately, it is ordinary voters and citizens who will pick up the tab.

However, because consumption is seen to be the engine of economic growth consumers are encouraged to exercise their full rights as individuals.

In the West, 1927 was a good year for individualism. While Heidegger described the experiential aspects of the self in his *Being and Time*, Henri Bergson received the Nobel Prize for literature, and Wilhelm Reich published *The Function of The Orgasm*. In the same year Coca-Cola introduced the first 'one-way' (that is, non-returnable) bottles for use on ocean liners. By 1948, non-returnable glass bottles were becoming standard throughout the US and elsewhere. Despite environmentalist protests about the growth of such practices, consumer lobbies (for example Nader, 2000) have tended to blame corporations, rather than individuals. However, the need to celebrate difference as a consumer also invites defiance, because the desire to be individual is often associated with a provocative or competitive spirit. The tagging of names, and graffiti, whether sprayed onto walls or etched aggressively onto the windows of buses is a symptom of this kind of assertive individualism, yet the modern individual enjoys the assumed right to choose whether to be courteous, moody, indifferent, or outgoing. In the world of accentuated difference, caring for society as a whole becomes more difficult. In the UK over the last few decades this is manifest in new patterns of conspicuous public selfishness. Many individuals appear to feel little responsibility or shame when shouting into a mobile phone, disposing of chewing gum mischievously, or putting their feet onto the vacant seats of buses and trains. This process reflects an extravagant economic system that is now overheated. Today public places are bristling with iPods, Blackberries, and mobile phones, and pavements are colonised by parked cars – often left with their engines running. The streets are also literally littered with litter. These habits are not just mildly annoying. Some pose a public health issue that transcends any standards of etiquette or social respect. For example, it is no longer rare to find the remains of fried chicken wings in take-away boxes that will encourage the carrion bird and rat population. Similarly it is now common for citizens to cough or to sneeze enthusiastically without attempting to find a handkerchief, paper tissue, or even a sleeve. All of these tendencies reflect a way of being that Chapter 2 will describe, in ecological terms, as solipsistic.

Many of the developments described have not led us to be satisfied, or proud of what we have achieved. In a stridently rights-centred world, if consumers work very hard they may feel perfectly entitled to a short vacation in a far-away country. This process is made easier by tempting them with 'treats', such as a carefully designed holiday package in another continent. Although our ability to orchestrate such a remarkable array of managerial and technological processes is remarkable, the end result falls short because it tends to erode the sense of playfulness of less affluent societies. We read of customers suing companies because of airport delays, the wrong kind of weather, or because they inadvertently spilt hot coffee over themselves. Psychiatric ailments seem to have increased in the richest countries, and the suicide rate is shockingly high, even for those of tender years, for whom life has scarcely begun. In many small towns and cities hedonism and reckless public behaviour leads to other health problems and a social nuisance in public places. Nor has an abundance of food and clothing enabled us to create an equitable society. While the number of millionaires increases each year, child poverty levels also continue to rise. We cannot focus all of the blame onto individual corporations. Nor can we simply make small adjustments to the current economic system. Ours is a complex and self-perpetuating predicament that cannot be remedied in a piecemeal fashion. Many possible solutions must be initiated and tested at the local level, but the best ones need to be endorsed by governments, banks and international agencies. At present, many of the most important things in our lives have come to seem remote and mysterious to us. The manufacture of goods, the generation of electricity, and the births and deaths of the animals we eat are all processes that take place at unknown circumstances, locations and dates. As producers, we may know a great deal about our particular professional skill or competence, but little about the adjacent practices that support it. For many people it is therefore a meaningless and humdrum routine that pays the rent.

How might we envisage conditions that are better than those described above? One obvious source is to be found in utopian literature that describes a prior golden age. However, some of its stories are symptomatic of a human folly that has emerged over the last few tens of thousands of years, or so. For example, the invention of agriculture evolved out of ancient practices of hunting and gathering, and entails the wholesale planting and harvesting of fewer and fewer cereal varieties. The bible (Genesis, Chapter 41) tells the story of a Pharaoh's dream of the ears of corn, an East wind, and other omens. In this well-known fable, Joseph interprets the dream as a portent of 7 years of good harvests, followed by 7 years of famine and pestilence. He wins fortune and power by advising the Pharaoh to stockpile grain, in preparation for hard times. Today the staple diets of our most prosperous nations still rely on cereal farming. Although these are perfect feeding environments for a wide range of edible creatures we see these as pests, and devote a great deal of energy in trying to exclude, kill, or eradicate them in order to feed other forms of livestock. In maintaining these unstable systems we also inadvertently erode the soil, use up non-renewable energy supplies, pollute our potable water resources, and attract damage by storms. While scientists are extremely well-informed about these problems, it is astonishing that we still fail to grasp the implications of Joseph's seven famine years. Most non-experts I speak to about this are unaware that deserts are the logical outcome of our agricultural and trading policies. They believe that the great deserts of Australia, US, and the Middle East are 'natural'. This is a moot point. In the past, most agricultural societies were able to ignore the long-term effects of de-forestation, pestilence, soil erosion, drought and desertification by moving to new areas. Joseph's vision was correct, but his diagnosis was merely a short-term fix. Indeed, other major civilisations have collapsed because of advisers like Joseph (cf. Ponting, 1991). It would be nice to think that a modern expert would have recommended re-forestation (Wood, 1976) and a more complex permaculture (Law, 2001) for supporting a rich variety of closely interrelated eco-industries. So far, this remains a dream.

Instead of developing a more stable ecosystem based more upon a vast variety of trees, shrubs and vegetables, scientists are still designing a handful of cereal crops to grow bigger or faster. In the last few decades, this folly has taken a more sinister turn with the development of gene 'sciences' that want to create 'super-plants' that will rise above the natural scheme of things. Although their developers claim they are founded on *bona fide* scientific research they do not appear to have followed the same strictures of human health testing that would be expected of the food industry (Smith and Smith, 2004), or the pharmaceutical industry (Ho, 1998). But if it is so difficult and expensive, why are we trying to do it? One answer to this question is that our society is driven to a large extent by the short-term profit-orientation of commercial companies, rather than by the long-term cost-effectiveness of everyone. Many vegetarians are proud that their eating habits require less land than that of meat eaters. In a global market economy, meat consumption is rising, especially in countries where the diet had previously been predominantly vegetarian. On the other hand, the rising concern for fitness and slimness has brought about the Atkins diet, which encourages the overweight to consume mainly proteins and fats from animals and fish. These new habits are made possible only by intensive farming practices and systems of mass distribution, which enable rich nations to live on resources that are often imported across great distances. What also sustains these habits, in the short term, is a belief that we deserve the best, rather than seeing that we are destroying a vital and limited resource. Either we need a miracle, or we must find a new dream.

In his 1931 book *The Epic of America*, James Truslow Adams explored the US's reckless craving for the good life, arguing that Americans 'were always willing to gamble their last peso on a dream'. Indeed, the book is said to be the origin of the term 'American Dream'. Although many US citizens are becoming aware of its limitations, the idea is alive and well. It seems to be an essential part of the

American brand identity, and is certainly its greatest export. The vision of new worlds without frontiers, or a money-based meritocracy based on hard work and ingenuity seem unashamedly American. The US is a pragmatic, money-orientated culture in which entrepreneurs create the jobs, buy the goods and 'live it large'. Dissenters will, perhaps, be more aware that it is also associated with the profligate burning of non-renewable fuels and an extravagant consumption of animal products. For example, the average US citizen consumes 1.5 times more than the average world citizen, with a diet that is high in animal protein. This is part of a vicious circle. Economic growth facilitates the American dream, and the dream is what sustains the economic *status quo*. This 'dream' inevitably reflects aspects of American history. In 1776, Thomas Jefferson, and others, drew up the American Declaration of Independence. This strongly humanist charter of individual freedom drew upon a mixture of sources, including North American Indian principles of governance, Utilitarian ideas from Britain, and ideas that emerged from the French Revolution. The earlier historical context for this constitution was that of mass immigration by the founding fathers. These were predominantly white farmers, miners and sailors, or unskilled and illiterate workers. This first wave of settlers found little merit in the habits of the indigenous population they encountered. Many of these tribes had lived modestly by following herds of buffalo and conserving the many species of plants, shrubs and trees. By contrast, the settlers found it convenient to slaughter huge numbers of buffalo for immediate consumption of the most accessible cuts of meat, often leaving the carcasses to rot where they fell (Jakle, 1968). No policy for restocking animal numbers was developed until a much later date. These unfortunate habits resemble some of the established practices of rainforest clearance in the Amazon and elsewhere. It is very hard to justify them in any way.

In the year that American Independence was declared, *The Wealth of Nations*, mentioned earlier, Adam Smith's influential blueprint for an economics of self-interest, was published (1776). The idea that diligence by the individual will produce wealth for the many is still a cornerstone of the American economic system. That the work ethic originally emerged from American Protestant values of unvarnished modesty is clear, but there is an irony inherent in hard work (cf. Schama, 1987). The more you produce, the more you have. Moreover, if you take Smith's logic too seriously, you may begin to value individual rights above individual responsibilities. Soon, simplicity was not enough. By the end of the 19th century designers were being asked to create new products that would appeal to different individuals (Forty, 1986). Since then, the artificial creation of new markets has become increasingly important for sustaining the new American Dream. By developing advertising, market research and promotional systems the US created a justification for desire, and then a desire *for* desire. The advent of an effective rail network and Henry Ford's development of the first mass-produced car created even greater potential for business and consumption on all levels. Greater personal mobility led to new vending opportunities and enterprise became rife. The American Dream became immensely appealing to the rest of the world, largely through the enviable charm, glamour and potency of the lifestyle that could be embodied and exported via novels, movies, automobiles and other products. By the 1980s it was very clear that this system was eventually going to eat us out of house and home. This is largely why we are in such a mess. It is why the Brundtland Report on 'sustainable development' was commissioned (Brundtland, 1987). It was clear that the American Dream might eventually kill us all and we had to look for an alternative. There is a sense in which consumerism is just the latest manifestation of this creed. But there is another unwelcome irony in America's vision of wellbeing. Despite the enduring Protestant tendencies in the US, the American Dream is not a million miles away from the old French Dream of 'liberty, equality and fraternity'. Both visions are aspirational, emancipatory and deeply humanistic. Each emphasises rights, rather than responsibilities. How is this relevant to the issues of climate change and the extinction of species on Earth? The clue is in the three guiding principles, liberty, equality, and fraternity. What is missing is 'Nature'.

In order to design viable 'micro-utopias' it will be necessary to ensure that we are all more aware of the way in which our style of living affects the eco-system. One way to achieve this is by measuring the area of land and water that a society, community, or individual requires to support itself indefinitely. This is called its 'ecological footprint' (Wackernagel and Rees, 1996). The implied supposition behind this method is the desirability of the American Dream. In 1995, London was estimated to have an ecological footprint of 125 times its own size. In 2000, this was re-calculated. The new figures suggest that it has increased to 293 times its size – roughly twice the size of the UK (City Limits London Report, 2002). Up to a certain level the global population will sustain itself without harming the ecosystem. However it has been estimated that if we were to share resources equally across the globe – at the level of the US – we would need several more planets, perhaps as many as four or five. At present, the enormous increase in economic activities such as those in China and India will add to the existing burden. How is the Earth coping with the additional load we are putting upon it? Unfortunately, we are currently living at the 'overshoot' zone, in which we are using up resources that will compromise our ability to survive in the future. Beyond this point, we risk depleting and damaging the ecosystem, perhaps irreparably. During the early 20th century, the Taylorist – or Fordist – principle emerged in the countryside as the intensive farming system. Like any other manufacturing industry, agribusiness focuses on the limited task of ensuring high volume yields, rather more than on the implications for shared benefit. In comparison with traditional methods, intensive farming practices consume large amounts of fossil fuel and water resources. They also emit harmful gases and chemicals because the approach of industrial farming systems is monocultural. They pose a threat to biodiversity because they represent a very poor habitat for wildlife.

In describing the advantages of this system, however, the word 'efficiency' should be used with caution. Grazing and grain-fed animals need far more water than grain crops. Almost half of the water supply in the US and 80 per cent of its agricultural land is needed for this purpose. Meat, milk and eggs deliver a mere quarter of the energy that went into producing them, and the protein output is less than a fifth of that which is contained in grains, vegetables, legumes, seeds and fruits. Where the advocates of the GM food industry warn us that we do not have enough land to feed ourselves, the energy industry is asking us to give up large arable areas for the growing of crops as bio-fuels. Part of this folly is the result of thinking from within the limited mindset of GDP, economic growth and a blind faith in Nature to remain endlessly benevolent, irrespective of our actions.

Some routine practices that make sense to professors of economics are sometimes inexplicable to non-experts like the author. One of these practices is the tendency to include all work-related activities as useful endeavours towards the GDP. A great deal of work, however, is either counterproductive or even damaging. According to a 2006 Report from the New Economics Foundation, in 2004 the UK imported 1,500 tonnes of fresh potatoes from Germany but exported the same quantity in the opposite direction. Likewise, it imported 9,900 tonnes of milk and cream from France exported 10,200 tonnes into France. This example shows that the principle of auditing the costs in financial terms is helpful, provided it includes a large enough sample of space and time. One economic study showed, for example, that a switch to organic production could save the UK economy £1.13 billion per year. Hence the wider distribution of farm and other food products has brought new costs, in real terms. At the time of writing, 28 per cent of goods transported on UK roads are agricultural produce. This adds an estimated external cost of £2.35 billion per year. The cost of transporting food from the shop to home adds a further £1.28 billion per year to total external costs. Of course, the shopper may not be aware of all these costs, because some are hidden within government subsidies. It has been estimated that the real cost of the weekly shopping bill could be reduced by 11.8 per cent simply by encouraging food production to be more local.

Unfortunately, consumer-driven economic growth is only the latest in a long history of systematically destructive habits that threaten the long-term wellbeing of other species. There are striking differences in how much research and expenditure go into transport, housing, food production and waste processing. For example, in the richest countries, the average person spends between 15 per cent (US Department of Labor Bureau) – and 25 per cent (Automobile Association (UK), 2004) of his or her annual income on owning, maintaining and running a car. On the other hand, the even higher cost of renting or mortgaging one's living accommodation attracts many workers into commuting enormous distances to and from work. This mobility has led to the dispersal of many families. In the UK of all car journeys over 50 miles, more than half are for social or leisure purposes. A quarter of car journeys are less than 2 miles and 59 per cent are less than 5 miles (DTLR Transport Statistics). One short-term solution to this problem might be to impose a commuter tax that would subsidise affordable housing. Despite enormous investment on R&D and significant advances in technology, car design has advanced surprisingly little over the last hundred years. Of course, this is not the impression that most consumers have, because much of the research is driven by competition over sales. Branding, capability to accelerate rapidly, styling and the number of technical features are what has seemed to motivate the development of car design. Hence, many vehicles now have on-board computers that regulate engine conditions; temperature, airflow, fuel consumption, and so on. Modern cars seem to bristle with electric motors and other servomechanisms. They are fabricated using sophisticated management systems, to tolerances of a fraction of millimetre. Despite all this, an increasing number of vehicles have satellite guidance systems that can add to the journey length. Virtually all cars have heat engines that deliver seldom more than 25 per cent efficiency when they are working properly. This figure is reduced when in normal use, because cars burn fuel even when the vehicle is stationary. To my knowledge, very few current models are smart enough to recycle lost energy regeneratively, when braking or travelling downhill.

Despite these shortcomings, the technological sophistication of car design and manufacture seems far ahead of the way that houses are built. Although we probably spend half of our lives inside our apartments or houses, we put up with very poor standards of design and manufacture (Woudhuysen and Abley, 2004). This is because housing is a seller's market. This means that the less scrupulous property developer can easily exploit the system without needing much entrepreneurial ingenuity. It is interesting to speculate how well a car might work if it were to be designed and built to the values, assumptions and standards of the average house or apartment. Richard Buckminster Fuller posed a similar question in the 1930s (for example Fuller, 1949) but we have made hardly any progress since that time. His 1933 Dymaxion Car had a fuel efficiency that exceeds the current US standard (Automobile Association, 2004) for cars. Compared with aeroplanes and motorcars, the average UK house is built to far lower standards of precision and resource conservation. The computing power in many digital toys, mobile phones, laptop computers and personal stereos is far ahead of those used to manage the average household. Again, while these devices could be put to practical use they are designed more for market forces. Although they could be built to last for many decades we design them to be discarded after a year or two, because they have become unfashionable or obsolescent. On the other hand, even the most prosperous individuals live in houses with a technological standard that has advanced comparatively little since the 19th century. This system is endorsed by most planning authorities who tend to err on the side of conservatism, if not downright anachronism.

The design of most new housing estates in the UK reflects a nostalgic, conservative and inward-looking society. On the other hand, corporate buildings and public structures such as bridges, high-rise buildings and pavements are made from materials and processes that are energy-intensive and cause around 5 per cent of global carbon dioxide emissions. These play a significant role in climate change, pollution, resource depletion, and worker health and safety (World Business Council for Sustainable Development Report, 2006). Building standards in the UK are improving, but we still have a very high proportion of low-skilled workers. The amount of waste produced by the building industry is equivalent to three or four times that which individual consumers produce as domestic waste. This probably means that job satisfaction and consumer expectations are low. It is difficult to understand why, in the age of computer-aided design and an increasingly sophisticated manufacturing industry, we still design most buildings using traditional rectilinear shapes that ensure very poor air circulation. This means that when the sun is warm we resort to using electric fans for ventilation. Together, these two factors cause unnecessary health problems because of the harbouring, and intermittent dispersal, of toxic substances. When we get too hot we dump the solar energy into the surrounding environment, using even more additional energy from noisy air conditioning devices. When we get cold we heat our buildings by burning non-renewal materials, such as oil, gas, or radioactive material. Most people I speak to seem unaware that we have only about 60 years worth of materials for nuclear power from current fission methods (Douthwaite, 2003). In the 21st century we use huge quantities of glass in new buildings. The manufacturing process is very costly in energy terms, because it requires enormous temperatures to transform sand and other chemicals into glass. On the other hand, glass is perfect for space heating, because solar radiation is abundant and glass is an almost perfect material for converting solar radiation into useful heat for space and water heating. However, this process is seldom adopted in an active way. In many high-budget modern buildings, air conditioning systems are installed to dispose of the unwanted solar heat into the local surroundings. Unfortunately, it takes more energy to cool a building than it does to heat it. Sunshine therefore seems to be an embarrassment to many planners, managers and architects, who circumvent the minimum legal standards of construction and energy management. Nonetheless, now that the natural environment has become sexy, I predict that these same people will want to install conspicuous solar panels on the side of their inefficient buildings. In the UK, many of the electricity companies still use wasteful methods that dump up to 65 per cent of their energy production as heat, before it is turned into electricity. The remaining third is distributed as electricity, using an outdated grid system that will need a major overhaul if it is to accommodate a more de-centralised production system that would help us to manage renewable energy sources effectively.

If the design of our energy, water and disposal systems were better integrated, the average person would be able to manage consumption better. While there is a small degree of consumer choice at home, office standards seem to be beyond the control of most employees. For example, each office worker in the UK flushes away an average of 36 litres of potable tap water per day. This reflects a culture of thoughtless extravagance, but it also derives from the poor design of most modern bathrooms. In any case, many office workers prefer to drink imported water from bottles. These are usually made from plastic that introduces chemicals to the body, and designed to be discarded after use. It has become 'natural' to us to take rainwater from the roof of the house and run it quietly away. We then dilute our sewage with fresh water, pumped in from outside, and return it to the donor with a little added chlorine, and some oestrogen from birth control pills. Most of the warmth and nutrients from our baths and showers are sent away via the same route. The practice of diluting sewage is, in itself, probably not the best solution anyway. Human waste is more quickly and hygienically processed using local air treatment, rather than by remote dilution using water. Commercial aerobic systems, such as the Clivus Multrum system are well established. They produce garden manure without fuss, and without encouraging diseases associated with subterranean vermin.

It is possible that the stronger odours that accompany water-based, anaerobic systems caused city dwellers to recoil from their own waste products. This may help to explain why they may be tempted to drive to the nearest out of town garden centre, in order to buy artificial fertilisers for the lawns and flowerbeds. It is a pity that today we speak of excrement in a demeaning sense that signifies worthlessness. This kind of alienation did not always exist. Some stories from pre-20th century Japan describe the anxiety that attended a dinner guest if he needed to use his host's toilet, as he may have been tempted to run home in order to keep his own manure for his own garden. Today, the more ardent DIY gardener maintains the neat appearance of hedges, trees and lawns, by using power tools that require petrol or electricity, and gadgets that automatically dispense fresh water from the tap. Some popular television gardening programmes have popularised the extravagant use of hardwood decking that is commonly sourced from rainforests in Africa or Asia. With car ownership rising, many house owners are paving over their gardens with concrete or tarmac to create impervious surfaces for cars and recreational spaces. Unfortunately, the replacement of soil and plants with heat-absorbing surfaces make violent storms more likely in hot summers. This can lead to serious flooding, if heavy rains cannot be absorbed quickly enough to stop them overwhelming the underground sewage systems.

As dutiful consumers we seem compelled to experience everything in ways that sustain a wasteful economy. Similarly, the political obsession with achieving 100 per cent employment is somewhat baffling when what is needed is a higher level of shared well-being. In the UK, for example, the wages bill for the National Health Service (NHS) is higher than that of any other state employer. However, we know that a very large proportion of this expenditure is dedicated to repairing the untoward effects of child poverty, poor housing conditions, unhealthy diets, work-related stress and lack of good exercise. Unfortunately, seeking to address these issues within the economic system usually brings further inconsistencies. For example, if we drive to the gymnasium we may then be able to run to keep pace with the power consumption of an electric treadmill, perhaps while watching 'lifestyle' television. This is a cliché that is rather too common to seem comical any more. In the rich nations we are increasingly concerned about 'risk' (Beck, 2004). Many children are ferried to and from school safely while strapped into the seats of monstrous 'Sports Utility Vehicles', or 4 x 4 transporters. This is because many parents feel that they and their children are safer in them. Ironically, the number of child injuries and deaths from SUV vehicles is two to four times higher than for smaller vehicles (BBC News, 2006). Perhaps not surprisingly, there has also been a steep rise in the number of childhood asthmatics living in the towns. This is to be expected, as cars emit their most noxious gases within the first 2 minutes of being started from cold, and a high proportion of children live, on average, only a couple of minutes from their schools. Statistics also show a significant increase in the incidence of heart disease and diabetes in young children, presumably because they do not get enough exercise or are given inappropriate food to eat or both. At this stage, some readers may feel that the points made so far are biased. Nutritional awareness is rising, building standards are being improved all the time, and we have designs for hybrid cars that promise a truly 'green' way of life. Unfortunately, the economic system militates against a holistic process of step change. This is mainly because, unless it is market-orientated, design has tended to be implemented at the local, rather than at the global level.

Several car manufacturers have been trying to make more energy efficient car engines a feature of their company's branding and marketing campaigns. This is attractive to an increasing number of motorists. Nevertheless, corporations are always tempted to see themselves first as 'customer-friendly', and second as 'environmentally friendly'. In other words, they want to please as many potential customers as possible, and not just those who are determined to lower their fuel consumption. Thus, one of the world's largest companies has spent a great deal of money on promoting a 'green car'. However it also offers an impressive range of other vehicles, some of which have less than impressive average fuel-efficiency in terms of miles travelled per gallon. Indeed, some of its SUVs have a level of fuel use that is little better than the old model 'T' Ford, designed almost a century before. Hence, although we may admire the tiny, but undeniable improvement in one car's fuel consumption, the growth of popularity for far larger, gas-guzzling, 'off-road' vehicles is alarming. The net result is truly disastrous. This is because the logic of economic growth means that nothing can survive unless it proliferates, expands, or becomes more conspicuous. In a consumer-centred economy, increasing customer comfort, speed and excitement are paramount. Even some of those companies who are desperate to appear greener than others are considering the new 'space tourism' markets. This would enable wealthy individuals to waste hundreds of tons of carbon-rich fuel in making sightseeing excursions beyond the earth's atmosphere.

Some critics of environmentalism in the northern European countries rightly suggest that it is driven by a Protestant sense of guilt. However, in the prevailing culture of 'consumer rights' the moral aspects of speed, novelty, accessibility and comfort are not the issue. It is simply that we need to put the biosphere first. Over the last century or two of industrialisation we have seen an increasing technical ability to produce more consumer goods than we need.

During this time designers have conspired in the development of convenience foods, non-returnable packaging, competitive advertising strategies and product endorsement in films. This process has also begun to involve innovative ways of exchange and payment. Welcome to the world of 'Easy-Everything', in which 'loyalty cards', 'air-miles', 'buy one, get one free' offers and branded systems of monetary credit have merged with online purchasing, 'vendor-to-shopper' home delivery and wireless credit card authorisation devices. The recent advent of e-money, for example, is but an incremental step beyond credit cards. This is an illusion. The actual (that is, environmental) damage remains, but it may be camouflaged by clever 'design'. The logical outcome of aspirations like this is seldom questioned, presumably because the promise and allure of instant comfort, gratification and wellbeing has proved to be such a powerful means of fuelling economic growth. Unfortunately, while it has so far appeared to be astonishingly effective in delivering prosperity to many by increasing the rate of consumption of natural resources to unprecedented levels, it has led to environmental pollution, reduced bio-diversity, and created adverse climatic changes.

Why have our modern citizens become so callous and discontented about their own actions and conditions? Most of the negative arguments above have a common element that can be summarised as the tendency to cynicism. The reasoning behind modern day 'cynicism' is what Zizek (1996) called 'enlightened false consciousness'. Where the early Greek cynics were ascetics who shunned vanity and excess, the modern cynic usually knows that a given action is wrong, but he does it anyway (Sloterdijk, 1988). In behavioural terms this resembles the actions of a 'solipsist', that is, someone whose world faces inward. Each consumer is encouraged to indulge himself or herself. As one advertising copy line explains, 'Because I'm worth it'. Unfortunately, if I believe myself to be a 'special case', I will be less able to work in a way that contributes to the total benefit of my whole existence. I may be concerned about the health of my children, and I may even read about the problems of global warming, or ozone depletion. However, at a time when the car manufacture and ownership of SUVs in 'developing' countries such as China and India is growing rapidly, I may more easily be persuaded to follow the trend. After all, one more car on the road will enable my child to get to school safely and quickly. According to Garrett Hardin (1977) this logic reflects the fact that the human mind evolved in conditions of low population in which technology was pretty ineffective. He describes it as the 'Tragedy of the Commons' because it probably first emerged when the overuse of common, or 'shared' land led to the depletion of net resources in a high density of population. It represents a pattern that is similar to many cases, whether in over-fishing, or in the pollution of water, air, or land.

It can be found in rain forest destruction, computer chip manufacture and in many situations that seem to invite a selfish response to a shared problem. As world population levels rise towards the nine billion mark, the perceived effect of one person's action seems increasingly insignificant. Each individual sees the same equation. What difference will just one more car, plane journey, or baby make, relative to the whole scheme of things?

In the early 20th century, developments such as psychoanalysis, hermeneutics, existentialism and many artist-orientated artworks enhanced the West's long-standing fascination for the idea of the subjective individual. In his discussion of the human tendency to indulge in conspicuously wasteful, irreversible actions, Bataille (1989) offers a basis for investigating the psychology of economic consumption. This theory of waste and extravagance may help to explain why many of the wealthiest individuals will choose the largest, most expensive cigar, burn a little more than half of it, and then discard the remainder. A similar pattern emerges in the way that exclusive golf courses are designed and used. These carefully manicured areas of land include some of the most expensive real estate properties in the world. In their layout and land usage they represent a conspicuous gesture that celebrates the right of an individual to use large private areas of land that might otherwise be utilised for food production, or other common purpose. In these vast areas of manicured turf, high-energy fertiliser is used to create a rich, blue-green tint. In some places, ornamental lakes are deliberately poisoned with chemicals that inhibit the growth of algae and make them a lighter, more turquoise hue. In the UK, golf courses are exempt from the law (1991 Water Resources Act) that stop other gardeners from watering their plants with a hosepipe, during a drought. This is what I mean by 'ecological solipsism'.

References

Abbott, J. S. C. (1876), *Daniel Boone: The Pioneer of Kentucky* (New York: Dodd Mead and Company).

Adams, J. T. (1931), *The Epic of America* (Boston: Little, Brown and Company).

Automobile Association (UK) (2004), 'Figures for Cost of Car Ownership'. Available at: www.travelcalculator.org (Department of Transport).

Bataille, G. (1989), *The Accursed Share* (New York: Urzone).

Beck, U. (2004), *Risk Society: Toward a New Modernity* (London: Sage Publications).

Brundtland, G. (1987), 'Our Common Future', Report of the World Commission on Environment and Development. Available at: www.are.admin.ch/are/en/nachhaltig/international_uno/unterseite02330/

City Limits London, (2002), 'Best Foot Forward – City Limits Report'. Available at: www.citylimitslondon.com/download.htm

Douthwaite, R, (ed.) (2003), *Before the Wells Run Dry: Ireland's Transition to Renewable Energy* (Dublin: Feasta in association with Green Books and Lilliput Press).

Forty, A. (1986), *Objects of Desire: Design and Society, 1750–1980* (London: Thames & Hudson).

Fuller, R. B. (1949), 'Total thinking' in *The Buckminster Fuller Reader*, Meller, J. (ed.) (1972) (London: Pelican Books)

Hardin, G. (1977), 'The tragedy of the commons' in *Managing the Commons*, Hardin, G. and Baden, J. (eds.), (San Francisco: W.H. Freeman and Co). Original article available at: www.sciencemag.org/cgi/content/full/162/3859/1243

Ho, M-W. (1998), *Genetic Engineering, Dream or Nightmare*: *The Brave New World of Bad Science and Big Business* (Bath: Gateway Books).

Jakle, J. (1968), 'The American Bison and the Human Occupance of the Ohio Valley', Proceedings of the American Philosophical Society, 112(4), pp. 299–305.

Law, B. (2001), *The Woodland Way: A Permaculture Approach To Sustainable Woodland Management* (East Meon: Permanent Publications).

Maturana, H. (1997), 'Metadesign', Available at: www.inteco.cl/articulos/006/texto_ing.htm (Santiago: Instituto de Terapia Cognitiva)

Nader, R. (2000), *Cutting Corporate Welfare* (New York: Seven Stories Press).

New Economics Foundation Report (2006). Available at: www. happyplanetindex.org/survey.htm

Ponting, C. (1991), *A Green History of the World* (London: Penguin Books).

Schama, S. (1987), *The Embarrassment of Riches: An Interpretation of Dutch Cultures in the Golden Age* (New York: Random House).

Sloterdijk, P. (1988), *The Critique of Cynical Reason* (London: Verso).

Smith, J. M. (2004), *Seeds of Deception: Exposing Government Lies about the Safety of Genetically Engineered Food* (Totnes: Green Books).

National Highway Traffic Safety Administration (NHTSA), Department of Transportation (DOT) (2004). Available at: www.nhtsa.dot.gov/cars/rules/ CAFE/Rulemaking/AMFAFinalRule2004.pdf

US Department of Labor Bureau (2006), 'Figures for Car Ownership Costs'. Available at: www.bls.gov.

Wackernagel, M. and Rees, W. E. (1996), *Our Ecological Footprint: Reducing Human Impact on the Earth* (Philadelphia: New Society Publishers).

Wood, J. (1976), 'Could tree farming answer world food need?', in *The Handbook of Radical Technology*, Harper, P. and Boyle, G. (eds.) (New York: Pantheon Books, Random House).

World Business Council for Sustainable Development Report (2006), Available at: www.wbcsd.org

Woudhuysen, J. and Abley, I. (2004), *Why is Construction so Backward?* (Hoboken, NJ: Wiley-Academy).

Zizek, S. (1996), *The Indivisible Remainder* (London: Verso).

The Rise of Solipsism CHAPTER

2

'Fashion is a form of ugliness so intolerable that we have to alter it every six months.'

(Oscar Wilde)

One of the problems with the policy of unlimited economic growth is that, as humans, we soon become disenchanted with what we have. Since the Second World War, although we have become far richer, on balance we are no happier (Veenhoven, 2007). While it is often true that wealth can make us more content this does not usually last long. We soon forget our last pay increase, and look forward to another one. Eventually, this becomes a routine. It is generally accepted that capitalism emerged from a Protestant culture that encouraged a particular kind of individualism. This Chapter argues that the emphasis on individual diligence that is typified by Adam Smith's writings (1776) also led to alienation, solipsism, and, more recently, instrumental rationality (Habermas, 1968), and 'enlightened false consciousness' (Sloterdijk, 1988). All of these developments may help to explain why well-informed human beings appear to ignore their role in climate change, and losses in biodiversity, and so on. This process has led to enormous problems such as a reduction in the earth's potential for supporting our needs. Beyond this book's primary philosophical and theoretical agenda lies a whole set of deeply interrelated issues that are more recognisable as 'design'. This chapter shows how the process of individualisation became a catalyst for economic growth. It therefore explores a style of self-awareness that has become indispensable within the consumer system. It relates this to the idea of 'self' that was initiated at the time of Socrates, and that has become intensified over the last few hundred years. In particular, it suggests that this idea continues to reward patterns of personal choice, which exacerbates over-consumption, and the kinds of alienation described at the end of the previous chapter. This process is based on a belief system. As such, it can be re-designed.

Some research suggests that 38 per cent of the population will be living in solo accommodation by 2025 (Williams, 2005). Unfortunately, family dwellings of two adults and one child only consume 8 per cent more energy and resources than an individual living alone. Nevertheless, this trend is the result of a strongly individual-orientated economics of consumption in which rapid mobility and freedom of choice are highly prized. As dutiful consumers we have therefore been encouraged to believe that we are unique individuals with special rights and few responsibilities. As workers, however, we must accept more responsibilities and become less visible or distinctive as individuals. If we are to achieve a better balance between productivity and well being, we may have to develop a more playful society in which work is seen as a pleasure for its own sake. In the future, perhaps we will all become designers, artists, or scientists. In this way the boundaries between production and consumption will become blurred. This chapter explores two key issues. One is the rise of a strident form of individualism that has become vital within a commercial society. The other is the tendency to separate 'human rights' from 'human responsibilities'. Both have contributed to a profound and, as we are seeing, mortal conflict between humanism and environmentalism, and this leads to serious confusion at the practical level. If I wish to be a good citizen it is not clear whether I should work to sustain the economy or whether I should work to sustain the eco-system. For this reason, it is unfortunate that many non-Western cultures seem to have been strongly influenced by the cultural belief systems behind this kind of confusion. If so, it is probably because capitalist economics has proved to be spectacularly successful within its own terms.

The perceived economic need for citizens to become 'consumers' has encouraged certain kinds of 'alienation' from Nature. In exploring the Marxist idea of 'alienation', I will also use the word 'solipsism'. This is a term that describes extremely self-centred behaviour. However, rather than discussing the social ethics of solipsism, my intention is to use this idea within an ecological context, for any organism that attends more to its internal state than to its external environment is at risk of losing its life in an unexpected way. The acceptance of a citizen's 'private' thoughts and actions as important is something we take for granted. It seems to have evolved within early Hellenic cultures, perhaps with Socrates (circa 470–399 BC). However, we may suppose that the idea of solipsism became strengthened by the emergence of silent reading that took place, according to the suggestion of Borges (1964) at the time of St Augustine (354–430 AD). Although today we take silent reading for granted, it was something that may not have developed until the 4th century. According to Borges (1964), in 384, St Augustine described how Ambrose, the Bishop of Milan could read in silence, without moving his lips. This is possibly the first recorded account of silent reading, although it could have been introduced as late as the 10th century. The exact date is of little importance; it has become one of the key skills of our individualistic society and a major factor in the rise of solipsism. This is where we might usefully reflect upon deeper issues concerning our place in the scheme of things. We can also illustrate the idea of 'eco-solipsism' by referring to the ancient myth of Echo and Narcissus; this describes a young man who was so absorbed in his own reflected image that he failed to notice the attentions of a female admirer called 'Echo'. There are many reasons why solipsists believe themselves to be separate from the whole. In the 21st century context solipsistic modes of consumption are encouraged, in order to increase economic flow. Today, this story has a poignant relation with the cult of celebrity, vanity, and self-presentation. This is evident in the popularity of reality television shows such as *Big Brother*, in which ordinary people watch ordinary people being watched by ordinary people. As 21st century citizens we are still enthralled by notions of individual genius, whether exemplified in the reductionist reasoning of the Enlightenment, or by the extravagant visions of Romanticism. Arguably, both paradigms continue to inspire the evolution of the global citizen as 'individualised consumer'. These processes were symptomatic of a new ethics of the individual in which the environmentalist responsibilities of citizens became eclipsed by their implicit rights as consumers. Clearly, from an ecological perspective we can see that few individuals could adopt this mode of living without causing enormous environmental damage. From where did this process originate, and how significant is it? It reflects the way that industry encourages the ordinary consumer's self-absorption in the act of consumption that is designed to sustain his, or her, self-image. The myth of Narcissus has an unhappy end. If we extrapolate the fable to a much larger, ecological scale, it alludes to the possible death of a species.

The tale of Narcissus can also be seen as a critique of the Socratic principles that bolstered humanism and eventually led to the rise of individualism. The terms 'society' and 'individual' are more than complementary to one another, as there are many ways in which the individual upholds the group, and *vice versa*. Neither term would make much sense without the other, but there are many ways in which the individual, rather than his or her social group, may be important. The way that an individual gains its autonomy is important. Whether he or she is defined more by reference to the group or to his or her self-image will affect how he or she might behave. However, it is more complicated than this. Individuals see themselves differently from how others see them. In other words an individual's identity is co-created by his or her role within in a larger context. As the 17th century poet, John Donne said, 'no man is an island'. In other words, it is theoretically impossible to have an identity that is entirely defined by one's interior predilections, but during the last 300 years or so, developments in our way of life have made it thinkable for individuals to become less forcefully defined by society, and more strongly defined by themselves. In extreme cases this is a kind of solipsism. In medieval society 'individuals' were usually identified and named by their occupation, rather than by any personal distinguishing features. In England in the late 16th and early 17th centuries the concept of 'the individual' changed to that of 'a kind of absolute, without immediate reference… to the group of which he is a member' (Williams, 1961). In Western modernist art we have seen conspicuous forms of individualism, often exemplified in peculiarly male genres. Over the last few hundred years, Classical Science and Romantic Art spawned new ideas of the human mind that served to make us feel distant from Nature (cf. Merchant, 1980). Intellectually, this notion was inspired, in part, by the cognitive theories of Descartes, Kant, Locke and Berkeley. Whereas non-solipsistic modes of individuation probably emerged from the need for role differentiation within a technological society, the myths and attitudes of extreme individuation (that is, solipsism) evolved within the rational mindset of Baconian and Newtonian science. To some extent we can look to Protestantism as the inspiration for much of the ideology behind Western, ethical, self-aware individualism. This was largely because the individual conscience was developed as an alternative to the externally imposed dogma of the Church of Rome. In Northern Europe, in the early 16th century, Calvin, Luther and Zwingli emphasised mankind's weakness of spirit whilst in Holland, Erasmus asserted the importance of freedom of will in securing eternal salvation.

In the early 19th century the rise of scientific rationalism and humanism also meant that fewer artists could enjoy the traditional patronage of the church. The subsequent rise of Romantic movements in art and science inspired a set of beliefs in which the proactive imagination was seen as an object of enquiry, or as the unique outpouring of the artist's mind. Coined in the 19th century, the word 'individualism' marks a renewed emphasis on the self. Today, in an increasingly consumer-centred society it has become indispensable. The word 'individual' originally meant 'indivisible', or 'inseparable'. Over the last two or three hundred years or so, the individuated citizen has come to stand as an archetype of the social realm. For this reason, we now tend to speak of the primary duties of industry as meeting the needs of individuated consumers, rather than supporting society at large. If we take a negative view of the ideology of economic growth we might say that it is a short-term ethics of greed and selfishness. If so, why do we put up with it? To some extent it is because we have been happy to interpret Adam Smith's famous argument (1776) to mean that, as consumers, when we spend money to enjoy ourselves we are supporting society. In trying to establish an individual-centred ethical system for design practice it is important, for individuals, to be able to monitor their individual actions in a self-reflexive way. This has a special resonance within Western thought. The notion of 'self-awareness' seems to have emerged from a pitilessly competitive (Hellenic) culture in which self-assertion, rather than 'self-satisfaction' was seen as a public virtue. Today, the term 'self control' may still sound austere and mechanistic, because it is reminiscent of militaristic attitudes. In the two and a half thousand years since Socrates it has diverged from the qualities or values that it once had. In the current technological era it can be seen to run in tandem with the development of self-regulatory machines such as clocks and thermostats. In mediaeval Europe, humanist thinkers such as Erasmus (1469–1536) introduced ideas such as 'self-regulation' to describe the moral conduct of the dutiful Christian. By using it as the basis of a rather specious enquiry into the nature of reality Descartes (1596–1650) exaggerated the solipsistic aspects of this idea (Descartes, in Veitch, 1907). In the 18th century, Daniel Defoe's novel *Adventures of Robinson Crusoe* (1719) created a literary genre that mythologised the individual as someone independent of society. This became a popular theme in modern sci-fi literature and we are still inclined to read it as a positive, if uncanny tale. Jonathan Swift's contemporary satire *Gulliver's Travels* (1726) offers a less favourable image of solipsistic alienation in which, for example, certain characters would swivel their eyeballs inwards, thereby losing touch with their surroundings. All of the above ideas contributed to the understanding of the self as an 'object' in its own right. Logically speaking, if one were truly independent of one's environment the question of social or ecological responsibility would be redundant. This is reminiscent of some modern 'freelance' consultants who believe that they should be ready to ignore their own ethical standards when working for a client.

Today, it is not uncommon for individuals to describe their feelings in terms of popular medical theories that refer to a single gland, or chemical in their body. This represents a curious form of reductionism that, by merely its suggestive powers, may make it difficult for some humans to get in touch with their full complexity of emotions. Moreover, it is a form of solipsism in that it fails to acknowledge the almost indefinable web of connections that enable emotions to serve to integrate us with our natural environment. This post-Cartesian idea is so familiar to most of us that we easily forget that, before humanism emerged, people in the Middle Ages attributed emotions like 'fear' and 'merriment' to their natural surroundings (Campbell, 1987), rather than to their own psyche or state. Between the 16th and 18th centuries, keywords such as 'self conceit', 'self-confidence', and 'self pity' came into use, and

Coleridge coined the term 'self-consciousness' in the 19th century. We should not see the emergence of this kind of individualism as value-free. Weber uses the term 'disenchantment' to argue that it coincides with a growing rift between mankind and Nature. Perhaps surprisingly, it can also be found in a fashion called 'Dandyism' that ran from the late 18th century until the early 19th century. Whereas, in the 18th century, a 'fop' was a figure identified with femininity and folly through 'over dressing'; the dandy originally exemplified elegance and self-restraint. Dandyism therefore epitomised a more masculine balance between fastidiousness and casualness. Under Byron's influence (1822) the Dandy looked nonchalant, but at the same time ill and tragic. As the style developed the Dandy developed an insolent look. The Dandy's rigid sense of protocol meant that his clothing must be exquisitely understated. More importantly, his sense of self-awareness needed to be refined.

Beau Brummel was the original dandy, who took enormous care over his appearance, and had no wife or lifelong partner. Here, he may be seen as the prototype for the 21st century (self) consuming self. He pretended to be amoral, passion-less, and disinterested in politics or ambition. His air of self-superiority was exquisitely balanced with a feigned disregard for what others might think. In some ways this was a militaristic pose. Just as Greeks in the time of Socrates competed fiercely to attain distinction and to bring honour to their country, so the Duke of Wellington urged his officers to be well-groomed and calm. Arguably, they are different styles of the same thing. However, this raises questions about how we maintain equilibrium between internal and external aspects of self-image. From a patriarchal perspective, the origins of Dandyism seem characteristically male. The idea of honour was one of the reasons for the rise of rhetoric and a pride in competition. There are tales of Spartan soldiers seen combing their hair before battle. When asked what they were doing they replied, 'We are preparing to die'. Samurai warriors and North American Indians have said similar things. Perhaps this is the 'boys' thing' that some countries call 'machismo'. However, another important precursor to the modern autonomous self was the mercenary soldier. As a freelance merchant he was independent of allegiance to any particular realm or kingdom and, as such, he was free to offer his services to the highest bidder. On the other hand, many mercenaries conducted themselves according to strict codes of self-discipline. Both tendencies can be found in European mediaeval codes of chivalry. Arguably, they informed the later idea of reflexive self-control that can be found in the Cavaliers, Dandies, Flaneurs and Romantics (Campbell, 1987). This led to a mode of fastidious individuation that is recognisable on the fashion catwalk and, by extension, in the public persona of the modern consumer.

Some of the conceits of the modern celebrity can be traced to the behaviour of Lord Byron and his claim that his life was probably more important than his work. This is a difficult area to understand because the tendency to deceive or play a role tends to mask the poseur's underlying motives. Similarly, Coleridge's (1772–1834) invention and use of the word 'self-consciousness' does not really tell us much about his inner experience of the psyche and whether this was more, or less, important to him than the way that it affected his fame or other aspects of outward appearance. By way of contrast, the Dandies drew attention to their image and presence rather than to their work or professional status. They had no explicit philosophy. They were neither rationalists of the Enlightenment, nor were they Romantics in today's popular sense of the word. These ideas helped to set the scene for the emergence of more recent terms such as 'positive self-regard' (Rogers, 1951), 'presentation of self' (Goffman, 1959), and 'self-actualisation' (Maslow, 1987). In all the above cases we may note that self-gratification is subservient to the goal of living up to one's image and chosen style. This is part of what constitutes the psychic make-up of the Dandy. All of the above ideas derived from the Western tradition of thought that led to the generic idea of 'human rights', a principle that has been adopted by international agencies such as the United Nations. Of particular interest is the idea of 'individual human rights' that may, today, seem self-evident, natural, or 'inalienable' to us although it is has yet to be theorised adequately as a universal truth. This is not to claim that the generic idea of human rights utterly polarises opinion. Indeed, the major religions all seem to agree that Homo sapiens is 'top banana' within the ecosystem. However, each culture has its own way of saying this, and it is important to respect the discursive differences that make it difficult to frame an unequivocal, common statement of belief. The disadvantage of a United Nations style of human rights charter is that it represents a compromise in which local wisdom may get overlooked or subsumed within a larger whole. Keown (1998), for example, argues that the concept of 'human rights' sits awkwardly within traditional Buddhist teachings. Similarly, many thinkers from Hinduism, Roman Catholicism, and Islam all remained troubled by the increasing tendency to disconnect individual human rights from the rights of each member within a family group. This is not to say that all collectivist cultures will necessarily become individualistic. Indeed, many Japanese citizens, for example, tend to regard consumption more as a duty to their national economy than as a celebration of their individuality. Many cultural exports from the Western entertainment industries continue to associate western individualism with a glamorous lifestyle. In other cases, different traditions can just as easily map onto consumerism. Although less individualistic cultures such as those of Japan and Korea may see things slightly differently, the idea that 'the customer is always right' is common to many modern industrial societies. Despite the important role of individual actions, consumer lobbies (for example Nader, 2000) tended to blame corporations for environmentalist problems such as climate change.

This was not a spontaneous development. It grew out of a carefully cultivated mythology developed by experts including designers and advertising designers. For example, the advertising and communication industries are contributors to a culture of product placement, cosmetic enhancement, and brand awareness. Some of these inducements artificially strive to make us look inward, mainly for commercial reasons, at the expense of social outcomes. Today the process is largely commercially motivated: designed to increase appetite or desire, rather than make us wiser. In the 17th century it was monarchic rights, albeit with few clear responsibilities, that inspired the idea of the 'self-owning individual' (MacPherson, 1975). In today's consumer world we may discern an additional level of self-confidence that is manifest in the circular performance that is epitomised in the expression 'feeling good, looking good'. In the fashion world this enactment of the self-contained self can also be characterised as a fetishist attraction between the rhetorical component of a product's appearance (Haug, 1986; Buchanan, 1989) and the self-image of the individual consumer. The vanity mirror has long played an important role in the Western construction of the individuated self (Lacan, 1977). It also plays an important part in the process by which anorexia, or bulimia, erodes the 'feeling good' aspects of being 'good enough'.

Although it was by no means unprecedented, the French Revolution gave new impetus to the ethical idea of individual liberty. It was part of a new order that sought to foster a sense of social cohesion and mutual support within society. This was not intended to promote individualism, per se, but it certainly had this effect. No matter how ingenious human beings are, their previous experiences and existing models always curtail their imagination. In this case, the new model of a republican citizen was inevitably inspired by the lifestyle of the monarchy. This can be illustrated by France's wonderful cuisine that was once the envy of every starving commoner in Paris. After the Revolution it came to exemplify the unquestionable right of every citizen. Whereas, for many decades, English cooking epitomised class difference and a system of privilege for the few, France's dining halls embodied a lofty vision of bonhomie for all. However, this unambiguous policy of equality has obvious ecological implications. At present, the idea of 'equal human rights' has tended to be equated with visions of freedom, and the American Dream. This idea of freedom implies that all citizens will have a right to eat colossal steaks and drive capacious cars, irrespective of whether there will be enough cows or gasoline to meet the demand. This ideology is increasingly difficult to uphold when humans are facing the possibility of extinction as a result of their actions, which is why the chapter uses the rather extreme word 'solipsism'. Just as, in the old Palace of Versailles, court officials were inclined to shield the monarchy from unpalatable truths, so today's producers, planners, and politicians cushion their customers from the ecological realities that nourish or threaten them. As a consequence, consumers enjoy strong individual rights of consumption but few responsibilities, apart from payment. Often, this rhetoric of 'consumer rights' treats customers like infants. The advertising industry is constantly seeking new technological techniques that will 'narrow-cast' product messages into the mind of each and every individual on the planet. Mobile phone technology is a good example of this approach. So are multi-channel radio communication, user-tracking satellites and databases that monitor each user's credit rating and shopping predilections. Digital systems will encourage more and more consumption at the most local, personal level. The way this works is strongly dependent on a hard, mechanistic (that is, Cartesian) model of the world, coupled with a softer, more organic notion of the self.

In the 19th century the first Industrial Revolution produced relatively few industries. Each was dedicated to the production of primary materials or basic products, such as soap, steel or sugar. In the quest for product diversification, design and marketing learned to cultivate consumer individuation. Without systematic customer individuation we would have fewer products to choose from. This meant catering to a wider range of individual preferences. This, in turn called for greater social and cultural individuation. In one example, an American mail order company (1895) advertised a knife in 131 versions, grouped in four customer categories of gender and age (Forty, 1986). The subsequent strategy of increasing product differentiation therefore led to a sharper differentiation of user types. Today, as markets expand and mature, products and customers must become increasingly interdependent, in order to facilitate economic growth that far exceeds what is needed for human wellbeing and happiness. By enhancing social individuation we catalysed economic flow, helping to diversify and expand all market sectors. As part of this process, the system needs to promote an ethic of individual self-gratification. In this system, people and things begin to behave as complementary, or equivalent entities. The rhetorical self-identity of products (Buchanan, 1989) regulates the self-identity of consumers, and *vice versa*. When the process takes place within a starkly competitive system of economic production it leads to the apparent self-management of consumption. In other words, it induces a process by which the flow of materials and energy is maximised within parameters that are, in the first instance, economic, rather than ecological. The foundational precepts for these developments are often attributed to the rationality of Socrates and the idealism of Plato. Early Socratic individuation identified self-knowledge and the soul as a unique centre of a person's ethical integrity within society. However, it is only after the time of the Enlightenment that Socratic reasoning joined forces with the atomistic or monadic notion (after Leibniz, 1951) of a self-defining and self-owning individual. At this point, the belief in self-possession began to qualify the individual and his or her 'own' ideas. Arguably, the developments of writing, moveable type printing, and, latterly, digital communication systems led to systems of representation that were progressively self-absorbing for their 'readers' (Wood, 1998).

In the mid-20th century the philosopher Martin Heidegger, and deep ecologists such as Arne Naess, responded to this issue with the Buddhist argument that humans must learn to 'let things be', suggesting that we can only learn to do so when we gain insight to the 'nothingness' that pervades everything, including ourselves. Only our radical 'openness', or 'emptiness' to things will enable us to see beyond the dualistic concepts that represent humans as separate from nature. In reflecting upon the 20th century Western mind, Heidegger suggests that our normal state is one of anxiety, because we do not like to face this predicament. The feeling is so unnerving that we absorb ourselves in busy lifestyles and hectic careers as displacement activities. The beliefs that maintain our sense of distance from Nature are exemplified in the 18th century theory of 'observation', which suggests a powerful, yet non-participatory role for the observer. When describing his dualistic notion of the human mind and its observation of the 'outside world', John Locke used the metaphor of a solitary judge 'in chambers'; that is, in his room, gazing outside. He argued that sensations are conveyed 'from without to their audience in the brain' to what he called 'the mind's presence room' (Locke, 1690). Richard Rorty compares Descartes' and Locke's philosophical position with earlier Greek and mediaeval thinkers, concluding that Descartes and Locke saw the mind as a separate 'inner space in which both pains, and clear and distinct ideas passed in review before the Inner Eye'. This idea may bring to mind Caspar David Friedrich's famous painting *The Wanderer Above the Mists* (1818) that pictures a solitary man gazing down into a sublime landscape.

This image acts as a perfect illustration for Kant's famous Enlightenment phrase, 'dare to know'. This defiant symbol of human supremacy did not emerge spontaneously. Its sentiments can also be found in many of the major religions, which reassure their followers that mankind is the most important of all species. In 1336, 500 years before Friedrich made his painting, the humanist Petrarch climbed Mount Ventoux and looked down on his town. What was his purpose? It is hard to see one, apart from the experience of doing it. Doing things without a purpose, or 'for their own sake' is something that has become essential to the modern consumer. Why? Today we might describe the purpose of Petrarch's journey as one of personal development, or growth. More recent paintings from, say, William Turner, to Pablo Picasso, to Jackson Pollock, to Damien Hirst, all testify to the artist's growing self-confidence in 'his personal vision', rather than requiring any deference to the 'natural' world around him. This is not to make any specific criticism of an individual artist, but to show how we, as a society have become worshippers at the shrine of unbridled, infantile, individual expression.

Early in the 20th century Paul Klee validated the notion of totally arbitrary license in his idea of 'taking a line for a walk'. Once you start moving your pen, you can choose to move in any direction. In the 1960s, Jackson Pollock did a similar thing, but on a bigger scale, and at a much greater speed. By the end of the century, Damien Hirst was making huge 'spin paintings' that needed even less intervention by the artist's hand. In today's world of celebrity, actions by famous people tend be seen as exempt from responsibility. To some extent this has become an ethics of who you are, rather than how you fit into the world of deeds and intentions. If a famous artist chooses to use vast quantities of precious or toxic materials to make a gigantic sculpture this is more likely to enhance his reputation as a naughty child, rather than a self -centred adult. Hirst's gigantic toy Hymn (1996), and Rachel Whiteread's installation, *Embankment* (2005), fabricated from 14,000 polyethylene casts of the insides of large cardboard boxes, were both criticised for their extravagant use of material resources. The decision by the artists Jake and Dino Chapman to purchase and then to deface a set of etchings by Goya led to their being short-listed for the UK's coveted 2003 Turner Prize. In the world of the shrinking taboo, what are the ultimate limits beyond which an artist would not wish to go? In the literary world the parallels may be less congruent with the end of the BritArt era, but the general public has been just as enthralled by a majestic ego, whether it be more introvert, or extrovert. We have enjoyed reading about it in the exploits of William James, John Steinbeck, Jack Kerouac, Norman Mailer, William Burroughs, and Ted Hughes. We can also discern it from the earnest egoism of Beethoven and Wagner, and the blind creative tenacity of Schönberg, Stravinsky, Cage, or Glass. Performers can celebrate creative heroism more easily than artists who only leave a trace of their presence. In its raw form, exponents such as Antonin Artaud, Charlie Parker or John Lydon (aka Johnny Rotten) brought an eccentric recklessness that is made more spectacular by unfolding 'live' before the audience. The world of fashion exploits our craving for individualism and our fascination with celebrity. Historically, it has clear connections to the pre-revolutionary French Court. The fashion designer Vivien Westwood has played with this idea in a wonderful way by alluding to it both explicitly and implicitly. Because of her vision, as an ordinary citizen I can purchase an ermine suit, sceptre, or crown and learn to walk and talk like Prince Charles. In a world of commoners, noble birth is not attainable, but if I buy the right accoutrements I can 'feel like a million dollars'.

At one time the celebratory enactment of wellbeing itself was enough in itself. Indeed, the golden years of Hollywood abounded with images of glowing self-contentment and power, as demonstrated in the charm and charisma of actors such as Clark Gable, John Wayne, David Niven, Dean Martin and Sammy Davis Junior. After a while, it became even more self-conscious with the notion of 'cool'. We may see this in the confident unflappability of Lou Reed, Frank Sinatra, Johnny Cash or the brothers from Oasis. It is usually male actors, such as Lawrence Olivier, Humphrey Bogart, Richard Burton, Michael Caine, James Fox, and Jeremy Irons whom we may be more likely to remember when we think about self-confident self-observation. Perhaps we can think of female examples such as Dame Edith Evans or Bette Davis, but these are comparatively rare. Most manage it less broodingly, and more coquettishly. Angela Lansbury, Elizabeth Taylor, Meryl Streep, Julie Andrews, Barbara Streisand, Goldie Hawn, Cher or Glenn Close come to mind. In more recent times, the insatiable demands of our global growth economy have encouraged us to focus upon desire, rather than its gratification. This is always good for business. Today, many of the most famous male stars in Hollywood are better known for their tireless enactment of disappointment and disdain. Here we may pay particular attention to the self-awareness that accompanies an uncomfortable sense of craving. Indeed, in the 'needy look' of on-screen, or off-screen actors such as Sylvester Stallone, Clint Eastwood, Al Pacino, Harrison Ford, Nicholas Cage, Mel Gibson, Madonna, Michael Douglas, or in some work by Samuel L. Jackson we see an infantile ego that seems to say, 'I deserve more'.

It is hard to over-indulge oneself indefinitely without feeling tired, bored, jaded or confused. Cynicism and irony therefore play a major role in our modern solipsistic world. In the last few decades, they have become indispensable ingredients of global capitalism. For this reason, we can also find that we are moving towards narratives that cannot be bound by their own internal structure and logic alone. In all cases, higher orders of feedback are becoming necessary to sustain continuity across the whole system of production. Irony is a convenient way to merchandise disconnected or inconsistent beliefs. It displays a sense of self-awareness in which the subject can appear to be 'of' the world, yet also above it. This can be seen in the ironic, self-aware productions of Mel Brooks,

Quentin Tarantino, David Lynch or George Michael. Many artists have long shown a natural flair for self-reflexive self-promotion. Salvador Dali, Marcel Duchamp, and Gilbert and George have all used it. Sociology, Constructivism and Cybernetics have given us additional tools and techniques to make the Dandy into an even more distinctively 'self-made' man. How many levels of self-celebratory smugness can we find in Ricky Gervais (a.k.a. 'David Brent', star of the British television series *The Office*) and in the sardonically self-effacing, self-analytical self-promotional tactics of self-made novelist Will Self? We now find it at an equally sophisticated level in the self-awareness of Cindy Sherman, Tracy Emin, Damien Hirst, Robbie Williams, or Tony Blair. Any such study of the self-observing observer raises methodological issues because observer, observed and observation cannot always be differentiated. This problem will become even more difficult when we encounter further levels of reflexive irony in the way we manage our self-identity as model citizens on the catwalk of life.

Being self-aware is not a crime. However, the quality of awareness is important if we are concerned about egoism. Let us take, for example, Rene Descartes' (1596–1650) famous questioning of whether he existed. Here, his model of self-reference is highly reduced if, by 'self' we mean a singular entity that conceptually defines its own existence. Leibniz's idea of the 'monadic self' emerged from a similar, rather cold and cerebral approach. George Berkeley (1685–1753) offered a counterpart to this idea, arguing that self-reference only makes sense when conducted in conjunction with another entity (for example a person) that is aware of you. Loosely speaking, nobody exists unless he, she or it is perceived by somebody, or by something else. This seemingly simple model lends itself to a fair degree of interactive complexity. It is likely that Socrates acquired a somewhat truncated account of Confucian wisdom and therefore began his arguments in somewhat reduced terms. This is what may have inspired the somewhat uncanny notion of Western dualism that has enjoyed a particular cachet after Lutherism and Capitalism. Perhaps this why seeing oneself as a machine is funny. In Western thought the notion of 'self-regulation' can also be traced to the individualistic roots of Christianity, and early humanism. Today, the modern Western self can be parodied as a digital, interactive gadget. Perhaps the humble thermostatic system merely reminds us of the moral lesson that every creature should get more closely in touch with itself. Half a millenium ago, Erasmus (1466–1536) challenged the Calvinist emphasis on Christ as the sole source of redemption. Instead, he espoused a belief in 'free will' and 'virtuous actions' as part of the equation. Within this humanist framework, our spiritual destiny became more answerable to the self. However, the Protestant license to become introspective led to a possible bifurcation between self-approval and self-criticism. This is one of the important boundaries upon which the Dandy does most of his 'conceptual surfing'. Crudely speaking, this system is a cornerstone of the 'self-organising self'. In 1973, looking distinctly pale and shaky President Nixon greeted reporters outside the courtroom of the Watergate hearings. 'How are you feeling, Mr. President?' a journalist called out. 'My doctors tell me I feel fine', Nixon quipped. The irony of this answer tells us two things that most of us may assume to be 'natural'. The first is that we always expect to have our own experiences. The second is that we can interpret our own experiences from the experience of someone else.

It is hard to escape from the reductionist mindset of Descartes and Locke. Industrialisation is also to blame. However, Foucault (1977) and others have shown that the mechanical routines of self-representation and self-projection also became internalised through militarism and the Catholic Church. Later, it was further individualised via developments such as psychoanalysis. Sloterdijk (1988) has argued that it is the modern citizen's 'enlightened false consciousness' that helps to maintain the *status quo*. At a popular level, our growing acquaintance with systems theory has made us more aware of the feedback paths that sustain our habits, and that make us cynical and manipulative.

This idea can be traced to early systems of power and presence that are embodied in Aristotle's discussions of rhetoric. Whereas the idea of individual self-control became conceivable during the 18th century, in the 20th century we increasingly refer to systems that regulate or create themselves. This idea derives from the disciplines of cybernetics that emerged during the mid-20th century. In the evolution of cybernetics, or Systems Theory (for example Wiener, 1948), the idea of regulation was based on the early Greek realisation that negative feedback can be used to control a given parameter in a system. It seemed to offer a nicely self-contained way to describe, for example, how rudders steer boats, or how thermostats regulate the temperature of things. Following this logic it appeared that robots would simply need to be able to identify and compensate for their errors in order to function like living beings. Several decades later it became clear that this view was inadequate to describe complex systems (for example Penrose, 1989). No system exists in isolation. A revised, or 'second-order' cybernetics began to emerge; one in which positive feedback played a vital role in the behaviour of large, complex systems found in nature. The attendant recognition that all systems are 'open systems' represents an implicit challenge to the solipsistic legacy of Descartes and Berkeley. However, their language lives on. Although Heinz von Foerster's (1911–2002) phrases, 'we think, therefore we are', and, 'to know is to be' (Scott, 2000) are indicative of a conscious attempt to exorcise the dualistic assumptions implicit in Cartesian solipsism, the individualistic mindset is hard to replace. Gordon Pask's theory of conversations (1975) appears to build from similar dualistic and solipsistic presuppositions. A more satisfying application of second-order cybernetics can be found in James Lovelock's *Gaia Theory* (1995), which points to the importance of interplay between positive and negative feedback. It also serves to illustrate that interdependence is necessary for collective survival.

How might one inspect this proposition from the standpoint of individualism? Where events in the so-called real world are complex and entangled, it is possible to simplify some of their salient features by mapping them in a diagram. Once things are mapped they can be used to focus attention on the way we experience things around us. In seeking an action-based self-mapping tool that is simple enough to use without the need for an instruction manual, we can start with an index that is confined to 'direction' and 'scale' (see Figure 2.1).

This enables us to map subjective feelings and to log their possible role in an actual situation. The chart can therefore be used in conjunction with a specific task. It may also serve as a guide for how to imagine events that are within, or outside us, no matter how large or small they may be. These dimensions correspond to the level or phase of action, and the scale of transactional involvement. The 'direction of action' relates to whether the action is more a fulfilment of 'rights' or 'responsibilities'. When the user looks at each of the possible qualifiers a meditative experience is possible, although the experience sometimes invokes an awareness of all of the things that co-exist within, and without us. This is a healthy way to avoid becoming too self-contained, egotistical, or isolated.

	Direction of Action	Scale of Action
RANGE:	Inward-facing ←•••→ outward-facing	Micro level ←••••→ macro level
		(local/topical/concrete) ←••••→ (general/abstract)
QUALIFIER:	Dependent on ethical balance required	Date/time in the site of the event concerned
Example:	Inhaling/ ←•••→ exhaling/	'Here and now' ←•••→ 'everywhere'
	Listening ←•••→ speaking	

Figure 2.1   Tool for self-enquiry that uses only two dimensions

References

Borges, J. L. (1964), 'On the cult of books' in *Other Inquisitions, 1937-1952*, Simms, R. L. (trans.), p.117 (Austin: University of Texas Press).

Buchanan, R. (1989), 'Declaration by design: rhetoric, argument, and demonstration in design practice' in *Design Discourse: History, Theory and Criticism*, Margolin, V. (ed.), pp. 91–109 (Chicago: University of Chicago Press).

Campbell, C. (1987), *The Romantic Ethic and the Spirit of Modern Consumerism* (Oxford: Blackwell Publishing).

Defoe, D. (2005), *Approaches to Teaching Defoe's Robinson Crusoe*, Novak, M., E. and Fisher, C. (eds.) (New York: Modern Language Association of America).

Forty, A. (1986), *Objects of Desire: Design and Society, 1750–1980* (London: Thames & Hudson).

Foucault, M. (1977), *Discipline and Punish*, Sheridan, A. (trans.) (New York: Pantheon).

Goffman, E. (1959), *The Presentation of Self in Everyday Life* (Garden City, NY: Doubleday Publishing and Company, Inc.).

Habermas, J. (1968), *Towards a Rational Society* (London: Heinemann).

Haug, W.F. (1986), *Critique of Commodity Aesthetics: Appearance, Sexuality and Advertising in Capitalist Society* (Cambridge: Polity Press).

Keown, D. (1998), 'Embodying virtue: a buddhist perspective on virtual reality' in *The Virtual Embodied*, Wood, J. (ed.) (London and New York: Routledge).

Lacan, J. (1977), 'The mirror stage as formative of the function of the I as revealed in psychoanalytic experience' in *Écrits: A Selection*, Sheridan, A (trans.) (London: Tavistock/Routledge).

Leibniz, G.W. (1951) 'Essays on the goodness of god' in *Theodicy*, Huggard, E. M. (trans.), Farrer, A. (ed.) (London: Routledge and Kegan Paul).

Locke, J. and Woolhouse, R. (1690), *An Essay Concerning Human Understanding* (published 1998) (London: Penguin Classics).

Lovelock, J. (1995), *Ages of Gaia* (Oxford: Oxford University Press).

Macpherson, C.B. (1975), *The Political Theory of Possessive Individualism: Hobbes to Locke* (London and New York: Oxford University Press).

Marx, K. (1988), *Economic and Philosophic Manuscripts of 1844 and The Communist Manifesto*, Milligan, M., Marx, K. and Engels, F. (trans.) (Amherst, NY: Prometheus Books).

Maslow, A. (1987), *Motivation and Personality*, 2nd edition (New York: Harper & Row).

Merchant, C. (1980), *The Death of Nature; Women, Ecology, and the Scientific Revolution*, (London: Wildwood House).

Nader, R. (2000), *Cutting Corporate Welfare* (New York: Seven Stories Press).

Pask, G. (1975), *Conversation, Cognition and Learning* (Amsterdam: Elsevier).

Penrose, R. (1989), *The Emperor's New Mind* (Oxford: Oxford University Press).

Plato (1990), *Gorgias: A Revised Text, with Introduction and Commentary*, Dodds, E. R. (ed.) (Oxford: Clarendon Press).

Rogers, C. R. (1995), *On Becoming a Person: A Therapist's View of Psychotherapy*, (Boston: Houghton Mifflin Co).

Rogers, C. R. (1951), *Client-centred Therapy: Its Current Practice, Implications, and Theory* (Boston: Houghton Mifflin Co).

Scott, B. (2000), 'A Design for the Recursive Construction of Learning Communities', Paper for the Second International Conference on Sociocybernetics, June 25–July 2, Panticosa, Spain.

Sloterdijk, P. (1988), *The Critique of Cynical Reason* (London: Verso).

Swift, J. and Vogel, M. G. (1995), *Gulliver's Travels* (New York: Baronet Books).

Veenhoven, R. (2007), *World Database of Happiness*. Available at: www1.eur.nl/fsw/happiness (Rotterdam: Erasmus University).

Veitch, J. (ed.) (1907), *The Method, Meditations and Selections from the Principles of Descartes* (Edinburgh: Blackwood).

Wiener, N. (1948), *Cybernetics* (Cambridge, MA: MIT Press).

Williams, J. (2005), 'One-person households: a resource time bomb?' *Ecosystems and Sustainable Development*, pp. 409–418. Available at: http://library.witpress.com/pages/PaperInfo.asp?PaperID=14806

Williams, R. (1961), *The Long Revolution* (London: Encore Editions).

Wood, J. (1998), 'Re-designing the present' in *The Virtual Embodied* pp. 88–101 (London; New York: Routledge). Simultaneously published in USA and Canada: ISBN 0–415-16025–1 (hardback); ISBN 0–415-16026-X (paperback).

Bureaucracy

'It is not necessary to accept everything as true, one must only accept it as necessary.'

(*The Trial*, Franz Kafka, 1925)

The previous chapter sought to explain why modern citizens acquired their license to individuate themselves as consumers; but in focusing upon this facet of the modern citizen it overlooked the fact that we also treat ourselves like anonymous cogs in a large machine. It is, perhaps, remarkable that these virtually opposite images co-exist in the consumer's imagination. However, where solipsism is comparatively recent, centralised management systems have been around for thousands of years. Today they are described as 'bureaucratic', a French word that derives from the baize that covers a writing desk. In a letter of July 1, 1764, the French Baron de Grimm declared: 'We are obsessed by the idea of regulation, and our Masters of Requests refuse to understand that there is an infinity of things in a great state with which a government should not concern itself.' Although in recent times bureaucracy began its rise in the 18th and 19th century, by the 20th century it was continuing to define new boundaries. Today, we have to contend with increasingly devious and intrusive styles of management from the major banks, utility companies and other commercial organisations. These organisations are sometimes, but not always, as conspicuously 'bureaucratic' as those described in Kafka's stories, although their desire for control may be similar. The culture of 'Quality Assurance' exemplifies it. While its advocates may fairly show that it can deliver something of what its name would suggest, bureaucracy seeks to satisfy the internal conditions for consistency, rather than confronting the realities of its external world. This is why bureaucracy is solipsistic, but where solipsists see no reason to change anything unless it threatens their interior equilibrium, bureaucrats want to homogenise everything in accordance with a pretext or plan.

This problem is worsening with the proliferation of management strategies that ask employees to trust machine data rather than human judgement, experience, or intuition. In essence, bureaucracy creates a form of chaos by enforcing rules, regulations and standards while the surrounding conditions and context undergo change. Feedback processes emphasise the past and present conditions within the context of an imagined goal. Once such a system is administered to a network of people who do not all work directly with one another, the rules have to be generalised (that is simplified) to meet the criteria of the lowest common denominator. At this point the perceived need to redefine the rules becomes stronger than the shared vision of the organisation. Without 'rules' that can be upheld, symbolic conformity is weakened. But rules are merely epistemological signifiers that operate as a pretext to actions. In other words, while they may emerge from real events, they always seek to prescribe events that have yet to pass. This is why Wittgenstein (1974) said, 'When I obey a rule I do not choose, I do it blindly'. It is possible to attribute this syndrome to the earliest origins of writing and accounting that evolved alongside the development of large-scale systems of production, trade, or military domination. In the long term, despite their obvious attraction to governments, armies and corporations, these would prove to be far more wasteful than smaller, more complex and more local systems. Digital, networked bureaucracies not only tend to make us dysfunctional, but they also alienate human society from the natural world, within whose auspices we survive. Today, some of this process has been enshrined within automatic systems that seem cheaper and more reliable than human beings. They exist as algorithms, machines and automata that tirelessly enact the rules of their masters. In the 19th century, senior administrators sent their orders to long lines of human computers. Now they are also aided by the new technologies of digital computing that enable customer management to become more automated.

Jeremy Bentham (1748–1832), the eminent jurist and writer on law and ethics tried to envision a utopia that was, to all intents and purposes, bureaucratic. In 1789, he argued that if legislators were cunning enough they could make society manage itself in an increasingly felicitous way. Up to now we have failed to find the perfect algorithms and recipes that would make this work. We might say that Bentham's vision embraces an attempt to regulate the ethical flow of a whole society by using precise meanings in language. There is some merit in this quest, although we would need to improve on the original model. This chapter suggests that our obsession with (written) 'consistency' has produced a culture of narrowness and inflexibility that adversely affects both business and education. Some of the discussion therefore continues the meditation on alphabetical writing. While the chapter concedes that the principles behind it are those that informed the development of useful systems such as computer programming, legislation and database design, it points out that they also create an arbitrary mode of inflexibility and conformity within politics, education and business. Some of these arguments also apply to assumptions behind number systems. They are therefore closely related to the discussion of clock design in Chapter 6. It seems clear that bureaucracy can emerge whenever a culture decides to diminish the importance of orality and pictographic writing in favour of simpler system of writing. Conversely, when a political power wishes to extend its empire it may find it convenient to 'dumb down' the subtleties of the culture and replace them with more primitive ideas that can be stacked up like boxes in a supermarket. Although there are examples of early bureaucracies that were sustained by pictographic systems of writing, bureaucracy seems more likely to flourish when an alphabetical writing is the lingua franca. This augments the comments about the dysfunctional and disconnected nature of our society that I made in Chapter 1.

We live in a world of flux but are governed by a framework of language that creates the illusion of stasis. We should not, therefore, blame everything on technology or bureaucracy. As the previous chapter argued, both Plato and Aristotle believed in the existence of an ideal world. In western thought, the ancient belief that (platonic) 'Forms' are immutable still influences the role of the designer. A legacy of this process is a habitual confusion between the 'real' and the 'imagined'. For example, when we build a new housing estate we create 'show houses' that fix the final forms as a way to raise expectations and to guarantee standards.

Although Aristotle suggested that we could, in a sense, recognise ideal Forms by observing the world that we see around us, he did not really challenge the belief that these Forms were immutable. In the way that the ancient Greeks presented it, it is not really clear whether the consistency referred to is at the ontological, or at the epistemological level. This confusion is perpetuated in the language we use to describe everyday events. This has become increasingly rational over the last few hundred years or so, because our technologies developed out of an understanding of absolute measurements, categories, and standards.

We say, for example, 'my idea will take the form of x, or y'. Admittedly, it is therefore hard to imagine how any sizeable utopia would be feasible without some kind of conformity, even if this is simply to ensure that there is enough goodness to warrant the description 'utopian'. Where the logic of written truth can make things seem neat and tidy, the world we experience is always more messy and complicated. Where writing can make relations seem fixed, the actual world is seldom so. In the last few tens or hundreds of thousands of years Homo sapiens has evolved certain abilities to read flat pictures and writing. What does it mean, in evolutionary terms, to be able to follow a serial text without deviating too far from its internal logic? Let us answer this question by reflecting on the traditional skills of literacy. Where writing tends to manage issues largely within its own formal constraints and terms of reference, the 'real' world is constantly producing and 're-writing' connections between everything and everything else. In comparison with the situated act of looking, writing often restrains the viewer from imagining things in different configurations. Indeed, the very ability to be able to imagine pictures, scenes and shapes from any angle is one that is advantageous in what is, at minimum, a four-dimensional world that sustains us. Alphabetical writing may be particularly frustrating in this respect because, unlike pictographic writing, it depends on the same, small set of arbitrary codes to represent different qualities and shades of meaning. Reading in a particular sequence of characters therefore becomes an important part of this process. I once met a dyslexic student who told me she was irritated by finding so much emphasis on the ability to differentiate between the letter 'b' and the letter 'd'. Surely, she said, it is merely the same shape viewed from a different angle.

Obviously, from a paedagogic perspective this is not how a normal reader is supposed to register alphabetical characters, because they operate as the ciphers in a code. However, where the meaning of codes is always unsituated, the logic of ecosystems is seldom so. The ability to interpret many simultaneous events, in their context, is more useful than being able to memorise predetermined codes. Imagine what it would be like to be abandoned deep in a rain forest without sophisticated technology or a team of helpers. In such a four-dimensional environment, what would be required to ensure a prolonged period of survival? Presumably, the ability to monitor and adapt to the whole situation is of primary importance. Compared with this, the ability to abide by an agreed grammatical and representational code would be of a far lower priority. Hence it is not surprising that wild animals lack the ability to maintain a punctual bus service or to maintain quality control on a production line or in an office. While they may remain acutely sensitive, creatively adaptive and spontaneous in their actions, their scheduling and sense of 'rigour' is therefore poor. If we wanted to improve our personal chances of survival in such a vastly complex ecosystem, what skills and aptitudes would be called for? Surely, the ability to visualise and process many simultaneous events operating at many levels would be an important one. Being experientially situated in the world means 'being in touch', and this is something that happens at the sensory, reflexive level. Hall's theory of 'proxemics' (c.f. Hall, 1968) accounts for the feeling of ease or discomfort that humans feel when they find themselves in physical proximity to others. How someone feels, for example, is subject to a number of cultural and other factors that guide the experience. In trying to map out the broad issue of context, Hall differentiates between 'intimate', 'social' and 'public' norms. It is unlikely, for example, that someone will feel comfortable when standing very close to a stranger; but this is dependent on context.

What is required is a system that reconciles oneself and the world in an active continuum of being and becoming. In developing this idea it is important to acknowledge the mental state of the subject and the particular language and context within which his, or her situation is framed, or 'reframed' (see Chapter 5). This may help to inform and elucidate an idea of shamanism that can serve as an antidote to solipsism. A key attribute of my notion of shamanism is the ability to be creatively responsive 'in the moment'. Ross Ashby (1903–74) was a pioneer in the understanding of complex systems. His 'Law of Requisite Variety' (1956) sought to define the minimum number of states by which a given system should be controlled. This suggests that it may be hazardous to reduce the number of variables within any situation if it is done without deep involvement. Real events are highly complex and it is easy to 'throw out the baby with the bathwater'. This is a common situation in management consultancy, where a reputable outsider is called in to make decisive observations about a failing, or ailing company. Ashby's Law warns that an outside observer of an existing situation seldom has enough wisdom to justify making a wise decision about the best way to maintain it, or improve it in its current form. Since Henry Ford's historic innovations within the factory system, many industries focus their attention on the internal consistencies of their operations, rather than on integrating their task within a larger social or ecological context. Instead of working to improve the net efficacy of human society at a meta-level, the factory system tends to concentrate on the logic of 'supply and demand', moderated within common economic and legal constraints. This process has produced a particular kind of bureaucratic, technological and target-orientated approach. For example, Ford's faith in mechanical processes meant that he did not trust individual workers to perform efficiently without applying his own 'scientific' rules of efficiency. While it has proved formidably successful within its own narrow frame of reference its net effects have also imposed a massive burden on the natural environment.

It is ironic that the factory system evolved from a puritanical concern for modesty, simplicity and precision because it led to cheap food, extravagance, and waste. Legend has it that President Herbert Hoover, when running for office in 1928, offered his would-be voters 'a chicken in every pot, and a car in every garage'. The historical accuracy of this story has become irrelevant, because it has left an indelible trace in the global imagination. It has rendered the American Dream almost palpable. But what is a dream? If it is what Plato or George Berkeley saw as an 'ideal' it is a somewhat materialistic, process-driven one. Its conformity is, perhaps, surprising, given the much-vaunted vision of rugged individualism within American popular culture. Its waspish, neighbourly conformity is also exemplified in the utopian 'Celebration Village', built by the Disney Corporation in Florida, or even in Prince Charles's model village at Poundbury in Dorset, UK. In both cases, their designers have opted for style codes that standardise the unpretentious colours and detailing on doors, windows, fittings, and so on. This approach may be satisfying, although not necessarily ideal, for any inhabitants who loathe untidiness, subversion, or deviation. Otherwise, it might seem almost alien to a politics of inclusion. Arguably, singular models of utopia will always produce a kind of aesthetic totalitarianism in which subjectivity is sacrificed in the interests of uniformity (Carey, 1999). As Chapter 5 will show, they are also fashioned from within the written language of qualities, names, descriptions and categorical boundaries. In short, we live mainly in a world of names and forms. One of the reasons why Bentham's 1789 model of 'felicitus calculus' (c.f. Bentham & Lafleur, 1948) did not achieve its purpose is that it embodies a 'top-down' process in which the rules are dictated by the legislators. One might therefore see this as a kind of 'design by algorithm'. In this approach, the laws would need to be understood and approved by most citizens. Conventionally speaking, this process is largely a negative one in which the limits of propriety are defined as categories. These categories are usually associated with penalties, taxes, or punishments of one sort or another. Normally, the designers of a legislative system would expect there to be a clear and appropriate grammar for the logic of governance. This has important differences with the domain of forms, in which actions are not demarcated by declaring negative limits, but are inspired by the pragmatic discourse of affordances (cf. Gibson, 1979; Norman, 1988). This is not to say that our lives are fabricated wholly within the language of forms, textures or colours, but that they are guided and monitored by the instructions and affordances they convey. Normally, designers work between the discourses of both name and form. For example, most of them spend a great deal of their time interpreting, clarifying, or trying to subvert design briefs and product specifications that are written. However, many designers feel more at home with the notion of 'form' as the significant domain within which they operate. Many are also happy to redirect the rules of a given grammatical structure at the same time that they work within it.

In the final chapter of Lewis Carroll's book *Alice in Wonderland*, it dawns on Alice that she had been working to a tiresome set of rules that were constraining her actions. 'You're nothing but a pack of cards!' she suddenly exclaims to the Kings, Queens and courtiers. At that moment it had become clear that what seemed to be a real predicament was really only a meta-level description left over from of an older set of power relations. Carroll's games with language exemplify the reverie of creation that can lead to a wiser understanding of our role in the scheme of things.

Would it be possible to extend this argument beyond the pages of a book and into the world in which we walk around and speak with others? May we assume, for example, that the scientific notion of 'laws' is dubious? What if complex living organisms were not bound by inflexible rules? Perhaps what we hold to be the laws of physics are merely epistemological categories that are inferred by scientists. Arguably, Nature has no 'rules' if, by this term, we describe dependable categories of meaning that remain constant throughout their utterance. Hence, although the Newtonian laws of ballistics were contradicted or, at least, amended by Einstein, they are still used by NASA and other agencies to ensure that projectiles land on their intended destinations. The role of rules and algorithms is a key issue within the quest for micro-utopias. For example, grammatical rules are never central to a language, merely adjacent to it. Nonetheless, many educators like to preserve the illusion that grammars are as 'real' as the languages they regulate. However, the rules of grammar are, at best, an emergent superset of the process of languaging. They work as a meta-language that functions, post-hoc, to uphold and conserve certain prescriptive values or processes. This is an issue that informs the health of democracy. How can we find freedom if we are unable to rewrite the codes that pertain to a given situated question or task? (cf. Minsky, in Horgan, 1994). The early Dadaist and Surrealist Alfred Jarry (1873–1907) postulated a 'counter-science' that he called 'Pataphysics'. Jarry sought to see each and every entity as totally unique and subject to its own laws. This idea may seem mischievous, or even baffling for many of us who, from our early years, have been steeped in the apparent certainties of mathematical and alphabetical writing. Indeed, Jarry's provocation is so unusual that it is hard not to see it merely as a joke. It is corroborated, however, by the later theories of Alfred North Whitehead (1861–1947); if true, this argument suggests that Jarry's claim cannot logically be disproved, because all 'laws' are merely propositions that would be subject to the same fluctuations as things in the so-called 'real' world. This is the central argument of the chapter. If we were to work towards a more micro-utopian TOE (that is 'Theory of Everything'), a Pataphysical approach is helpful because it puts the citizen into a kind of devotional stance that invites reverie

and wonderment. This is a tall order, as it soon leads to an idea of holism
that resists any definition within a factual (that is atomistic) framework. If we
were to write down some secrets of survival in the wilderness they are most
likely to prove dangerously incomplete, in practice. This is why 'wisdom' is
probably too mercurial and emergent to be encapsulated in the rigid codes
of alphabetical writing. It seems likely that the development of quantum
computing will transform the way we use logic. Where the binary logic of
digital computers applies a dumb, categorical approach to meaning, quantum
logic accommodates a more situated, pluralistic notion of truth. Heraclitus was
clear about the lack of constancy that he observed in the world. One version
of his aphorism states that, 'we both step, and yet do not step into the same
river'. But, if constancy were a false assumption, we would only know about
it if there were a close correspondence between the experiential realm and the
language that describes it. Without such a correspondence, we would not be
able to verify what we think we see. Interestingly, the myths that emerged after
Heraclitus were formulated within the culture of alphabetical writing. As such,
they opened the way for solipsistic thinking and 'modal thought'. It would
seem that we have Aristotle to thank for the logic of 'modes' in which things are
assigned to a fixed category and dealt with only within that category.

It is important to realise that the post-Heraclitean legacy of thought
has tended to overlook the entanglement of ontology and epistemology.
In philosophy, 'epistemology' means, in effect, a concern for the domain of
meaning, signification, or truth. By contrast, 'ontology' describes the domain
of what exists or, simply 'is'. In believing that bureaucracy is a 'reality' one
withdraws from the ecological domain in order to emphasise the artificially
rigid domain of nomenclature and codes. To those who have placed their faith
in the dependability of such coding systems, Heraclitus appears as a minor
forerunner of intellectual giants such as Socrates, Plato or Aristotle. This is a
common apprehension. Others who acknowledged the central importance of
the fact that the world is alive and mercurial are less dismissive. Nietzsche
(1966) said that 'The world forever needs the truth, hence the world forever
needs Heraclitus'. Although no written text by Heraclitus survives, he was
born less than a century after the Greeks adopted a version of the Phoenician
alphabet in 480 BCE. This means he was almost certainly aware of the transition
from a pictographic form of writing to an alphabetical one. The Greeks had
a great trading empire to run, so they had decided to use a simpler writing
system in order to make international commerce easier. The new alphabet was
a phonetic system that worked (more or less) additively – that is 'brick-on-
brick'. Unlike pictographic writing with many levels of meaning, it was more
reductive, working as a code with only a vestigial meaning of its own. This story

is not unique to ancient Greece. Many other cultures have undergone a similar transition. Indeed, this process has been part of the history of imperialism and the need to do business across the barriers of culture and language. It represents what we now call a 'trade-off'. In a thriving commercial empire, by 'dumbing-down' the meanings and value-system of the local discourse it is easier to trade with outsiders. A simpler and less ambiguous grammar might lead to a lower common denominator that enriches the common currency across a larger market. It is interesting to read Heraclitus within this context.

Several generations after Heraclitus (390–322 BCE) Plato (427–347 BCE) acknowledged the implications of his arguments, complaining that books are 'like the painted figures that seem to be alive, but do not answer a word to the questions they are asked… the teacher selects its pupils but the book does not select its readers, who may be wicked or stupid.' It is a fair point. The propensity of writing to defy the multifarious and unstable nature of the world has proved to be a mixed blessing. On the one hand, we can record agreements in such a way that they remain beyond dispute for a long time. However, in a litigious world riddled with libel and copyright laws we may sympathise with Clement of Alexandria who complained (in 200 AD): 'To write all things in a book is to leave a sword in the hands of a child' (in Borges, 1964). Objections to the introduction of writing are legendary. Poster (1990) comments that writing promotes forms of spoken grammar such as lists, formulas and recipes and that these forms are rare and less conducive to reason, freedom and equality than speech. He quotes anthropologist Jack Goody's description of alphabetical writing that 'tends to arrange terms in (linear) rows and (hierarchical) columns in such a way that each item is allocated a single position, where it stands in a definite, permanent and unambiguous relationship to the others'. From a similar perspective, Baudrillard observes that the culture of writing has an alienating effect upon the writers and readers themselves: 'Speech constitutes subjects as members of a community by solidifying the ties between individuals. Print constitutes subjects as rational, autonomous egos as stable interpreters of culture who, in isolation, make logical connections from linear symbols.' From this perspective, bureaucracy is maintained by its fidelity to written alphanumeric codes.

Alphabetical systems are not equally arbitrary. Many other writing systems convey parallel meanings that serve to enrich and inform their use. For example, although ancient Egyptian hieroglyphs were alphabetical, each character had a pictographic meaning that also guided the reader's attention around the page. Likewise, in both Arabic and Hebrew each letter also conveys a numerical meaning. However, in the evolution of writing from early Greek through Latin to the modern western alphabet, each letter has lost virtually all of its original meaning. Broadly speaking it merely serves to generalise and record the succession of sounds uttered by a given speaker. While this has loosened the function of writing and has made it more accessible to readers across different cultures this also tends to reduce the intensity or poignancy of discourse. Hence, it is normal for modern readers to adopt the position of someone who is, by default, always already outside the writer's circle of friends. It feels natural to adopt anachronistic modes of writing in which our readers are unknown to us as actual people. Obviously, we have become highly adept at using the alphabet as a way to imply meanings, rather than to state them explicitly. Hence, we may create text messages, poems, aphorisms, riddles, bank statements and political promises. These are often more suggestive than declarative. They are therefore intended to work on different readers in different ways. They operate rather more connotatively than denotatively. However, by introducing a representational system that depicts the world using 'sets' of exactly equivalent categories or units (that is, accountancy) and by using alphabetical writing to standardise international systems of management and trading, we risk impairing the vital synergistic and creative nature of social intercourse. Like bureaucracy, the alphabetical system replaces (that is, 'rationalises') existing modes of thought and action with a drastically reduced range of meaning. This was intentional. The advent of 'Business English' and 'word-processor English' is like a common carrier wave that appears to unify the world's business communities. Of course, the process is sub-optimal because it tends to introduce English concepts into its users' native languages, rather than the other way round. This means that the professional language remains as a lowest common denominator, rather than as its highest common multiple.

Like dictionaries, the above systems offer a lowest common denominator because they are designed to function in isolation from their context. Today this seems utterly reasonable to us, yet it would probably have alarmed Plato, who was wary of the alphabetical book's innate tendency to separate the speaker from the listener. One type of bureaucratic logic derives from Aristotle's 'system of categories'. While it has proved useful in the design of database systems and search engines it has also affected the way many people now think. In the last few years, political and managerial scandals have highlighted an increasing trend in the way many professionals utilise the logic of category to avoid blame. And then there is the kind of wilfully applied rigorous argument we may have seen in countless television courtroom dramas. It is also part of a litigious culture of routine post-hoc justification and evasiveness that is fuelled by a fear of commercially inspired, opportunistic and even predatory use of the court system in the US. While these genres have become a source of scorn and amusement for some, they also generate real fear and misery in public, political debates and in some 'issue-centred' journalism. All of these eventualities have brought home the fact that bureaucratic procedures such as 'Cost-Benefit Analysis' and 'Quality Assurance' may intensify accountability, but often at the expense of a fully distributed ownership of due responsibility. Moreover, it may even be apparent to very many of us that an over-dependency upon procedures and rules can erode trust, human involvement, altruistic initiative, creativity, willingness and capability. While we may be amused or even horrified by these processes, it is sometimes hard to avoid being sucked in by them, especially in the workplace.

Alphabetical writing works in a qualitatively different way from that of pictographic writing. In order to uphold an extreme consistency within categorical logic, we must ensure that, for example, a particular name does not get confused with a similar or identical word. This is part of the approach that the young Bertrand Russell (1872–1970) believed would enable us to achieve a perfect language, in which every signifier has a unique and distinct role in the whole set of signifiers. Hence, in everyday speech, if two words are spelled the same they are called 'homologues'. We usually regard them to be the same word, even though the writing of this word is always used in different contexts. This idea makes more sense in the context of alphabetical languages, rather than pictographic ones. The era of mechanical printing gave it additional credibility and it was underpinned by several important theories. In the 14th century, William of Ockham (1285–1349) established an argument known as 'Ockham's Razor' (1330). This is the principle that we should never make more assumptions than the minimum needed. To put it another way, one should not increase, beyond what is necessary, the number of entities required to explain anything. Four hundred years later, Leibniz (1646–1716) added to this his theory of the 'identicality of indiscernibles'. Loosely speaking, this argues that if two entities are similar enough to be indistinguishable, then they may be able to be assumed to be the same (see Chapter 6). In the age of digital logic, this now sounds reasonable to us, but may not always have done so, even though the principle is similar to that of moveable type, which has been with us for around a thousand years. Perhaps it pre-dates all of these precedents, if it is also intrinsic to western grammar which emphasizes differentiation, rather than integration within the whole. It also sharpens the boundaries between, for example, 'inside' and 'outside', 'self and other', 'observer and subject' (Wood and Taiwo, 1997). It therefore leads us to emphasise a gap between individual author (or designer) and the writing (or design) task itself.

Some of the above arguments may seem rather remote and philosophical. They inform the book's underlying concern with the dystopian tendencies that threaten the ecosystem of the planet. However, the idea of Utopia seems to speak to a long-standing feeling of loss, or 'fall from grace' that may have arisen from the development of systematic modes of agriculture, urbanisation and imperialism. It was the scaling-up of these methods that necessitated bureaucratic procedures such as accountancy and written legislation. Each characterises the other. For without a language system that creates fixed categories we may have firm beliefs, but it is more difficult to have intellectual certainties that can be demonstrated to exist in their own right. It is hard to imagine an empire without artificial certainties, and facts or axioms are far weaker without alphabetical writing, but we risk diminishing utopias by over-defining them or by over-prescribing how they should work. Plato describes the moment when alphabetical writing was offered to the ruler of the day, King Thamus. As Plato put it, the King was reluctant to implement this New Invention because, to him, it was clear that it would corrupt or distort the essence, the structure, the elements, the connections, the balances and the tensions of the prevailing culture. Why was he so concerned about such a simple change? Well, for one thing, the change was more qualitative than quantitative. Secondly, there is a greater tendency in categorical thought to chunk complex situations into 'channels', or 'modes' of activity. This always loses value and meaning. Whereas in complex pictographic script, each flourish of the brush may carry special nuances, in an alphabet with a restricted number of letters each is utterly distinct from each other. Unlike pictographic writing, alphabetical letters act as arbitrary codes that no longer resemble the sounds they depict. Because pictographs derive from pictures they are always hand-made. Psychoanalytically speaking, they therefore reflect the situated context from which they emerged. By contrast, alphabetical letters are merely 'codes' that must conform to their own rules of identity. Hence, when you choose a font for a particular screen-based text you make no change whatsoever to the underlying letters that were selected from your keyboard. For example, a 'b' is always a 'b', irrespective of its typeface, layout, or colour. When scribes copy alphabetical documents the only way to lose meaning is when a wrong letter is used. The practical advantage of this system is that the textual essence of the message is not lost when it is transferred from one place to another. Where the logic of codes is absolute this is not the case when we try to remember what someone said yesterday. Nor is it the case with pictographic writing, because the forms of the characters may still carry nuances of pictorial meaning. As such, the way they are written may add nuances of meaning that cannot easily be copied by another human being. This is because humans respond emotionally to forms before they can depict them, thus enabling a great deal of knowledge to be conveyed as tacit wisdom that cannot easily be recorded alphabetically.

The domains of computer programming and jurisprudence come to mind, here. In software authoring, alphanumeric codes are used to set up (internal) rules and procedures that become enacted within the working system and those parts of the actual (external) world to which it is connected. The legal system has an even greater sphere of co-creative influence. Jurisprudence is the name given to the philosophy of law and it's working. Because it lays down the probable conditions for legal statutes and case law, some legislators could even see it as a mode of metadesign. Although the law is a set of rules that are intended to provide justice within society, legislators act within the certain knowledge that these rules will be challenged, bent and broken. Nevertheless, in our increasingly bureaucratic society we have tended to use this process in an instrumentally rational way, in order to maximise profits, maintain power and elicit maximum compliance with the *status quo*. This has encouraged us to believe that the 'truth' resides in documentary 'facts', rather than in the experiential 'flow' of events. It is offered in the hope that we can return to a more fluent, relevance-centred and integrative way of living. If this were so, why would society have wanted to introduce such an alienating discourse? The short answer to this question is that alphabetical writing helped to facilitate imperialism and international trade. Historically, its introduction makes it easier for governments or corporations to implement clear operational boundaries that make unequivocal distinctions between individual items of property or discrete actions.

More recently, the culture of global consumption has influenced a political approach that encourages more of a more eudaemonic, or 'feel-good', ethics, rather than an uncompromising morality of 'right' and 'wrong'. Optimistically speaking, this opens up the possibility of governance by laws designed to bring about shared well-being. If we follow the advice offered by religions such as Hinduism and Buddhism, we may seek to develop an experiential discourse of 'flow', rather than seeking to focus on names and on other categories of being. This is also the conclusion of Csikszentmihalyi (1990) who explored the source of happiness in many individuals from many different social strata, cultures, and countries. In contrast to the logic of 'flow' it may be clear that design is a highly intrusive activity that creates or shifts categories in order to create new meanings and 'affordances'. The following chapter criticises the bureaucratic metaphor of 'rigour', hoping to encourage a form of 'design shamanism'. Rigour cannot helpfully be applied to circumstances in which change influences the mode of logic that has worked previously. This is because relevance is at least as important as rigour in informing the complex synergetics of the actual. Where, for instance, an epistemology such as mathematics may show a high level of coherence within its own terms, there is usually an arbitrary relationship between the systems it is used to model, and the truths that it is deemed to express. When this occurs, non-rigorous (for example abductive, heuristic or contingent) logic must be summoned in order to choose, modify and apply relevant algorithms to problems at pertinent times throughout their unfoldment. To summarise, in practical or purpose-centred problems, whereas relevance without rigour may sometimes be immediately helpful, this is seldom true of rigour without relevance.

As I have suggested, the relationship between humanity and Nature has become increasingly dominated by technological and other modes of instrumentalism. This can be characterised by the mechanistic Galileian and Newtonian paradigms of cause and effect, rather than by more organic models of reciprocal co-sustainment. This serves to explain, for example, why many people in the prosperous nations may feel that their quality of life does not equate with their level of income. Ultimately, the current epoch of competitive overproduction can be characterised, briefly, by the constant technological quest for increased productivity, ubiquity and invisibility of supply. For the individual consumer, the delivery of these attributes can be summarised as the implicit duty to attain comfort, satisfaction and self-respect at all places and at all times. Today, rather than rewarding ecologically solipsistic behaviour we need citizens who are more shamanistic. Here, I would define shamanism as a state of being in touch with everything around one, while being immediately and acutely reconciled with everything within one. Being a shamanistic citizen would therefore not only mean being deeply, positively and actively in touch with one's own feelings and reactions; it would also mean being in immediate touch with the feelings and reactions of society. A shamanistic master planner, civil servant, healer, or architect, for example, would act more imaginatively, holistically and contingently within a local context. This new criterion is what is needed for many of us, as designers, planners, politicians and citizens if we are to live more rewarding, meaningful lives at the local level.

References

Ashby, W. R. (1956), *Introduction to Cybernetics* (New York: Wiley).

Bentham, J. and Lafleur, L. J. (1948), *An Introduction to the Principles of Morals and Legislation* (New York: Hafner Publishing Company). Available at: www.la.utexas.edu/research/poltheory/bentham/ipml/index.html (University of Texas at Austin's Classical Utilitarians website).

Borges, J. L. (1964), 'On the cult of books', in *Other Inquisitions, 1937-1952*, Simms, R. L. (trans.) (Texas: University of Texas Press).

Carey, J. (1999), *The Faber Book of Utopias* (London: Faber & Faber).

Csikszentmihalyi, M. (1990), *Flow: the Psychology of Optimal Experience* (New York: Harper & Row).

Gibson, J. J. (1979), *The Ecological Approach to Visual Perception* (Boston: Houghton Mifflin Co).

Hall, E. T. (1968), 'Proxemics' in *Current Anthropology*, 9:2/3, pp. 83–108. [DOI: 10.1086/200975].

Minsky, M. (1994), Interview in Horgan, J. (1994), 'Can science explain consciousness?' *Scientific American*, July, pp. 88–94.

Kafka, F. (1925), *The Trial*, Muir, W. and Muir, E. (trans.) (New York: Schloken Books).

Nietschze, F. (1962), *Philosophy in the Tragic Age of the Greeks* (Washington DC: Regnery Publishing Inc. Eagle Publishing Company).

Norman, D. A. (1988), *The Psychology of Everyday Things*, pp. 87–92 (New York: Basic Books).

Poster, M. (1990), *The Mode of Information* (Cambridge: Polity Press).

Wittgenstein, L. (1974), *Tractatus Logico Philosophicus* (Routledge and Kegan Paul).

Wood, J. and Taiwo, O. (1997), 'Some Proprioceptive Observations of 'Being-With'', paper given at the Problems of Action and Observation Conference (Amsterdam: University of Amsterdam).

Academic Rigour

'From the fact that in Einstein's point of view no signal faster than light is possible, it follows that the concept of a rigid body breaks down.'

(Bohm, 1980)

One of the underlying aims of this book is to challenge the current political preference for short-term pragmatism at the expense of long-term vision. Where Chapter 3 questioned the role of bureaucratic governance and management, similar questions are posed here for educators. Over the last few decades, rather than developing a sense of the deep purpose of education, universities and schools have become preoccupied by equity and impartiality. This is reflected in some dubious concepts, such as 'academic rigour', 'level playing fields' and 'transferable skills'. All of these ideas represent a basic misunderstanding about how humans cope best with a world in flux. Similar issues emerge with terms like 'sustainable consumption', and 'sustainable business'. All reflect a misunderstanding of the way organisms learn, adapt and evolve in the natural world. What is urgently needed is a discussion of the profound purpose of education. According to Handy (1998) corporations tend to forget that, ultimately, they are servants of society. If service to society is the purpose of business, what is the deep purpose of education? In my view, it should be to enable learners to become more harmoniously integrated with their habitat. This is illustrated by describing some of the many layers of intelligent adaptation that go towards enabling integration and wholeness on different levels; for example, sensory, linguistic, social, cultural, biological, ecological, or spiritual. On the one hand some students are able to cheat their teachers by buying ready-made essays online. On the other hand, their teachers may speak of 'scholastic rigour' yet be deceived. Previous chapters of the book have suggested that the responsible citizen of the future will need to become more like a 'shaman'. In other words, he or she must become more imaginatively in touch with the ebb and flow of the living world. While this will mean thinking and writing in order to deepen his or her understanding of the world, 'rigorous' writing is more affected by codes and constraints that reflect the internal and arbitrary logic of learning and teaching.

This chapter asserts that the idea of academic rigour is at odds with the mysterious, situated, opportunistic judgements involved with good citizenship. It is therefore addressed at educators and other professionals who continue to emphasise the role of rigour in 'good' practice. Why do we continue to do this? There is nothing intrinsically wrong with learning to read, write and add figures. However, much of our obsession with literacy levels, or with the memorisation of names and facts, 'tick-boxes', attainment targets and the political obsession for fairness still drives the school system and, to some extent, our universities. Although young learners will spend their subsequent lives learning to work in cooperation with others, educators still insist on testing their development as solitary candidates who have been removed from a situated context. Moreover, they also tend to apply external, faceless and arbitrary standards of attainment. These are all symptoms of the bureaucratic and solipsistic society. It may be helpful to consider the culture of design education, because it highlights the issues well, albeit from a somewhat eccentric perspective. Historically, in the way they have been taught, all of the art school practices represent an uncomfortable fusion between the meditative mediaeval culture of the printed word and an atelier system based on 'learning by doing'. While it is clearly a special case it is, nevertheless, a useful basis from which to reflect upon all other modes of teaching and learning. Schön (1985) has shown that the methodologies of design practice and scholastic research evolved from two historically distinct traditions of thought. Loosely speaking, whereas the university 'research' tradition stemmed from the cloistered scriptoria of the monasteries, studio traditions evolved from the mediaeval craft guilds. In effect, the monasteries became the prototypes for libraries, universities and laboratories (that is the 'research' tradition), and the Craft Guilds were the antecedents of today's design studios (see Figure 4.1). This has meant that, whereas we associate scholastic knowledge mainly with 'truth' claims, design knowledge is orientated to making practical, appropriate and elegant interventions within actual situations. For this reason, it took a long time to integrate both modes of knowledge in design education. Common misunderstandings about 'scholastic rigour' are symptomatic of this confusion. As I will show, this has also become symptomatic of larger problems that are beyond the use of the term itself. This background goes some way towards explaining the moral panic about plagiarism in schools and universities. It derives from the irrational insistence on paraphernalia such as written examinations that test individuals, rather than self-managed teams. This is the context of terms such as 'academic rigour' (Wood, 1998).

Monastic truth-oriented knowledge	Crafts-guilds result-oriented knowledge
i.e. text-based knowledge that serves to validate and to fortify belief	i.e. task-based knowledge that facilitates situated actions and judgements

Figure 4.1   Differences in monastic and crafts-guilds modes of knowledge

In the academic context the idea of 'rigour' stands for 'logical accuracy and exactitude' and derives from the Latin word 'rigere' – to be stiff. According to the *Oxford English Dictionary*, it stands for 'severity, strictness, harshness… strict enforcement of rules, and so on (with the utmost rigour of the law); extremity or excess of weather, hardship, famine, and so on, great distress; austerity of life, puritanical strictness of observance or doctrine, whence rigorism'. When Karen Armstrong, the celebrated authority on religion, did her degree at Oxford University, examiners stood and applauded her viva and awarded her a first class honours. She then began teaching at the University of London while continuing with her studies as a research student at Oxford. However, although her supervisor believed her thesis to be 'brilliant', the external examiner rejected it and she eventually left academia without a doctorate (Armstrong, 2005). Although the reason for her academic failure was later agreed to have resulted from a probable travesty of academic judgement, the rules of the university were rigorous. They stated that no candidate would be allowed to re-submit for a PhD after once failing. This is not just a story of gratuitous power. It reflects a strict enforcement of rules within Judeo-Christian Puritanism. St Ignatius Loyola (1491–1556) taught his followers to accept the maxim 'henceforth as a corpse' on entering the Jesuit order. In Loyola's prayer, self-denial is expressed as a total bodily submission to the assigned task: 'to give and not to count the cost; to fight and not to heed the wounds; to labour and not to seek to rest'. Importantly, such associations reflect a Christian recoil from the sensual body and it is no accident that we use the term 'rigour' to describe the stiffness of dead bodies. We should not underestimate this association because scepticism exemplifies a denial of immediate sensory experience that may lead to a repression of certain emotions and feelings. This is important for the idea of rigorous writing because we are increasingly aware of the important role of the emotions, where learning is concerned.

As science has become so well popularised by the mass media, most readers will be familiar with the theory that the universe is a homogeneous whole. Science has tended to assume, or at least has continued to search for, evidence of 'universal laws' that permeate the universe. The term 'consilience' was coined in 1840 to claim that there is a unity across all the disciplinary boundaries of knowledge (Harper, 1989). A few years ago it was extended to suggest that the world is orderly and 'can be explained by a small number of natural laws' (Wilson, 1998). Over the last few hundred years this debate has been dominated by scientists such as Galileo, Newton, Einstein and Hawking. Although Stephen Hawking, for example, has shelved his quest for a 'Theory of Everything', the assumption behind his quest is commonly held. The principle of 'rigour' underlies our attempts to fix knowledge within autonomous truths that can be 'disembodied' from the opportunistic apprehension of their living, breathing authors. However, if failure is an important aspect of learning, could rigorous assessment be too consistent? In practice, those who believe they administer 'rigorous' methods may be deluding themselves about the attainability of rigour itself. Today, although the word is routinely used within claims to clarity and propriety, it is surprisingly under-theorised. Why is this the case? Why is the word 'rigour' still 'de rigeur' in the broad professional context of communicating, thinking and doing? Most pathologists would confirm that, in the case of a living body we couldn't predict what might happen to it over the next 3 days. When it dies, however, the level of certainty rises to almost 100 per cent. We may concede that our intuitive belief in the sensation of firmness and consistency runs in accordance with a particular bodily understanding of dependability and safety. On the other hand, we may also agree that this reflects particular cultural values that have been discredited on many levels. In short, the metaphor is not one that is easy to corroborate by exploring Nature as we find it in the Earth's biosphere. Nevertheless, intuitively speaking, our emphasis on hardness and stasis may be less unnerving. It may be often be more appealing, or compelling to us than our awareness of how things actually run. It is largely for this reason that we sustain its use. This is not inevitable. The idea of 'rigour' is only a symptom of the problem. It has become a lazy conceit that reproduces and sustains itself by its own rhetoric; and in so doing, it perpetuates a methodology that has tended to assert text before author, procedure before experience, arrival before travel, means before ends, standards before outcomes, algorithms before heuristics, rhetoric before task, consistency before inspiration, quantity before quality and bureaucracy before efficacy.

Logically speaking, if we define 'rigour' as the regulated invariance of relations or terms within a given task, this may show what it has in common with bureaucracy. It means, for example, that it will not assist us in addressing complex or synergistic elements that cannot be managed unless they, themselves, are rigid. The idea of rigour reflects an early Greek anxiety that if the world were not rigid then we could never understand it in a factual, generalised way. As Aristotle said: 'There is no knowledge of things which are in a state of flux'. In other words, it is the emergent nature of life that resists relevant analysis using categorical and symbolic logic. If we analyse rigour in terms of explicit consistencies within a system, we would need to decide which active points in its network of relations are the most important. This is not a straightforward task because relations among these properties are manifold, rather than discrete. In a ceaselessly unfolding world, the more we assume that a given quality is fixed, the less we can know about it. In this regard, the metaphor of 'rigour' is of limited usefulness in 'real' situations. It is only operative either as a theory, or as a simplified model. This is because more complex theories of rigour generate additional concerns about the solipsism that underpins our internal resistance to adaptation. It is increasingly difficult to justify to any degree of complexity, whether or not it has been modified in the light of our current understanding of ecology, biology, chemistry, or physics. Ironically, early 20th century scientific thinking showed that the concept of rigour is more applicable to waveforms, rather than to materials that are 'hard'. Information is meaningless without flow, and flow cannot occur within the context of rigour. In short, the way we invoke the metaphor of rigour is not rigorous, except in a narrowly reflexive or institutional context. This is because successful actions cannot take place without communication, which is a kind of flow that changes things in several places at once. From these assumptions, it follows that situated actions are antithetical to the fundamental principle of rigour. This critique of the idea of rigour raises issues about how an organism's internal properties communicate with those around it. However, we may infer that most of the body's intelligence during the rigorous phase would be devoted to maintaining internal consistencies, rather than communicating with the surrounding environment.

There is a difference between the behaviour of a shaman acting as a stone and a real stone. Logically speaking, the presence of rigour would seem to deny sensitivity. However, in the case of the cybernetically rigorous body, this is not so, as it simulates a rigorous state through active obstinacy. A rigorous body can therefore be said to be either intrinsically inert, or somehow able to regulate itself using negative feedback to attain an apparent state of imperviousness. Where, in an inertly rigid body there is no adaptive rapport between its internal and external conditions the cybernetically active body must act out its state of immovability. When a soft body conveys the illusion of hardness it can only be said to be soft in theoretical terms. Initially, that is at the moment (or just before) it comes into contact with something else, the cybernetically rigorous body must become receptive. This is necessary for it to know how to deny its own softness in form or location. If the intruding body continues to invade its space it must harden itself accordingly. When the threat abates, it may resume its non-rigorous state. A true shaman should be able to emulate the habits of a bureaucrat, just as he or she would be able to empathise with, and adapt to, the habits and behaviour of a businessman, fox, rabbit or stone. This is an important lesson for designers. The story of why escapologist Harry Houdini (1874–1926) died illustrates this point graphically. One of Houdini's stage acts was to invite any member of the audience to come up on stage and punch him very hard in the stomach. His reflexes and muscle control were so well tuned that he was able to simulate a rigorous target. One day, a fan that confronted him in the street unexpectedly hit him in the midriff. As he was taken by surprise he did not roll with the punch. As a result he sustained internal injuries that eventually proved fatal. In cybernetic terms, in order for a soft body to sustain, or attain a given state of apparent rigour, timely feedback signals are needed. Used in a practical managerial context, rigour is often part of an attempt to guarantee a desired outcome, or to maintain continuity in time. Many managers are proud to attain a faithful match between plan and outcome. However, this may require a rhetorical slippage between those conditions that are expected to change and those that contribute to change. Although written text may be static, what it describes is not. Consistency is therefore more likely to exist at the level of text, rather than at the actual level. This points up the need for a flexible genre of writing, rather than for a truly rigorous approach.

What I have described here is a temporal mode of 'rigour' that corresponds to the way academics commonly perceive the task of research and writing. It also seems characteristic of how we, as a species, perceive the world. It is because we are so contaminated by the temporal hegemony of writing that professional managers commonly act as though bureaucratic 'truths' were more 'real' than the proximal, actual and biological realms that enable them to exist. Such behaviour would probably have been impossible for pre-literate cultures to comprehend. Indeed, it is only when we concentrate on the artificial residues of actions (for example written texts) that the notion of rigour begins to make any sense.

This is not to say that designers or other practitioners do not really need to write. On the contrary, designers are strategically important for re-designing the world as a safer, saner place. They therefore need to inform their practice via some form of scholarship that will sensitise them to philosophical, political, ethical, ecological, technological, economic and other issues. This is easily said but difficult to achieve. Competitive professional practices do not facilitate long periods in the library, and many designers succeed commercially without much contextual reading and writing. This is a cultural, as well as a practical problem. While this chapter stresses the educational importance of writing and reading it also identifies some limitations to the scholastic mindset that informs them. How are the received models of essay writing appropriate to designers? In traditional doctoral research projects there is usually a great emphasis on the form or, rather, the style of presentation of the thesis itself. This approach has given us assessment criteria in which written and 'source-remote' information eventually assumes the status of a body of knowledge in its own right. Here, writing, rather than the candidate's wisdom, remains the primary site of appraisal, albeit supplemented by a relatively brief viva voce examination.

Edward de Bono once said: 'Scholarship has become little more than the triumph of form over content. You take some tiny part of the field of knowledge and examine it with immense detail and concentration. In the end it is your workmanship which is praised and not the importance of the subject.' (de Bono, 1973); this suggests that its underlying purpose is to enable the writer to celebrate his or her non-tacit knowledge of the topic and to win approval from senior academicians. Moreover, although traditional academic approaches can lead to profound and novel design outcomes, the scientific tradition of deductive enquiry tends to inspire robust truth claims, rather than to facilitate the intensification of an author's competence. As such, it may tend to proceed from hypothesis to theory, rather than from practice to theory to practise: and so, even though the knowledge gained may be vitally important it can easily get archived and forgotten. Today, new alliances between industry and academia continue to foster a more entrepreneurial, outcome-centred idea of aptitude. Designers will need to demonstrate both practical and theoretical aptitude in a creative combination (Cooley, 1987) if we are to make design practice more ethically and ecologically accountable. This would evaluate the terms within which their embodied knowledge is likely to be effective within a realistic context. School education still appears to emphasise the self-justifying and rhetorical aspects of writing, rather than their auto-didactic and reflective capabilities in the context of other practices. It is easy to see how a series of de-contextualised 'facts', such as those we may find in a heavy reference book were valued for their apparent durability and hence exalted within the learning process. By solidifying information into facts and storing them in great books we attributed huge kudos and importance to the 'library' culture. Later, we extended the great libraries into government-sponsored academies of learning that stood as keepers of wisdom. Very recently digital technology has enabled us to revive Diderot's 18th century vision of the Encyclopaedia as a receptacle for all human knowledge. A similar metaphor would be the idea of having a vineyard and a cellar of fine wine. A connoisseur of wine will ensure that bottles are kept at the proper temperature and labelled with the wine's provenance, year, and the name of the vintner. However, as Perry Barlow said: 'Information in a digital medium is like wine without bottles' (Barlow, 1994).

As this epithet suggests, the rigorous culture of the Book is weakening in the face of hypertext. In 1974, Ted Nelson coined the term 'intertwingularity' (Nelson, 1987) noting how people 'keep pretending they can make things deeply hierarchical, categorizable and sequential when they can't. Everything is deeply intertwingled.' If Nelson was right we have good reason to celebrate the rise of free Internet services such as Wikipedia or Amazon Book Search. Unfortunately, many academics seem to regard them more as obstacles than as benefits. Basically, because Wikipedia is not 'rigorous' it is seen as a temptation to err, rather than as an attractor of good quality thinking. There are several reasons why this situation has emerged. For one reason, the technology behind digital publishing was designed mainly for selling, managing, archiving, finding, accessing and reading texts, rather than for authoring them. In many important respects the companies who dominate the market in authoring software have fallen far behind some of the amateurs and enthusiasts who have introduced new thinking within the hypertext domain.

Although Google Searching, Blogs and 'Wikis' are useful, they represent relatively feeble advances in regard to what digital computers can do. Nevertheless, they have revolutionised the way that students read and write. Likewise, because academia has failed to discuss the deep ecological purpose of education, it has not managed to revise the assumptions on which students are taught and assessed. This has led to an absurd situation in which small, clandestine companies are making profits by selling essays to students. This would not be a problem if academics would reflect upon the reason, purpose and potential for education in the 21st century. A great proportion of students are still examined away from the context of their studies, when we know that factual knowledge is of very limited use without 'tacit knowledge' (Pascal, 1670; Polanyi, 1969; Dreyfus and Dreyfus, 1986). In the 21st century, students are still made to sit alone at desks, in rows, while writing answers to generic questions posed by anonymous examiners. This process encourages them to memorise convincing arguments that often have little bearing on how they will act in the workplace or home. A more cynical reader might argue that the written examination process trains lively minded individuals to become solipsists of the modern office.

The underlying ideologies of the UK school system still reflect the values of what used to be taught exclusively to a ruling elite in which, in turn, power was exchanged discursively through rhetorical claims and repudiation. This is why we still encourage young school students to emphasise linear, dialectical modes of argumentation in which they 'narrate' the salient features of a topic and develop it into a well-rounded and unassailable conclusion (see Figure 4.2). Indeed, scholastic rigour has itself become a central, yet largely unchallenged paradigm of academic rhetoric. The 'thesis—> antithesis—> synthesis' model has come to seem so 'natural' that it is sometimes difficult to persuade students to adopt alternative structures. Admittedly, this rhetorical, adversarial and discursive model can be versatile and engaging because it can help students:

- To recognise their own insights

- To identify with other facts, arguments and views

- To clarify their own position

- To evaluate their own knowledge

Its advocates would probably remind us that, where the task of marking becomes blurred with the task of facilitating learning, it is difficult to maintain administrative consistency over time. I would accept this. A familiar format of common procedures can be helpful for a group of learners who are sharing the same teacher or curriculum.

However, the cardinal purpose of education is to facilitate learning, rather than to ensure fair assessment. Ultimately, there are two conditions

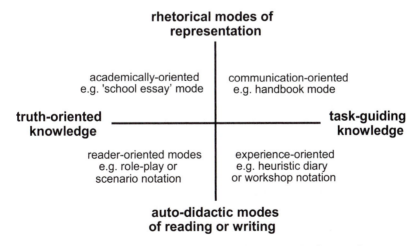

Figure 4.2   Academic writing techniques evolved from the monastic tradition

that predetermine all others in a rigorous, quantifiable assessment system. It is necessary to distinguish between the 'inside' and the 'outside' of an assessment process, and it is also necessary to make a pass or fail that is understandable to both parties. Self-assessment is therefore different from external assessment in that the self-assessor must imagine the 'outside' perspective. The world no longer believes that everyone thinks in the same way, yet we still appear to educate our children as though we did. When the marks are elicited from an actual script, if an apparent inconsistency is noticed, observer entanglement may ensue. Entanglement is therefore common because different learners have different learning styles, aims and experiences. This invalidates or impairs any claim to rigour in the strict Newtonian sense of an organism remaining impervious to the changes that might impinge on its agenda or demeanour.

One reason why we still hold onto the myth of rigour is that it is so well established.

Almost two and a half thousand years ago Aristotle (384–322 BC) believed that moving bodies naturally tend to slow down and stop. While this misapprehension is understandable, it remained unchallenged for two thousand years. Nor was Aristotle the first to find the metaphysics of rigour somewhat more appealing than that of flux. Stronger claims to rigour can be found in the writings of pre-Socratic philosophers such as *Parmenides* (born 515 BC – 450 BC) and Melissus (probably born around 470 BC). These thinkers were influential, not only for emphasising the importance of clear argumentation but also for their associated claim that we live in a single, 'rigid' universe. The quality of rigour they describe combines monogeneity and immobility, as shown here in this seemingly inconsistent description by *Parmenides* (Barnes, 1979):

> *And you must ascertain everything –*
> *Both the unmoving heart of a well-rounded truth*
> *And the opinions of mortals in which there is no true trust*

These arguments have influenced Western thought for more than 2,000 years. Of course, 'rigour' is only a metaphor. However, it is a centrally important one for both Judaism and Christianity. Perhaps this helps to explain why it enjoyed an almost axiomatic status until the arrival of 20th century science. This might in turn help to explain why we tend to confuse 'sloppiness' with a refusal to ignore the dynamic and situated context of a given case. Newton's First Law of Motion was an important step in undermining this idea because it proved the non-existence of absolute rest. Albert Einstein took the idea further and showed that space and time are dynamically interdependent (Einstein, 1920). With this insight, the idea of rigour became, if not indefensible, then anachronistic. As David Bohm explained, 'From the fact that in Einstein's point of view no signal faster than light is possible, it follows that the concept of a rigid body breaks down' (Bohm, 1980). It is interesting that the idea of a non-rigid universe troubled Einstein. Perhaps this is not so surprising because, as a Western thinker, he found it hard to accept. Stephen Hawking suggests that, in 1922, Alexander Friedmann was possibly the first modern person fully to embrace the idea of a non-static universe when he anticipated Hubble's discovery, in 1929, that the universe is expanding away from us in all directions. He muses that Friedmann's idea 'could have been predicted at any time in the 19th, 18th, or even 17th centuries. Yet so strong was the belief in a static universe that it persisted into the early 20th century' (Hawking, 1988).

Even though Quantum Physics and Chaos Theory became topics of popular interest, we continue to speak of 'firm foundations' and use metaphors such as 'concrete' and 'material' to elevate the status of thoughts and opinions. Around the time that Friedmann and Hubble were coming to terms with an expanding universe, Bohr, Dirac, Heisenberg, Planck and Schrödinger were formulating the strange laws of the Quantum world that confounded Western models of linear causality and observation. These developments have also taken their toll on epistemology and seem to coincide with Freud's emphasis on the analyst's active role of 'listening' in psychoanalysis, and with the reader theories of Ricoeur, Barthes, Lacan, Derrida, Foucault and Gadamer; who all, in different ways, argued that belief systems are unstable, therefore transient, and will perish without the support of insight and innovation. This is why, although hardly anyone really believes that the universe is solid, our desire to believe in 'rigour' coincides with a popular idea of rigidity as a paradigm of the so-called 'real' world. But if rigour is such a dubious metaphor, why has it survived into today's culture of design education? For one reason, the idea of rigour is compatible with the mediaeval corporate power structure, which led to the founding of the modern universities.

In seeking self-evident rules of fairness by which to ordain and to promote their members, the universities developed a rhetorical form in which claims to power could be tendered and considered within a fairly clear set of protocols. Here, the underlying metaphors often sound militaristic (for example, defending one's claims of truth against attack) or geological (for example, Tectonic plates as rival schools of thought). It has been argued in the past that large academies tend to regulate the flow of new ideas, in order to protect the particular doctrines that sustain their own interests. Thomas Kuhn has depicted this process as a series of plateaus and sudden troughs. The latter are described as 'paradigm shifts' (Kuhn, 1962) in which these changes of belief eventually happen suddenly, when they become so compelling that they may no longer be held back. In effect, this is an inertial metaphor that could be modelled, perhaps, using catastrophe theory or Newton's second law of motion. Feyerabend's (1975) subsequent enquiry into similar issues showed that these institutions also tended to underestimate, or ignore, the moment of insight or ideation, preferring to define the protocols and procedures by which truth claims are verified. Both tendencies seem to imply that new knowledge is ossified by the inertia of the most powerful research bodies. This has encouraged a bureaucratic culture of research that prefers proven methods rather than bolder, more imaginative innovation. Up to now this approach has proved successful in attracting large funding grants, because a tried and trusted approach is more likely to achieve predictable outcomes, even if the outcomes are of modest importance. There are signs that this lesson has been learned, although there is still some confusion about the relative role and purpose of knowledge, adaptability, innovation and discovery.

In the first part of the 20th century scientists arrived at several dramatic conclusions about the nature of certainty. In 1927, Werner Heisenberg published a paper that shows that certain aspects of the quantum realm cannot be measured. For example, he showed that it while it might be possible to know the position or the momentum of an elementary particle, it would never be possible to know both at the same time. Intuitively speaking, this is not much different from what happens when we photograph someone jumping off a table. In other words, it is impossible to record both the jumper's trajectory path (that is with a 'blurred focus'), and spatial location (that is with a 'sharp focus') at the same time. After Heisenberg published his theory, Gödel's theorem (1931) showed that in any axiomatic mathematical system there are propositions that cannot be proved or disproved within the axioms of the system. Again, although Gödel's work was not intended to be extrapolated beyond the precision of number systems, it finds resonance with the world of puns, riddles and jokes. For example, Sufi stories about the Mullah Nasrudin also play with the interdependencies and incompatibilities of 'truth' and 'consistency'. Arguably, in philosophical terms, these findings validate the fluxist arguments of Heraclitus, and confirm the entanglement of epistemology and ontology. Ironically, this is because of consistencies that are paradoxical, rather than because of inconsistencies that are transferable. By emphasising flux they tried to reflect the profoundly laminar relationship between what we can show to others, and the role of our situated presence when doing so.

In Western dualistic terms we could say that this view entails a refusal to separate language from the (so-called 'external') world. If we describe something as part of our 'living presence' we cannot also logically describe it from a standpoint of 'rigour'. This misunderstanding also reflects a mediaeval conflation between our belief in a rigid universe and the idea of the Book. When Galileo described Nature as 'a book written in mathematical language' he combined an assumption of consistency in the practical world with a corresponding assumption that the Book was an ideal form that corresponded with the form of the universe. Underlying this logic is the aesthetic principle that unless we can show that all parts of a representation, argument or proposition are monolithic or, in other words, that they share the same style that is, the whole work may be spurious. This may generate an understandable discrepancy between the culture of the academic library and that of the design studio. All of these findings put the idea of scholastic rigour into a new context that invites better modes of learning and assessment. Yet, despite these, and other insights from quantum physics, Psi research, chaos theory, and so on, our education systems continue to dumb down complexities and to design systems that are likely to deliver certainties. In my experience, many learners often find the complexity of actual relations more understandable than the artificial logic of an isolated 'law'. In a written exam, for example, it is harder to guess the 'right' answer when the context, intention and author of the question are hidden.

Another reason why the culture of rigour has endured is the influence of the tradition of monastic book production. In the closeted mediaeval monasteries where scribes painstakingly copied books by hand, errors of detail must have had an immense significance. It is hard for universities to be aloof from such ideas when they have to administer 'scrupulously fair' systems of assessment and to manage the implications of equal opportunities litigation and the reactionary logic of Quality Assurance. One possible reason for the idea of 'rigour as perfection' is the Christian belief system that incorporated the practice of writing into mediaeval monastic life. Panofsky (1968) argues that the idealised form of the Book was assumed to be homologous with the architectural form of cathedrals. Behind this morphology is the idea of the body of Christ as the prototype for truth. Hence the 'perfect', or completed book had qualities that can still be found in the classical structure of the modern scholastic thesis, with its emphasis on such familiar features as: perfection, consistency, comprehensiveness, personal detachment, linearity, objectivity and explicitness. Many of these qualities have also emerged within a Western framework of philosophical scepticism. I shall examine each of the above attributes in turn.

In this context we may understand rigour as a teleological idea of human actions, rather than as a quality of the world's natural 'becoming'. Hence a striving for perfection may be said to require rigour because we always assume that there is an ideal outcome (for example the Platonic ideal form to which craftspeople may aspire in vain). The Western idea of perfection (Blanchette, 1994) therefore refers mainly to a state of final accomplishment. This idea carries with it the notions of skill and our capacity to complete tasks without leaving any blemish or flaw. However, such an idea only makes sense within a previously agreed context and therefore is a managerial idea that raises aesthetic and other subjective questions. In today's research era, although automatic spell checking, 'cut-and-paste' and grammar guidance have altered our idea of 'perfection', there is still a residual academic suspicion that typographical errors must be symptomatic of a fundamentally flawed piece of work. Both Einstein's finite limits on the ultimate velocity of light (1915) and Heisenberg's uncertainty principle (1927) imply that the moment information arrives, it always fails to match what we expected. This imposes limits to the consistency of relationships between parts of a general argument, when seen within their full context.

Gellrich (1985) speaks of the rigid mediaeval writing style that eventually became the object of its own scrutiny, and in doing so, had to itemise – in totality – all its constituent parts or 'members', taking care to retain a structural coherence among those parts. There is a logical limit to such an exercise, however, because the integrity of linear argumentation becomes increasingly problematic as document size increases to meet the need for completeness. This is an issue in systems modelling where, because all modelling media have idiosyncrasies of their own, the model can eventually become more complex than what it was designed to emulate. Indeed, comprehensiveness also becomes inconsistent where, for example, what is being represented seems correspondingly inconsistent. This issue is illustrated by the idea of 'transferable skills'. In practice, skills are always situated within genres of practice and their actual context. They are therefore impervious to the rigours of textual equivalence. In this sense, skills may be 'adaptively re-mapped' but not 'transferred'. Here, rigour confined to the level of language may remind us of the limitations of encyclopaedic, textual or categorical logic in comparison with the situated logic of orality. This equates to what Panofsky (1968) referred to as the mediaeval 'scholastic mind'.

The idea of academic rigour is usually exemplified as argumentation in a narrative sequence rather than in aphoristic, diagrammatic, pictorial, or hypertextual form. This idea probably originates in oratory and story telling in which text became used to claim plausibility, respect, trust and belief in the speaker's case. Although narrative structures may inspire readers or listeners, we cannot easily 'write' explicitly and comprehensively about human 'attitudes' or 'postures'. Unlike the practices of reading and writing, design practice is richly non-linear. Since the Enlightenment, the vision of an objective perspective has encouraged authors to create a sense of detachment from what they address. The stylistic conceits that it produced have discouraged us from using the first person singular, and verbs in the active tense. This represents a dangerous legacy of denial about the ownership of, and therefore responsibility for, knowledge. Objectivity is only meaningful from within a dualistic mindset and it is more pleasing to imagine the universe as a unified whole. Following from the arguments above, the principle of 'bounded rationality' (Simon, 1969) confirms that a decision-maker in an actual situation will never have all the information necessary for making an optimal decision at the right time. The assumptions behind this idea of optimal decisions also raise deep questions about power and its political limits in the finite world of material culture.

In describing the habits of mediaeval scholarship Panofsky talks of 'clarification for clarification's sake', saying that it required a '...maximum of explicitness' and a 'gratuitous clarification of thought through language.' Techniques such as 'comparisons' and contrasts evolved into methods familiar to modern scholars. However, as suggested above, there is a limit to what can be made explicit. We are fully sensuous mind-body organisms in a fluent and contiguous multi-dimensional time-space world. We are therefore neither omnipotent nor dispassionate. Much of the dogma of rigour derives from the ancient Stoics who were careful to avoid their own passions. We can define scepticism as a regime of doubt, especially with regard to our own senses and opinions. This is usually seen as an intellectual issue but it has important emotional implications. Scepticism shows itself as a kind of incredulity as to the truth of supposed facts or claims and we sometimes personify this trait as an inflexible and bemused academic. Descartes was a formative influence on the development of (scientific) research methodology in the West. In his rigorous and mistrustful approach to the pursuit of knowledge he advocates the value of scepticism whose '...greatest benefit lies in freeing us from all our preconceived opinions, and providing the greatest route by which the mind may be led away from the senses'. It is at the Cartesian extremes of self-doubt that we may notice the psychoanalytical aspects of scepticism, especially where it leads us, at different levels, into an ambivalent state that oscillates between certainty and uncertainty. Ironically, while sceptics aspire to a permanent condition of stasis, their quest necessitates a dynamic process of vigilance and adaptation. In 1640, Descartes wrote: 'I realised that it was necessary, once in the course of my life, to demolish everything completely and start again from the right foundations if I want to establish anything at all in the sciences that was stable and likely to last' (Descartes, 1951).

The Cartesian aspects of the research tradition are usually associated with a logical and sceptical methodology of argumentation. This has been refined for the practices of framing answer-seeking questions that do not include the author's views, skills, or standpoint. On the other hand, responsible and thoughtful modes of design practice are less dependent upon permanent 'truths', in the academic sense. The practice of research is too time-consuming, so they are usually governed by informed and situated acts of judgement in which there is seldom a predictable – that is 'stable', 'durable' or 'certain' – answer to a given design-related question. Similarly, in the world of practical endeavour what may look like individual achievement is, almost invariably, the outcome of collaborative activity. It is interesting that education does little to teach methods such as co-authorship. Nor does it routinely assess the self-reflexive and emotional skills involving collaboration. Indeed, another symptom of our lack of attunement to educational purpose is the anxiety surrounding plagiarism. Arguably, if the learning criteria and assessment methods were to be more student-centred (for example author-reflexive) and situated, then plagiarism would be unthinkable and pointless. Instead there is a concern for grade competition, standardisation, league-tables and attainment targets. If we explore the way that creative individuals read and write we may find many anomalies. Everyone thinks and learns slightly differently. Yet an anomalous aspect of State education in the UK is the standardisation of curricula in the name of 'fairness'. Where this happens, the deeper purpose of reading is overlooked because the logic of writing is used mainly to ensure the transparency and internal consistency of assessment.

Because much of the orthodox grammar of academic discourse is generalised, both reader and writer tend to give up their identity to be part of an 'objective' claim to truth that is deemed acceptable to the academy. The seldom-acknowledged role of the rhetorical writing tradition also tends to emphasise aspects of the document's structure and style, rather than its usefulness as a process and its ultimate outcome. Significantly, in orthodox modes of academic rhetoric the modern (design) essay is not designed to address an actual reader. Today, students assume that a faceless manager of academic standards will judge it. In my experience, even when students know the actual individuals to whom they will submit their papers they seldom make any explicit concession to their particular interests, understanding or demeanour. Likewise, those tutors who have been assigned the task of reading will usually try to repress their personal position and adopt the assumed academic values and standards of the academy. More disturbingly, many design students are assigned tasks by specialist theoreticians who necessarily expect them to relate their writing to their studio practice.

If we are to raise our level of ecological attunement, the importance of propriety is only high if the value system is well attuned to the prevailing ecological conditions. One of the effects of alphabetical writing systems was to elevate idealism in space-time systems. This was probably because of the rise of very large or dispersed communities that needed organising. This may often have called for abstract instructions to be carried out by unknown operatives. This form of writing tends to alienate authors and readers from their proximal domains of time-space. As with all static, noun-centred, fixed-code writing systems it is virtually impossible to represent change effectively in the embodied present tense – that is during the change of which it is a part. With a greater emphasis on codified, unsituated text, it was possible to develop a system of logic that was more symbolic than indexical. In other words, change came to be represented in a way that detached description from event. As such it was therefore less self-reflexive. Arguably, this in itself is a form of spatio-temporal alienation that has also been attributed to thinkers such as Plato (Wood, 1998).

One of the dangers of living in a fact-orientated culture is that you begin to depend on deductive, rather than inductive or abductive (Pierce, 1958) forms of reasoning. Where deduction works by adhering to the rules and integrity that can be demonstrated within a given text or equation, abduction and induction cannot function without implicating the internal state of the thinker and the way things work elsewhere. In other words, the tradition of deductive reasoning makes more sense within the text than beyond it. In reality, 'real' situations are always more situated, actative and holistic than the way we present them in writing. Although the logocentric idea of 'exegesis' makes most sense from within the culture of literacy, printing and digital 'search' technologies, it seems more dubious at an ecological level. Without the deductive capabilities of printed text, abductive reasoning might have become more important. De Nicholas (1986) claims that if Western thought had not taken such a strongly Aristotelian direction, imagination would have become far more important to our culture. Where reading tends to emphasise static relations, hierarchies of meaning, un-situated values, serial temporalities, linear causality and a largely internalised order of meaning, the ecological domain is holistic, dynamic, opportunistic and polymorphic. Where most writing focuses the reader's attention inward, the 'real' world makes its inhabitants pay attention to one another, most of the time. In short, while it has brought certain benefits to humanity, the reading culture has also encouraged the illusion of self-dependence that probably inspired virtual worlds such as the cinema, television, VCR, Walkman, and so on. The ability to scan alphabetical characters in the appropriate direction is of limited use. Indeed, it seems more likely that heuristic skills of adaptation would be more helpful.

Writing has therefore become more and more a part of a technological culture of power and control. Instrumental rationality is the tendency to see something merely for 'use', usually as a means of achieving one's own goals. What is 'used' might be virtually anything, from object to ideology, individual, or opportunity. A formative design innovation that relates to instrumentalism is Rene Descartes' (1596–1650) invention of the 'A-to-Z' grid, as used today in almost all geographical maps. Descartes is said to have had the idea while lying in bed and watching a fly crawl up a wall. He visualised a grid of lines surrounding the fly and realised that its position on the wall could be described by assigning letters and/or numbers to the vertical and horizontal coordinates on the grid. However, just as alphabetical writing offers a completely arbitrary code for connecting us to the world, so the Cartesian grid is also an alienating 'tool' that emerged from a kind of fanatical scepticism. Later, cyberneticians such as Von Bertalanffy (1968) have implicitly criticised the kind of systems thinking that puts technological expediencies above human values. Nonetheless, it should be remembered that military, industrial, and state sponsorship inspired the early epistemology of cybernetics as a discipline. As such, some of the concepts that led to cybernetics derive from classical science and inspired modes of technological determinism (Ellul, 1964) that traded human experience for certainty and control. In particular, this paper notes the scientific tendency to frame cryptic generalisations – that is 'laws' – that are un-situated from the spatio-temporal complexity of immediate observation. It argues that this tendency alienates us from our ongoing (human) present and therefore makes us less sensitive to our 'presence', and thereby to the environmental damage that we continue to wreak in the name of progress and comfort.

In an education culture that is keen to develop 'bona fide' research methodologies, situated models of writing such as notative, fictive, aphoristic or diaristic approaches are unlikely to resemble what we would expect to see. Normal modes of essay logic are, however, of limited use except to focus the writer's attention upon issues and topics, or to represent existing design thinking in a more self-justifying and persuasive way. In short, these modes of writing are better for putting previous 'thought-actions' into words than they are at responding with new ones. Where algorithms conform to most of the qualities of 'rigour' detailed above, heuristics is concerned with discovery, rather than with proof. As Einstein intimated, the rigour of logic is not enough: 'To these elementary laws there leads no logical path, but only intuition, supported by being sympathetically in touch with experience' (Einstein, 1920). How might we teach writing in a more enlightened, ethical, and helpful way? It is important to remember that the purpose of authoring is both auto-didactic and rhetorical. Unless this is made clear, these requirements can easily impede one another, but I have yet to find students who have been taught how to separate them. This is probably because the competitive learning culture values persuasion and self-image so highly. When learners write academic essays they feel moved to convince their readers that they are right, even when they are unsure of their ground. I presume that this rhetorical bias is ingrained within the essay genres we teach in schools. If so, perhaps the form and style of writing could be made more subordinate to its outcome. In my own teaching I emphasise the imagining of a scenario and the self-reflexive mapping of relationships within it. Only after these steps have been followed is the issue of narrative and its effect given much attention. This is normally initiated by the nominating of a needy reader and the building of empathy, or a working rapport with this reader, whether as problem-holder, interest-holder, question-holder or stakeholder. I normally advise against choosing a reader that is simply an expert in the topic.

This approach is different from traditional methods of academic writing, which in my view tend to encourage an alienation from the author's whole experience and responsibility. The practice of distancing the author from the events that he or she observes can be traced back to the foundational thinking of Socrates and Aristotle. It became more analytical with the intellectual devices of mediaeval thinkers such as Duns Scotus and William of Ockham, and was endorsed by the technical innovation of Gutenberg and others. In the Enlightenment period, the wilful and intrusive minds of Bacon, Descartes, Locke, Leibniz, Galileo and Newton further extended it. Diderot and Dr Johnson took this detachment still further with their invention of the encyclopaedia and the dictionary, which routinely strip most of the context from their claims. Ironically, Plato's alphabetically inspired idealism also contributed to the development of the virtual realm in which 'types' of form are regarded as identical, rather than similar. This tendency is a crucial part of the heresy of alphabetical text. Whenever a letter is erased from a computer screen, another will replace it just as well. In practical terms there is no difference. However, this only makes much sense in a world of Platonic archetypes in which we underestimate the way everything emerges and mutates over time.

In a famous essay of 1936, Walter Benjamin alludes to the uncanny nature of technological reproducibility in the print industry. By applying the Marxist notion of 'alienation' to the process of making facsimile images (c.f. Benjamin, 1989), Benjamin generated a critical framework that has remained influential to this day. His development of the idea of 'aura' as a signifier of immediate experience is helpful in tracing possible 'micro-utopias'. Benjamin describes his somewhat enigmatic concept as a 'strange web of space and time' that he qualifies by saying that 'natural' aura was the 'unique phenomenon of distance, however close it may be'. This is a useful benchmark for engagement with the world. One of the issues that Heraclitus reminds us about is that of the epistemological entanglement of speaker and listener. With writing it usually has to be simulated, or 'faked' for the pleasure of the reader. As I have argued, the print culture has taught us how to write to the unknown reader and how to read the impersonal author. These are, now, matters of routine. Where speaking and listening used to be an intricately balanced, relational event, alphabetical writing tended to encourage the dominance of data. In the world of business-English (cf. Microsoft Word) a fact is a fact, is a fact. In the digital era, information presented in this form has become a commodity that can be traded without fear of 'data loss'. However, what Heraclitus reminds us is that, just as we cannot put our foot in the same river twice, so we change things by asking a question. Hence, we can never ask the 'same' question again. This is similar to how works of art are created. It is also similar to the way that quantum computers operate. The work of Heraclitus may also remind us that professional designers must use situated judgement that calls for multi-dimensional maps of understanding. This is where dyslexic wisdom may come in useful. If we can develop writing that will seek to map the dynamic world self-reflexively, it might bring us a little closer to building a multiplicity of micro-utopias.

The following section comprises an analysis of one particular text from Heraclitus. It has been chosen because it is so unusual in the way it brings together key players within a short sentence. It is important to remember that his words derive from the written quotations of later writers, as there are no surviving texts by him.

> When you have listened not to me but to 'λογοξ' (the 'way of things'),
> it is wise within this context to say: All is one.
>
> (Heraclitus: FRAGMENT 50.)

(N. B. The difficult Greek word 'λογοξ' is usually translated as 'discourse', utterance, speech, logic or reason. Here, I have assumed it refers to what nature tells us about itself, if we are attentive to it. I have therefore taken the liberty of interpreting it as 'the way of things'. In terms of relational thinking it is an important and interesting text, because it emphasises grammatical relations that exist strongly in situated story telling, but are seldom encountered in writing.

It raises issues concerning ethical relations. Here is my own, slightly optimistic interpretation of the same text:

> *When you have listened not just to my account, but also to the λογοξ ('way of things'), it is wise within this shareable account to say: All is one.*

Arguably, this aphorism seems to utilise several levels of meaning that cannot satisfactorily be put into any type of writing. In this case, the use of the word 'listened' implies that part of the meaning must be imparted from a face-to-face presentation of the text. Moreover, the summary content of Fragment 50 would suggest that it addresses the loss of situated meaning that can be attributed to writing and its failure to pay due respect to a grammar of becoming, rather than a set of rules for fortifying declarative knowledge. One way to redeem part of this loss is to establish a four-fold grammar that can map the text's implied agencies in a convenient three-dimensional form. This approach also removes the linear, temporal problem of narrative, in which the need for a 'beginning' and an 'end' imposes a false sense of priority, succession, or hierarchy within the text. It seems to me that Fragment 50 speaks to this issue. Finding an alternative to the written version is therefore a helpful step to take.

After the discussions in previous chapters it may be clear that the more important skills of creativity are those that may cross the grammatical boundaries between noun and verb, 'form' and 'content'. They may also operate beyond the constraint of number and category. If the world exists as a set of wave relations, then we live in a world of qualities, rather than quantities. Maybe imagination exists as a kind of vernier scale that crystallises ideas or 'facts' at the intersection of waves. One of the things that a wave-based approach teaches us is that living beings reside in a ceaseless continuum of relations, where 'being right' may be less important than being 'in phase' with what is happening. This calls for an understanding of 'phase-space' in which any semantic adjustment must always, also, be seen as an act of 'self-adjustment'. This brings us back to the importance of self-reflexive awareness within an ethical domain of shared actions. While theories like those of this book can be developed quietly in libraries, artists and designers must more often make judgements that have to work in 'real-time'. The following chapter will resume the exploration of Fragment 50, after it has outlined the importance of language within the quest for micro-utopias.

References

Armstrong, K. (2005), *A Short History of Myth* (Edinburgh: Canongate Books).

Barlow, J. P. (1994), 'The economy of ideas: a framework for rethinking patents and copyrights in the digital age', *Wired*, 2:3, pp. 85–90.

Barnes, J. (1979), *The Pre-Socratic Philosophers*, Vol. 1 (London: Routledge and Kegan Paul).

Benjamin, W. (1989), 'The work of art in the age of mechanical reproduction' in *Commerce and Culture*, Bayley, S. (ed.), p. 36 (London: Design Museum/ Penshurst Press).

Blanchette, O. (1994), 'The logic of perfection' in *Thomas Aquinas and his Legacy*, Gallagher, D. M. (ed.), pp. 194–206 (Washington DC: Catholic University of America Press).

Bohm, D. (1980), *Wholeness and the Implicate Order* (Boston and London: Routledge and Kegan Paul).

Cooley, M. (1987), *Architect or Bee? The Human Price of a New Technology* (London: The Hogarth Press Ltd.).

de Bono, E. (1973), *Po: Beyond Yes and No* (Harmondsworth: Penguin Books).

de Nicholas, A. T. (1986), *Powers of Imagining: Ignatius de Loyola* (Albany: State University of New York Press).

Descartes, R. (1951), 'Meditations on first philosophy', in *Library of Liberal Arts, No. 29* (New York: Liberal Arts Press).

Dreyfus, H.L. and Dreyfus, S. E. (1986), *Mind over Machine* (Oxford: Basil Blackwell).

Einstein, A. (1920), 'Ether and the theory of relativity', in *Sidelights on Relativity* Einstein, A. (Canada: General Publishing Company) (1983).

Ellul, J. (1964), *The Technological Society* (New York: Vintage Books, Alfred A. Knopf, Inc. and Random House, Inc.).

Feyerabend, P. (1975), *Against Method* (London: Verso).

Gellrich, J. (1985), *The Idea of the Book in the Middle Ages* (London: Ithaca and Cornell University Press).

Handy, C. B. (1998), *The Hungry Spirit: Beyond Capitalism - A Quest for Purpose in the Modern World* (London: Arrow).

Hawking, S. (1988), *A Brief History of Time* (Toronto: Bantam Books).

Harper, W. (1989), 'Consilience and natural kind reasoning' in *An Intimate Relation*, Brown, J. R. and Mittelstrass, J. (eds.), pp. 115–52 (Dordrecht: Kluwer).

Kuhn, T. (1962), *The Structure of Scientific Revolutions* (Chicago: University of Chicago Press).

Nelson, T. (1987), *Computer Lib/Dream Machines* (Redmond, WA: Tempus Books of Microsoft Publishing).

Panofsky, E. (1968), *Gothic Architecture and Scholasticism* (Cleveland: World Publishing Company).

Pascal, B. (1660), *Pensées*, Trotter, W. F. (trans.). Available at: www.ccel.org/ccel/pascal/pensees.html

Peirce, C. S. (1958), *Collected Papers of Charles Sanders Peirce, Vols. 1–6*, Hartshorne, C. and Weiss, P. (eds.), Vols. 7–8, Burks, A. W. (ed.), (Cambridge, MA: Harvard University Press).

Polanyi, M. (1969), 'Tacit knowing' in *Knowing and Being* (London: Routledge and Kegan Paul).

Schön, D. (1985), *The Design Studio* (London: RIBA Ltd).

Simon, H. (1969), *The Sciences of the Artificial* (Cambridge, Massachusetts: The MIT Press).

Wilson, E. (1998), *Consilience* (New York: Knopf).

Wood, J. (1998), 'The culture of rigour: does design research really need it?', *The Design Journal*, 3, April 1, pp. 44–57.

Writing the Design

CHAPTER

5

'Thought does not report things, it distorts reality to create things, and, as Bergson noted, "In so doing it allows what is the very essence of the real to escape." Thus to the extent we actually imagine a world of discrete and separate things, conceptions have become perceptions, and we have in this manner populated our universe with nothing but ghosts.'

(Ken Wilbur, 1980)

Previous chapters have claimed that the most dogmatic forms of fundamentalism somehow derive from the invention of writing. On the other hand, our society would not have survived in its present form without a system of writing or discourse that can make assertions that appear to be axiomatic. However, it is hard to imagine an equivalent to the written axiom in the way that ecosystems work (Bateson, 1973). Nor are written axioms equally important within all human cultures. What are the salient features of language that de-sensitise us, and induce us to 'dumb down' our sense of reality? More importantly, in order to understand what we are doing to the world, would it be possible to re-design language in order to see things more sensitively, lucidly, sympathetically, or adaptively? Many academics would probably argue that existing modes of writing already do this. Whoever is right, the principle itself is an ancient one. The idea that language sets the boundaries for thought probably came into Western thought from Indian writings of the sixth century (Bhartrihari, 450–510). It led, via von Humboldt (1767–1835), and others, to the famous so-called 'Sapir-Whorf hypothesis', or the concept of 'linguistic relativity' (Whorf and Ikegami, 1956). This argues that the grammatical categories of a given language have a guiding influence over the way its users understand the world, and therefore behave in it.

In order to make constructive changes, we may need to explore issues at a level that is below what seems obviously practical. In a materialistic culture does the structure of our language encourage us to see the world more as actions, or as things – and does it matter? In looking for answers to these questions, the chapter experiments with some bold ideas about the fundamental purposes, tenets, and effects of alphabetical writing and counting. The last chapter argued that an over-emphasis on 'rigour' discourages us from being adaptable to our changing environment. If we describe the highest level of intellectual enquiry or scholarship we are probably more likely to speak of 'rigour' than of curiosity, spontaneity, ingenuity, and adaptability. Similarly, the current educational consensus still teaches and assesses the individual learner, rather than fostering constructive synergy and collective wisdom. Unfortunately, many of our society's myths show how individuals get away with being obstinate, aggressive, and solipsistic. Indeed, outdated Darwinian myths and a glamorised history of wealth and power have made these attributes desirable. However, although individual societies may have perished because they did not adapt to the prevailing conditions, it has proved difficult to learn from their experience. History shows many examples of societies that perished because they over-exploited their natural environment (Ponting, 1991). This can easily happen when people become more interested in ideological and religious dogma than in surviving as a species.

In the next chapter I will ask why modern citizens seem to believe that clock-time and mathematical systems are more 'real' than their own experiences. Indeed, Maturana's (1995) account of the temporality of living beings offers a helpful foil to this idea. 'Living takes place in the now, in the moment in which it is taking place. Living is a dynamics that disappears as it takes place. Living takes place in no time, without past or future. Past, present and future are notions that we human beings, we observers, invent as we explain our occurrence in the now' (Maturana, 1995). This also implies that, within living systems, cognition, language and consciousness interact without axiomatic boundaries set up by the logic of writing and belief. This chapter therefore discusses issues of language, context, and intertextuality and their role in designing for micro-utopias. It introduces the tetrahedron as a more relational and self-reflexive figure upon which to map the most important players. Once again, the background to this exploration is ecological, rather than economic or political. For this reason, some familiar issues are reframed within a generalised context. For example, if an organism cannot attune itself to the prevailing conditions it will die. Given the ecological importance of adaptability it is surprising, therefore, that we have few words with which to describe it. Today, the claim to being a 'global economy' implies that we have become a single organism, society, or culture. If so, this differs from previous situations in which one tribe would die while another would live. Today there is a growing awareness of the shared limits of a small planet. Nevertheless, we have some way to go before we will act in a self-orchestrated way. Even the current threat of total extinction has yet to frighten us into being sufficiently receptive, ingenious, or resourceful. Perhaps it is because of our 'rigorous' mindset that we tend to think of terms such as 'opportunistic' and 'manipulative' in a rather moralistic, or negative way. Where the logic of 'rigour' continues to reinforce a belief in wasteful, durable and arduous practices, this chapter suggests that a more situated, creative and adaptive approach would be easier and better.

Texts such as Sun Tzu's *The Art of War* (Sun Tzu Cheng, 1992), and Macchiavelli's *The Prince* (Macchiavelli, 1955) are relevant to this discussion, even though they may emphasise political intrigue, diplomatic protocol, or even bloodshed.

To say that someone is 'Macchiavellian' usually means that he or she is self-serving and unscrupulous. In some ways, however, this can be seen as a positive exemplar in that it describes successful actions that do not require great effort. We might conclude that Macchiavelli and Sun Tzu offer a discourse that values watchful adaptability. In other words, they show us how to transform the *status quo* using a minimum expenditure of energy. In this sense, their advice can be said to embody ecological principles. From a different perspective, later thinkers such as Lovelock (1979) and Maturana and Varela (1970, 1980) have made an important contribution to this issue by offering a model of the whole 'living system' that may prove useful in practical terms. This idea is a counterpoint to the descriptions of solipsism in Chapter 2. According to Maturana and Varela's model, a living organism – whether it is an individual life form, social group or corporation – only survives by maintaining its identity (Maturana and Varela, 1980). Here the term 'identity' includes both its integrity in terms of its persona (it is perceived) and its attendant capabilities, structure, resources and so on. Hence, although an organism may see itself differently from how it is seen, its context will determine whether this really matters. In short, the two must somehow be reconciled in order for it to survive. There are no pretexts or 'rules' although, in general terms, it may appear as though there are. For example, I may believe that I am a tiger and travel to the African savannah to have lunch with my relatives. Unfortunately, it is more than likely that one of my four-legged 'cousins' will perceive me as lunch, rather than as a distant relative. Unless I am rapidly able to reconcile the difference between my self-identity and my perceived identity I may lose my life, but there are many ways in which I might achieve this, perhaps by modifying or losing the identity that is in danger. I may therefore camouflage my human appearance, or become 'invisible' by hiding or running. In theory, if I can work at a highly shamanistic level, perhaps I can persuade the tiger to meet for lunch by sharing a gazelle with me on the grass. This may mean that I could retain my self-identity as a tiger, albeit with some adaptation.

Maturana and Varela's theory defines the pre-requisite conditions for what we usually would call 'communication'. However, they point out that communication can only take place once the two organisms have established habitual values or terms of reference that are shareable. They call this pre-communication stage 'structural coupling'. Again, this is a largely unpredictable process until cultural values and habits are established. Another innovation by Maturana and Varela is the use of the word 'language' as a verb, rather than a noun. This makes sense if we consider the way infants 'language' what they want, rather than saying things 'correctly'. This raises the issue of the relevance (Sperber and Wilson, 1986) of a given utterance, and how well a given language can reflect the 'situatedness' of its time of writing (Gee, 2004). Where the idea of rigorous academic discourse is usually intended to be verifiable outside its full context, the act of languaging is highly context-situated, embodied, and outcome-driven. It is creative, opportunistic, and adaptive. In other words, it is part of an ecological interplay of resources that facilitates shared wellbeing.

When artists and designers work with others they often rely on a highly situated discourse that can be called 'saying-at-the-site-of-showing' (Wood, 1997). In design studios this is called 'show-and-tell'. Where a professional critic is likely to adopt a distant standpoint in order to write a commentary,

Table 5.1   A comparison of two approaches to writing and researching

Implications of Academic 'rigour'	The idea of Ecological Attunement
Emphasises permanence and ideals	Emphasises situated context and change
Emphasises the plan over adaptability	Emphasises adaptability before strategy
Emphasises consistency of method	Emphasises coherence of client relations
Emphasises presentation over content	Emphasises shared interest with reader
Emphasises notion of 'truth'/ 'facts'	Emphasises notions of discovery
Emphasises transgressive innovation	Emphasises incremental improvements
Emphasises 'best method' approach	Emphasises collaborative compromise
Invites individual correctness	Invites symbiotic sharing of knowledge
Focuses on analysis and specificity	Encourages relational, holistic approach
Emphasises epistemological form	Emphasises purpose and application
Emphasises clarity and quantification	Emphasises situated human judgement

'show-and-tell' encourages a more 'embodied', situation-dependent and therefore holistic form of critical reflection. In 1962, the UK government commissioned the first Coldstream Report in order to validate the degree status of art school diploma courses. Until this time many art students were not obliged to prove their writing abilities in order to obtain a degree-equivalent diploma. One of the conditions of legitimisation was that all subsequent degree students must write a dissertation of between five thousand and ten thousand words. For many students at that time this dramatised what they had perceived as a division between theory and practice. Despite its good intentions, Coldstream was a largely negative experience for many students because it now expected them to narrow their cognitive focus and to adopt arbitrary writing conventions that seemed to be disconnected from their understanding of the world. In hindsight, the policy had been framed without considering the possible role of dyslexia within the visual culture. Subsequent surveys (for example Cairns and Moss, 1995; Wolff and Lundberg, 2002) have shown that there seems to be a significantly higher incidence of dyslexia among art students than among other students. Although each dyslexic has an individual profile of cognitive and learning skills, there are certain positive features that may be found in a high proportion of dyslexics. For example, some observers have claimed that they are more imaginative, better able to use all of their senses and are therefore more aware of their environment. Many prefer to think mainly in pictures rather than words, and can modify the way they perceive things. They are also highly intuitive and insightful and are strongly curious about how things work. Admittedly, I have focused on dyslexia rather than on other cognitive conditions (Wood, 2000; 2005). I have also chosen to present only the more positive features of a complex condition. However, by definition, a dyslexic is someone of higher than average intelligence, but who may find it more difficult to cope with tasks that are deemed important to learning. Current legislation does not deny that there are positive aspects to dyslexia but it has yet to take these very seriously. In short, dyslexia tends to be seen more as a disability rather than what Ronald Davis refers to as a gift (Davis, 1997).

What would happen if the education system were to be radically revised to favour dyslexics, rather than 'normal' students? Would this put others at a disadvantage? Perhaps it would enable us to transcend the myopia of bureaucratic thinking and political 'spin'. Even more importantly, would it be of greater benefit to society as a whole? Perhaps there is a 'bureaucratic gene' that characterises the modern mindset; attracting us to one-dimensional certainties and blinding us to the multi-dimensional reality of Nature. This may account for the fact that many dyslexics are said to have 'abnormally symmetrical' brains (Habib, 2000). Whether we understand the world in one, two, or in 29 dimensions, we are beginning to realise that there are limits to the generosity of the biosphere. This dawning of awareness in Homo sapiens, however, has so far confined itself to the cerebral regions of the brain. The rest of our body-mind must catch up at the procedural level, in order to address our new situation.

In practical terms, one of the most significant factors of writing, whether it be for the purpose of design philosophy or, more directly, for 'writing the design', is the importance of context. No ecological issue can be resolved without referring to the eco-system of which it is a part. In the twenty-first century, whether we are looking at designs for ideas, designs for books, or designs for kettles, we need to ask how the system in question is 'embedded' within another system or systems.

Designers are not directly to blame for conducting their professional tasks in isolation. For one thing, rather than being given a broad and deep understanding of their role in the more destructive aspects of capitalism, most are trained to work within a small bubble of specialist competence and verve. Sometimes life in the bubble is dull. At other times it is euphoric. At present, many design educators appear to see their task as meeting the current demands of industry, rather than offering industry the kinds of skills that will be needed in a more viable future (Chapter 9 will suggest ways in which designers might become less trained as corporate cannon fodder, and more as entrepreneurs for ecological change). Hence young designers soon become pawns for industries that are in the thrall of competition by price, novelty, and speed of availability. Where the corporations may dream of working in a less damaging way, they have little time or incentive to work out an alternative. What we need now is a new form of metadesign that will enable sensible decisions to be made. Designers are often put into an invidious 'double-bind' whereby whatever they do will have a strong negative component. If a designer is asked to design a 'green' car or airline branding system, how should he or she do it? Neither task is likely to lead to a net improvement for the world as a whole, yet if he or she walks away, someone else may do a worse job. This is where even the finest universities have failed to deliver. Most are paid by government or industry to conduct their research. Their business is to support society by discovering new ways to design the world. They do have time to write innovative courses. They do not have to compete simply on price and turn-around. Despite all of these factors, designers have not really made things much better. Research has shown that the societies who have the smallest ecological footprint also have spiritual and cultural values that sustain the 'style of living' that produces it (Drucker, 1978). A key feature of this kind of society is that conflict is reduced to minimal or optimal levels because it is potentially wasteful of precious resources and energies. It leads to the conclusion that synergies at the material levels must be synergised with synergies at the phenomenological, social, cultural, somatic and discursive levels. This idea is developed more fully in Chapter 9.

Where communication by the spoken word can be immensely articulate, it is virtually impossible to remove it from its original context unless the sound and images can be faithfully and meticulously recorded for later scrutiny. Similarly, where communication via pictures may be convincing and even compelling, it remains open to broad interpretation. Hence, without alphabetical writing it is more difficult to share intellectual certainties. Without certainties that are rendered immovable via chiselled stone, printed parchment, indelible ink, or other 'atomistic units' we cannot have facts or axioms. Without unequivocal – therefore potentially incontrovertible 'facts', laws or axioms – we may not have the kind of fundamentalism that justifies turning political rhetoric into legal chicanery, or that enshrines cultural or aesthetic chauvinism within an intractable code of law. More importantly, how could we develop more innovative and ethical practices of designing without having an effective means with which to reflect deeply upon the world? Some authors have emphasised the political and cultural significance of books and speech. Generally speaking, a critical and negative scenario (e.g. Ray Bradbury' *Fahrenheit 451*, or George Orwells's *1984*) is more common than a positive one. In both cases, the reader is invited to consider what might happen if we were to erase certain words from our minds. This does not need to happen. Indeed, this book invites designers to work more positively and strategically by inventing new key words and making them useable. It is interesting how certain terms become alternately fashionable and unfashionable, seemingly irrespective of their possible value at the time.

Under the present system, how do designers intervene in the flow of things? Despite the current rhetoric of consumerism in which they are understood to design a user's 'experience', in reality they are only able to provide for the user what certain cognitive psychologists call 'affordances'. For example, James J. Gibson used this term to describe the opportunities for action that a given object offers (Gibson, 1982). Norman (1988) uses the word to describe those opportunities for action that are noticeable or perceptible to the 'player' or 'actor'. This term accounts for accepted codes of meaning that objects seem to have, at the same time as we put these readings to use within a situated and opportunistic logic of action. By understanding this domain of opportunity and perception, designers can alter the way that materials are apprehended and used. However, 'affordances' do not reside merely within the physical domain of spaces and things. They also include the use of language. It is fairly obvious that the popularity of a given product is often affected by its name, not just its functionality and appearance. In reality, an appealing name becomes very closely associated with the form that makes it recognisable. One way to address the above problems is to expand the perceived horizon of possibility by introducing new words and grammatical affordances into the language. This would encourage a two-way process. If there is an interdependence of language and thought, it will operate in both directions. This tells us that the 'design' of new words can help to create new ways of thinking, and that new ways of thinking can inspire different behaviours. We are both constrained and empowered by our range of vocabulary, and by the grammar that enframes the way we think. Although some highly prominent education institutions still see writing as peripheral to proper design practices, this assumption ignores the fact that the 'design' of names, voices, texts, and verbal concepts is now an integral part of today's commercial design agenda. Indeed, there are methods that help designers to combine design factors from different levels or domains into a whole experience. For example, in Japanese the term 'Jinba Ittai', literally meaning 'horse and rider as one' is used to describe the way that design affordances (for example in Norman's more phenomenological sense) can be evaluated, adjusted, and made to work in harmony with one another. Within certain intrinsic boundaries, 'affordances' can be designed (see also Chapter 9).

The experiential reality of our world is not only informed by physical and socio-cultural factors, but also by language. Lakoff and Johnson (1980) have argued that our emotions and experiences are guided by the metaphors and structures within language. This is a powerful idea, because one of the criticisms of the psychoanalytical theories of the Freudian approach is that it offers only a one-way account of the relationships between actions and feelings. In this sense it works reactively, by looking back in time for possible causes of a given behaviour or psychiatric condition. By contrast, neuro-linguistic programming, or NLP (Bandler and Grinder, 1982) is a looser framework of techniques and theories that acknowledge the ways in which 'cause' and 'effect' may reverse roles. Loosely speaking, it therefore brings together several entities in an active continuum that reconciles subjective 'realities' with human behaviours. In considering the mental state of the subject, it considers the particular language in which her situation is framed, or 'reframed'. In other words, the relationship between, for example, actions and beliefs is two-way. In practical terms this means that certain actions, if repeated in the right context may make us feel different. Conversely, when we feel different about something it may change our behaviour. This may help to elucidate the idea of shamanism. However, for many people, radio or television weather reports are avidly followed in order to ensure that they 'have a nice day'. If we were able to re-design the linguistic values that are latent in these assumptions we might be able to change our habits. In the future, it will be important to integrate language management with design strategies. This would be a positive alternative to the rather indirect, retrospective and often proscriptive way that taxation or legislation works. For example, over the last hundred and fifty years, turning on electric lights has become more an unquestioned habit rather than a pleasure. Partly as a result we now have serious light pollution and global warming. To some extent this is an aesthetic issue. Tanizaki's 1933 publication *In Praise of Shadows* (Tanizaki, 1977) used descriptive prose to heighten the reader's respect for natural light, thus disparaging electric lighting. In many rich countries we have developed a rather polarised aesthetics of weather conditions in which rain means 'bad' and sun means 'good'. For some people in the wealthy countries, the mere prediction of so-called 'bad' weather can kindle negative feelings, even in sunny times. This often has even more important implications at the practical level. For example, if we were to see rain as a blessing or gift we would feel happier to walk, rather than driving to the shops when it is overcast or drizzling. Hence, merely by enhancing the perceived value of a natural phenomena like twilight and rain it would be quite possible to reduce energy use and the number of cars on the road.

Another creative way for designers to make a creative intervention is by designing names for key issues that were previously overlooked. In this way we can make the nameless more visible. Once they become visible they will be less likely to remain ignored. A good example of this is the word 'Genocide', which was coined in 1943 by the Polish legal scholar, Raphael Lemkin (1900–59). For years, Lemkin had tried unsuccessfully to draw world attention to the military excesses of certain nations. Eventually, he carefully designed a new term by combining the Greek word 'genos' (family, tribe or race) and the Latin word 'occidere' (to massacre). Only after his word was made public did many people begin to use it. Once adopted, he was able to convince the Geneva Conventions to include it within a new international law. Although his definition was quite narrow, everyone now uses the term. Where, previously, genocide had not seemed to exist, it suddenly became irrefutable to everyone. Today, it would be virtually impossible to deny, or to ignore genocidal behaviour without seeming ignorant or reactionary. Today, there are many words missing from the received repertoire of terms that mean 'killing x'. While most people probably know the word for the killing of a father, a mother, a sibling, a king, queen, or even, now, a race of people, the word that describes the killing, or endangering, of a species is less well known, and rarely used. Presumably we did not previously see the need for one. History is not so hot on this. As children, the reality of 'giant killing', 'dragon slaying', or 'wicked witch' killing is made to become frightening real, but because it does not exist within familiar terms, the eradication of a whole species is less real. In some respects it is literally unthinkable. This is astonishing, given that between 1990 and 1995 there was a net loss of 56.3 million hectares of natural forests (SOFO 1997 report), and the 'manslaughter' of many species at an alarming rate. James Lovelock has used the word 'culling' as a way to discuss what will happen to the human species when it goes too far in its environmental onslaught. Perhaps if we were to introduce an invented term such as 'non-human genocide' people might wake up to what is happening. The word 'genocide' is hardly sexy, but it is nicer than many. What may be more important is the advent of new words that describe the positive aspirations for increasing, rather than decreasing biodiversity.

This raises the issue of the clumsy way that certain terms are used, which dumbs-down the subtleties of meaning. All of the major religions since Zoroastrianism seem to have myths of opposition, such as 'good' versus 'evil'. This has given us the dubious and often unhelpful habit of polarising concepts that are not really opposites. Light is not opposite to darkness. Rain is not opposite to sunshine. 'Good' is virtually as relational a concept as 'evil' in that both are defined in great measure by the perspective taken at the time. Nor are they equal in qualities. Some years ago, I introduced the term 'entredonneurship' and have since found it helpful in my teaching. In a Design Journal article (Wood, 1988) I argued that 'the entrepreneur; fixer, trouble shooter and exploiter should give way to the more socially responsible entredonneur; the giver, not the taker.' One way in which we use the term is to place these words at opposite ends of a continuum that reconciles the 'entrepreneur' with the 'entredonneur'. This would enable us to chart a gradient of values with 'taking' at one end, and 'giving' at the other. This kind of innovation can be seen as a helpful intervention that may be integrated within a 'metadesign' process. At the experiential level it will be important to afford ourselves the scope for many new feelings, meanings, possibilities and behaviours. At present we are constrained by an artificially restricted set of possibilities.

Swann (1994) collated a large body of separate (published) studies into the body's capability to monitor various phenomena. He concludes that there may be at least twenty-seven 'senses'. For the human organism with this number of sensory 'channels', any separation of purpose between channels becomes improbable. Although the idea of 'intertextuality' is commonly seen as a positive enrichment of meaning and value in the social sciences, in engineering and science we may be more likely to see it as offering difficulties for monitoring (for example because of 'cross-channel modulation'). Swann interprets the collected findings in a way that affirms the scientist's sense of presence and denies the positivistic tendencies in science: 'we are our senses', he concludes.

One major contribution of cybernetics is that it offers a discourse that describes the interconnectedness between individual working entities and their context. (e.g. Von Bertalanffy, 1968) It has therefore enabled us better to acknowledge that anything can be understood as a 'system', whether living or dead. However, in identifying systemic similarities between animate and inanimate systems, cybernetics draws a comparison between things that may, or may not share the same order of complexity. Hence it may have inspired a false sense of wisdom that is sanctioned by an efficacy of outcomes (that is, the black box approach) rather than by the emergent values that resist being modelled in systematic terms. Hence it would be difficult to develop a viable cybernetics of human presence if, by this term, we mean the reflexive ontology of becoming that exists within the human experience of being.

In order to help designers to think in a similarly self-reflexive and dynamic way I have tried a number of methods. Ultimately, they all depend on the designer's ability to memorise and embody a set of relations in a way that is personally meaningful. Heraclitus's *Fragment 50* (see the end of Chapter 4) also emphasises a dynamic set of relations, and it is possible to reflect upon them using role-play. However, another useful way to model the relevant issues is by using a static polygon to guide the user's memory and imagination. It is ideally suited to one particular figure, that is the tetrahedron (see Figure 5.1). One of Plato's famous solids, it has a number of unique features that are described in Chapter 8.

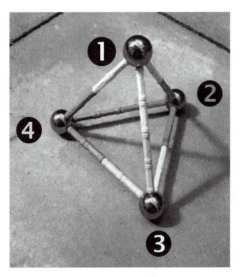

Figure 5.1   The 4 nodes of a tetrahedron

The tetrahedron affords parallel, self-reflexive, relational representations. It provides an almost ideal basic format for representing a manageable (that is 'thinkable') set of relations. As such it can be used to map situations that are more down-to-earth than other genres that use more lengthy, linear, narrative, or academic forms. This is because a designer's predicament can be expressed as a parallel, simultaneous set of relations. It has been chosen because it is difficult – although not impossible – to theorise more than four interdependent perspectives in a discussion. In short, unless we are attempting to stretch the designer's imagination beyond four parts, the tetrahedron is a convenient system. Some further thoughts on the tetrahedron are offered in Chapter 9.

With four interdependent parts we have an optimal structure, mnemonically speaking. According to the engineer and inventor Richard Buckminster Fuller, the mind may be tetrahedral (Fuller, 1975). Is it a coincidence that there are (only) four codes in the DNA? Systems with the quality 'four' are certainly familiar to many human societies. The idea of North, East, South and West or Earth, Wind, Air and Fire are handy examples. In his description of the way that humans co-exist with the space that their dwellings provide, Heidegger (1978, p. 346) speaks of four key elements – 'earth', 'sky', 'divinities', and 'mortals'. He calls them the 'fourfold'. When humans satisfactorily embed themselves within a dwelling place they experience all four as a unified whole. Whether or not we see the number four as magical or just conveniently auspicious may be of little importance to its usefulness. It certainly offers the basis for systems that are easy to conceive and to remember.

Using a tetrahedron as a primitive conceptual 'map' we can assign four interrelated players, values, or perspectives to a system that can be orientated in any position without compromising its integrity.

Practising artists and designers can also use this system as a reflexive mapping technique. It is useful because it contains enough rudimentary relations to represent a generalised predicament. As such, it may offer the basis for a new mode of design ethics. We can, for example, assign one node to:

- The author (for example, the designer)
- The topic (for example, the product, idea, system, outcome)
- The reader (for example, the recipient of the design)
- The context (for example, the biosphere)

Having assigned them, we can start at any of the four nodes and look for their relationships to the other three. As in the previous version, this very simple process merely reminds us to explore the six links implicit in any group of four things. In another configuration it may be helpful to assign two nodes to the self. By taking one as a personal self and a second as a professional self it serves to remind the creator that by learning to practise as a professional she or he may have suppressed personal desires for the world. It is probably more productive to explore the personal self first, then to explore the professional role, in order to rehearse what entrepreneurial actions may be possible.

Table 5.2   Four inward-facing and four outward-facing consequences of learning

VALUES that Can BE Self-MAPPED in HOLISTIC RELATION to each other
1a.   **SELF-KNOWLEDGE** (inward)
How much have you shown that you know yourself, your strengths and your weaknesses? (Preferably in a self-reflexive way, that is knowing how much you know within this particular context)
1b.   **READER-SYMPATHY** (outward)
How well have you shown that you can be effective on behalf of the named reader(s)? (Reflect upon how much you have understood your reader(s)' mission, standpoint, way of thinking, and value system)
2a.   **CURIOSITY MANAGEMENT** (inward)
How well have you shown your reader(s) that you can arouse, stimulate, develop, broaden, deepen, and moderate your own sense of curiosity and understanding for things?
2b.   **COMMUNICATION** (outward)
How well have you shown your reader(s) that you can organise and present relevant and helpful knowledge to others in a way that engages, informs, inspires, and supports them?
3a.   **STUDENTSHIP** (inward)
How well have you indicated to your reader(s) that you were receptive to a range of knowledge and insights of others while attending this course?
3b.   **RESEARCH SKILLS** (outward)
How well have you shown reader(s) how imaginative, creative, sceptical, and well organised you are, by your inclusion of relevant notes, documentation, and other information?
4a.   **PROFESSIONAL FOCUS** (inward)
How much have you shown your reader(s) what you are currently doing to clarify, focus, and prepare yourself for an effective future role in the professional world?
4b.   **ETHICAL AWARENESS** (outward)
How fully have you shown your reader(s) that you are in touch with the environment (that is intellectually, emotionally, and/or actively) in such a way that you could help sustain the ecological world that sustains you?

The attributes listed in Table 5.2 can also be used to map the relations implicit in Fragment 50 from Heraclitus (see also Chapter 4). This proposition, with its four grammatical elements and their resulting relationships can be parsed into four dynamically interpenetrating parts:

1.   Nominative co-subject (that is, the text's author/speaker)

2.   Significant proposition or event in question (that is, the publication/ speech itself)

3.   Dative co-subject (that is, the text's reader/listener)

4.   Discursive and all-pervasive context (that is, λογοξ ('logos'))

This chapter has sought to reframe the existing academic protocols for writing within a multi-dimensional framework that would encourage a new, and practical framework for ethical practice (Wood, 2005). The next chapter continues with the challenge to our existing atomistic framework of thought. It will develop this further by questioning the purpose of number systems. It will refer to the design of clocks as a way to exemplify the arguments, and because temporality and the culture of speed are important issues within environmentalism.

Table 5.3   The 4 Grammatical Elements

1).   Nominative co-subject (author/speaker)
The 'me' (1.1), that is this mortal human being (who has listened and who has reflected on many things)
The 'me' of 'I' (1.2), that is the living person you are listening to, and who now speaks
The 'I' of 'me' (1.3), that is the speaking voice that is part of this mortal being
The 'me and I' (1.4), that is this person/thinker who is moved to say 'All is one'
The 'me and I' (1.5), that is this person/thinker who claims, after being attentive to the λογοξ (logos), that the proposition 'All is one' is a wise conclusion
The 'me and I' (1.6), that is this person/thinker who advises you not to trust his words without reflecting upon his proposition for yourself
2).   Dative co-subject (the reader/listener)
The 'you' (2.1), that is the mortal human being who has listened and reflected on things
The 'you' (2.2), that is the human, mortal 'you' (2.1) who, at this moment, listens to me
The 'you' (2.2) who listens to what I am saying, rather than to my performance as a speaker
The 'you' (2.3) (including the integrity, awareness, honesty, and astuteness of your listener/ thinker-identity, and your readiness to listen to, and to reflect wisely upon my words) before you may, or may not, have reflected wisely upon a shareable significance of what I say
The 'you' (2.4) who, after fulfilling the above conditions, chooses to agree that 'All is one'

Table 5.3 *Concluded*

3). Significant proposition or event in question
The proposition that this mortal human being makes in saying: All is one
The proposition, 'All is one'
'All is one'
The integrity of what I say in terms of my astuteness, honesty and awareness
The coherence, in-and-of-itself, of these words
The coherence, in and of itself, of what my words propose
4). Discursive and active context (λογοξ or 'logos')
The context (that is, language entangled by world, and *vice versa*) of this (shared) proposition and how it is part of the λογοξ (or 'logos')
The totality of one
The unity of everything that is the case
The meaning of this discourse as truth in and of itself
The connoted + denoted (that is shareable) significance of the whole utterance as a proposition

Table 5.4 **The six relations formed by the four grammatical elements**

INTERPLAY between 1 and 2
The utterance from me (my mouth) that now reaches you (your ears)
INTERPLAY between 1 and 3
How what I say resonates with that to which I (implicitly) relate it; that is, the harmony between my perspective/experience and that of which I claim
INTERPLAY between 1 and 4
The rhetorical plausibility between me and the subject of which I speak
INTERPLAY between 2 and 3
The meaning of this discourse for you ('logos 2') assuming you have listened wisely and reflected upon what I am saying
INTERPLAY between 2 and 4
The pertinence/relevance of what I say for other things that are unsaid
INTERPLAY between 3 and 4
The λογοξ ('logos') that is implied and that reveals itself in my words

References

Bateson, G. (1973), *Steps to An Ecology of Mind* (London: Paladin Books, Granada Publishing).

Bandler, R., and Grinder, J. (1982), *ReFraming: Neuro-Linguistic Programming and the Transformation of Meaning* (Moab, Utah: Real People Press).

Cairns, T. and Moss, W. (1995), *Students with Specific Learning Difficulties/Dyslexia in Higher Education* (London: Goldsmiths College, University of London).

Davis, R. L, and Braun, E. M. (1997) *The Gift of Dyslexia, Why Some of the Smartest People Can't Read and How They Can Learn* (New York: Perigee Books).

Drucker, B. (1978), *The Price of Progress in the Philippines* (Portola, CA: Sierra Books,) 63, pp. 22-26, cited in *The Synergism Hypothesis; On the Concept of Synergy and It's Role in the Evolution of Complex Systems*, Corning, P. A., (1998). Available at: www.complexsystems.org/publications/synhypo.html

Fuller, R.B. (1975), *Synergetics: Explorations in the Geometry of Thinking* (New York: Macmillan Publishing, Inc.).

Gee, J. P. (2004), *Situated Language and Learning: A Critique of Traditional Schooling* (New York: Routledge).

Gibson, J. J. (1982), *Reasons for Realism: Selected Essays of James J. Gibson*, Reed, E. and Jones, R. (eds.) (Hillsdale, NJ: Erlbaum).

Habib, M. (2000), 'The neurological basis of developmental dyslexia: an overview and working hypothesis', *Brain*, 123:12, pp. 2373–2399 (Oxford: Oxford University Press). [DOI: 10.1093/brain%2F123.12.2373].

Heidegger, M. (1978), 'Building, dwelling, thinking', in *Basic Writings* Krell, D. F. (ed.) (London: Routledge, Kegan and Paul).

Lakoff, G. and Johnson, M. (1980), *Metaphors We Live By* (Chicago: University of Chicago Press).

Lovelock, J. (1979), *Gaia, A New Look at Life on Earth* (Oxford: Oxford University Press).

Macchiavelli, N., Marriott, W. K., Fuller, N. and Hobbes, T. (1955), 'The prince', in *Great Books of the Western World. v. 23* (Chicago: Encyclopædia Britannica).

Maturana, H. and Varela, F. G. (1980), 'Autopoiesis and cognition: the realization of the living', in *Boston Studies in Philosophy of Science* (Dordrecht, Holland and Boston: D. Reidel Publishing Company).

Maturana, H. and Varela, F. G. (1998), *The Tree of Knowledge: The Biological Roots of Human Understanding* (Boston and London: Shambhala).

Maturana, H. R., (1995), *The Nature of Time.* Available at: www.inteco.cl/biology/nature.htm

Norman, D. A. (1988), *The Psychology of Everyday Things* (New York: Basic Books).

Ponting, C. (1991), *A Green History of the World* (London: Penguin Books).

Sperber, D. and Wilson, D. (1986), *Relevance; Communication and Cognition* (Cambridge, MA: Basil Blackwell).

Sun Tzu Cheng, T. (1992), *The Art of War* (Taipei: Li Ming Cultural Enterprise).

Swann, I. (1994), 'Your Seventeen Senses – The Crumbling Mainstream Resistance of the Paranormal and New Scientific Confirmation Regarding the Existence of Certain Psi Faculties', paper given on, 21 March at the United Nations on behalf of the Society for Enlightenment and Transformation (SEAT).

Tanizaki, J. (1977), *In Praise of Shadows* (New Haven, CT: Leete's Island Books).

von Bertalanffy, L. (1968), *General System Theory: Foundations, Development, Applications* (New York: George Braziller).

Whorf, B. L. (1956) *Language, Thought and Reality*, Carroll, J. (ed.) (Cambridge, MA: MIT Press).

Wilber, K. (1980), *The Atman Project (A Transpersonal View of Human Development)* (Wheaton, IL: Theosophical Publishing House).

Wolff, U. and Lundberg, I. (2002), *Prevalence of Dyslexia Among Art Students in Dyslexia*, 8:1, pp. 34–42 (Chichester: John Wiley & Sons Limited). [PubMed: 11990223]

Wood, J. (1988), 'The socially responsible designer', *International Design Journal*, October.

Wood, J. (1997), 'Situated criticism and the experiential present', in *The Special 'Criticism' Edition of the Journal of Design Issues*, Whitely, N. (ed.), 3:2, pp. 5–15. ISSN: 0747–9360.

Wood, J. (2000), 'The culture of rigour: does design research really need it?', *Design Journal*, 3:1, pp. 44–57.

Wood, J. (2005) 'The tetrahedron can encourage designers to formalise more responsible strategies' *The Journal of Art, Design & Communication*, 3:3, pp. 175–192. ISSN: 1474273X.

Clocks Beyond Number

*'As far as the laws of mathematics refer to reality, they are not certain;
and as far as they are certain, they do not refer to reality.'*

(Albert Einstein, 1920)

This chapter continues the book's general critique of coding systems that are autonomous to their surroundings. In extending this criticism to mechanical tools, it focuses mainly on the influence of clocks, showing how their design and use in the 21st century is strange, anachronistic and ecologically damaging. It does so by showing how the arguments relating to alphabetical writing can also be used to challenge common assumptions about the use of numbers. In contrast to the temporality of organic systems, clocks invoke a mechanical and unidirectional model of change. This condition has evolved over the last 600 years to introduce a tyrannical mode of industrialisation. In exploring the use of clock-time, and its current role in the more dystopian aspects of living, this chapter asks whether languages such as mathematics are really helpful within a possible 'micro-utopian' context. Many experts on eco-design have expressed concern about the acceleration of modern lifestyles, and suggested that we find ways to slow down (for example Fuad-Luke, 2002). This critique of industrial 'speed' is not new. In the 1840s, the flâneurs (literally 'strollers') are said to have walked around with pet turtles as pacesetters, and Marx (1988) saw the clock as the main exemplar for industrial capitalism. Later writers such as Benjamin (1992) and Mumford (1934) reflected in more detail on subsequent developments, such as the 'atomising' of clock time into discrete hours, minutes and seconds. The clock has played a key role in speeding up the pace of life in the industrialised world. In more recent times the Slow Food movement (founded 1986 in Italy) found popularity in many cities around the world and remains as a positive and beneficial influence.

This chapter goes further, arguing that unless we also change the design and purpose of clocks, 'slowing down' and 'down-shifting' will not be enough. It might therefore mean re-designing clocks as a way of integrating many parts of our lives in a more effective way. In Chapter 2 the concept of solipsism was used to illustrate how individual consumers become alienated from their environment. It pointed out that this kind of alienation creates damage to adjacent parts of the ecosystem and that, ultimately, it is also fatal for the solipsist. This would be equivalent to a parasite that is so self-absorbed that it kills its host within a very short time. Of all the machines invented it is hard to think of one that is more self-absorbed and more detached, and therefore more solipsistic than the clock. Nonetheless, few people seem aware that clocks do not 'measure' time, but are self-governing machines with virtually no connection to the ebb and flow of daily life. Nonetheless, citizens in nearly all countries ardently obey the many watches, timers and clocks that clutter their environment, whether awake or asleep. In short, clocks rule our lives. This chapter asks how this happened, and offers suggestions for how designers might contribute to a revolution in how we live. Since mechanical clocks acquired their 'minute' hands, then their 'second' hands, digital technology has played an increasing role in fostering our belief in number systems as a form of 'reality'. The use of clocks and other mechanical regulators is therefore not just a technical detail that can be addressed in terms of functionality and logistics. Clocks are also objects of power that carry emotive messages that work at the social and aesthetic level. Because numbers are often associated with this form of power, time itself acquired more of a cachet by being displayed on alphanumeric screens.

In other words clocks are 'sexy' instruments that remind us of the great achievements of science and technology. The 17th century mathematician Blaise Pascal (1623–62) is famous for personalising the rhetorical power of 'time' when he began walking around with a clock tied to his wrist. Hitherto, only the most powerful cities were rich enough to display their importance by installing a clock in a prominent public place. By virtue of science's subsequent glamour, Pascal's fashion statement can therefore be seen as a conspicuous claim to power. Another way to explain society's enduring faith in clock time is by discussing a corresponding faith in rationality, as exemplified by the way that finite numbers are used and perceived. By 'rational' I refer to a logic based on the belief that the world is essentially regular, and therefore bound by a rational number system. This assumption can be traced back many thousands of years but is probably best known in the claim by Pythagoras (525 BCE) that 'all things are numbers'. Some might interpret this to mean that reality consists of, and is wholly commensurate with a numerical domain that exists as the very essence of the world. Does this mean that the reality we experience is somehow numerical? In repudiating the wholehearted acceptance of rule-based number systems I also challenge, by implication, the atomistic view of the world that conforms to an alphabetical, as opposed to a more fluent, pictographic logic.

This reflects a very old debate that stems from the assumption that the world is a unified entity with a single quality. It therefore asks, in effect, whether this quality is either this, or that.

Where Heraclitus argued that the world was 'an ever living fire', some of his contemporaries believed it to be made, for example, of water or gas. Heraclitus is often contrasted with his near contemporary Parmenides (515–450 BC), who believed the world to be made of atoms. Atomism therefore can be associated with numerical certainty. Since this ancient debate began, the atomists have dominated the discussion, especially in the era of digital computers. Here, I am using the term 'atomistic' to describe a belief in 'particles', in preference to 'waveforms' or 'fields'. I believe that the reductionist approach within research methodology is one of the stumbling blocks set up by scientific discourse. While it is now being dismantled in many disciplines, and while it proved highly effective in certain practical terms after Galileo, it nevertheless strengthened the popular belief in atomism. The atomistic view is enshrined in the Pythagorean belief in mathematics as a central truth. Today it is echoed in the widespread acceptance of dubious terms such as 'transferable skills' and 'transferable knowledge', that encourage the application of training regimes, in preference to education systems. As I implied when discussing transferable skills in Chapter 4, the idea of transferability is untrustworthy because it implies that each atom is isomorphic to any other. This assumption is very hard to justify without an *a priori* belief in mathematics as a kind of reality. It represents a feat of self-induced alienation from the world of ubiquitous flow, to which Heraclitus alludes. A. N. Whitehead's reflections on mathematics endorse this view. Referring to mathematics as '...a refuge from the goading urgency of contingent happenings' (1925) he argues that it represents mankind's most original creation because of its high level of detachment from the emergent, immediately proximal world (c.f. Hall, 1968).

Only when we learned how to ignore the context of a given issue did it become possible to see different types of relations, such as those that take place in different times and places, as identical. In western thought this has been a long and fairly inexorable process. Perhaps the most prominent steps in this process are those of the early Greek logicians who spoke of 'universals', and who inspired the 14th century (c. 1285–1349) thinker, William of Ockham to propose that a logical argument should always ignore everything superfluous to what is essential to its proof (see Chapter 3). This idea had a huge influence on classical science, and lingers on in the academic world. It makes good news for anyone wishing to make general claims that are true, but it also encourages us to ignore the larger context of a given study. Leibniz (1646–1716) later developed

Ockham's theory of the 'identicality of indiscernibles' (c.f. Ashby, 1956). This stands as another piece of expedient logic that privileges the argument, rather than the conditions that co-created it. In effect, it licenses us to assume that those things that have no discernible difference can be treated as though they are identical. It is no coincidence that this principle became the cornerstone of digital culture. In mathematical terms, a string of digits is either identical to another string, or not. There is no in-between state. In the binary world of digital data it has meant that whether something is identical or different is beyond question. However, this has led to logical errors in the presumption of guilt, where DNA samples are used to identify individuals. For example, Sherman's 'prosecutor's fallacy' (Halgh, 2000) is the confusion between two probabilities, for example, the probability that an innocent person's DNA would match that found at the scene of a crime and the probability that someone whose DNA matches the crime scene sample is innocent. This has important philosophical implications for the way we value employees, students, citizens, or exam results. For example, it made it easier for the crime of 'identity theft' to become such a lucrative business.

George Boole (1815–64), the mathematician who developed binary logic, did more than create the rules that make digital electronics function at the technical level. He also claimed that his identification of a binary (that is 0 and 1) logic was the fundamental basis for what he called the 'Laws of Thought' (1854). In the 20th century, George Spencer-Brown (1923) took the argument even further by asserting that 'distinction' is the simplest imaginable form or structure. As such, a distinction is the cardinal act of cognition. His Laws of Form (Spencer-Brown, 1969) asserts that it is in this phenomenological sense that distinction operates. This is reminiscent of William of Ockham's notion of an 'intentional distinction' (that is, mental) that is different from 'real distinction' (that is distinction at the level of material things). In other words, we assign distinctions whenever we observe subjective relations. While Spencer-Brown's conclusion emerged from a study of a wide range of disciplines including medicine, computing, mathematics and psychoanalysis, it is a truism that can only be verified within by its own linguistic terms. The biologist and cognitive scientist, Francisco Varela (1946–2001) appears to go even further by arguing (1969) that the act of making a 'distinction' is the living organism's primary act of cognition. Both set theory and number systems rely on the same idea (that is, 'boundary crossing'). However, this idea should not be over-emphasised because any given distinction is always a subjective event.

Nonetheless, many have been swayed by Spencer-Brown's idea, including Niklas Luhmann (1927–98), and Jacques Derrida (1930–2004), who said, 'unless a distinction can be made rigorous and precise it isn't really a distinction'. This may seem surprising, given that Derrida made a career out of declining to get to the point (cf. Derrida, 1978). Nonetheless, if designers are to develop a wiser repertoire of practices, they may need to question the tendency to see the world in these 'either-or' terms, or at least to go beyond where distinction is seen as categorical truth. A similar duality is the distinction between 'epistemology' and 'ontology' (see Chapter 3), which represents an artificial distinction. According to *The Upanishads*, the ancient Sanskrit scriptures, the universe is without 'name' or 'form'. This means that distinctions are a mere expediency. The interpretive domain of language projects difference onto the world by invoking categorical boundaries that differentiate between 'name' and 'form'. In other words, Indo-Germanic languages divide the world into separate objects, even though it is all Brahman (that is 'matter-energy'). This may be why sages traditionally seem to seek refuge in interventions that seem deliberately enigmatic, rather than precise or dogmatic. However, making the act of 'distinction' is precious within Western thought. Where Pythagoras valorised number, Aristotle developed a way of compartmentalising the world into what we know today as 'categories'. Both approaches remain enormously important to most aspects of our bureaucratic and technological world. To be fair, the structural tenets of bureaucracy are not all bad. At the practical level, many of us can hardly remember a world in which we managed without databases, digital programming languages or Google search engines. It is therefore an important issue that needs careful exploration. Philosophically speaking, it is good to remember that categories only exist because of the process of naming. Moreover, in Western cultures, names attract greater status and permanence because of the invention of alphanumeric writing.

This was a factor in establishing the symbolic importance of heavy books and libraries. According to Ong (1982), the introduction of sound recording and broadcasting became a new way to delay the gradual loss of importance of words uttered within a given context. Now that we have microphones and digital recorders, the relative importance of the book has begun to wane. It seems clear that power is delayed by symbolic events in the mind, rather than by the endurance of physical objects in the material world. The advent of digital logic has therefore revived the ancient importance of numbers. Moreover, it has been a process of reciprocal development in which a belief in numbers inspired the computer, and the efficacy of digital technology endorsed the Pythagorean claim to number as the stuff from which the world is made. It was largely Kant's thinking on this issue that paved the way for Charles Babbage's mechanistic, code-orientated innovations. Babbage (1791–1871) is an important figure for several reasons. Although better known for his pioneering work with development of the first digital computer, he also worked with Frederick Taylor on a reductionist system of management (Taylor, 1911) for factories. This is better known as 'Ford-ism'. It combined a Newtonian idea of time and a Cartesian idea of space to create a mechanistic and alienating method of production. The name Charles Babbage gave to his early prototype for a computer is significant. In calling it the 'Difference Engine' he gives a clue to the thinking behind the modern digital computer. In effect, the notion of 'difference' means the same as 'distinction'. Where some early computers were developed as 'analogue computers', Babbage's machine used cogs to perform complex counting tasks. Like all modern computers, it used a small, discrete set of arbitrary codes (that is numbers) that could be re-assigned to new tasks. This means, as a basic principle, that the numerical input will determine its output. This could be achieved by building in error-compensation processes that are mathematically precise. This was never true of analogue computers because they had no absolute way to govern small shifts, or drifts of value. Importantly, at some levels, Babbage's machine works on the basis of judging 'absolute distinctions' and processing them without questioning them in the light of subsequent or attendant information.

By contrast, analogue computers usually worked using mechanical or electrical components to simulate other processes such as the dynamics of fluids. Sometimes they would even use fluids in a model that was scaled down, or up, in order to simulate larger, or smaller events. It meant that they could perform tasks without having to use internal distinctions using an artificial language, such as programming. As such, they were, quite literally, not ideal. In a sense they are therefore more attuned to the chaotic logic of Heraclitus or Cratylus. Where digital computers can simulate the principles of balance or flow, they usually do so by idealising the parameters in a very precise way. In 'real' (that is analogue) systems the presence of noise is endemic, and this always affects the calculations. However, the programmers of digital computers can sidestep this problem by choosing to omit noise from the system. Following this hypothesis, one should be able to predict the future using precise enough numbers to make distinctions that are sufficiently 'fine-grained'.

Unfortunately, this does not hold true. We now know that numbers are never precise enough to simulate nature. Around 1963, the scientist Edward Lorenz noticed that a precise beginning did not always lead to clear, repeatable outcome. As Richard Feynman later asked himself (Feynman, 1965), 'Why should it take an infinite amount of logic to figure out what one tiny piece of space/time is going to do? So I have often made the hypotheses that ultimately physics will not require a mathematical statement, that in the end the machinery will be revealed, and the laws will turn out to be simple, like the chequer board with all its apparent complexities.' Here, it is vital to distinguish between simplicity and numerical precision. Lorenz's famous work on Chaos Theory emerged from studies of weather forecasting in 1960–61 (cf. Gleick, 1988). His initial experiments showed that, like many systems, the future states of a complex system are too sensitively dependent on its initial (that is first monitored) conditions to be fully computable. He therefore suggested that the weather would remain unpredictable. A popular figure used to illustrate Lorenz's argument is that of the 'butterfly effect', whereby we might conjecture that a butterfly flapping its wings on one side of the world could, conceivably, trigger tiny turbulent effects in the air that would, in turn, trigger larger and larger effects that lead to a hurricane on the other side of the world.

More than a century before Lorenz's insights, Charles Babbage's young assistant, Lady Ada Lovelace, realised that we might be able to encrypt attributes of 'quality' into calculating machines. Nevertheless, as history shows us, Babbage's emphasis on a quantified notion of 'difference' was probably more influential, notwithstanding the later advent of more visual, 'user-friendly' gadgets. It evolved into a further mathematical invention of a base-two number system by George Boole (1815–64). Clearly, George Boole's role is a vital one, especially as he advocated the separating of symbols used to 'operate' mathematical functions from those of the quantified 'data' itself. Arguably, by treating the 'operators' of calculation as distinct from the numerical values they operate on, Boole had made another step towards systemic alienation (Boole, 1958). This alienation stems from the essentially dualist idea that 'distinction' (in the sense alluded to by Spencer-Brown) is a cardinal property of the natural world. While it may be reasonable to agree with Kant that human beings need to make distinctions, this does not necessarily mean that they will have an autonomous existence in nature. When one living organism apprehends another there are likely to be separate processes of distinction that may align in specific ways. This is a way to explain structural coupling, but it is only an explanation. However, the practical success of digital computers seems to vindicate their theoretical limitations at the more philosophical level.

This rhetorical claim proved to be a decisive factor in the 'digital' lobby's struggle for research funding, almost a century later. One part of this story relates to the findings of Warren McCulloch, Walter Pitts and others, which appeared to prove that the nervous system operates in a simple 'binary' way (McCorduch, 1979). As we know, Claude Shannon's theory of communication (Shannon, 1963), combined with Warren Weaver's understanding of telephone systems led, quite unintentionally, to an implied generalisation of the philosophy of human discourse. Where binary logic might have looked like a travesty of how the world flows, it nevertheless offered certainty and power to its research sponsors in the military world.

Just as the digital world turned alphabetical writing into keyboard codes based on 0s and 1s, so late 20th century tabloid journalism pushed up the contrast on the grey-tones of the analogue world. In a fairly conspicuous way, some qualities have given way to quantities. If we explore the genres of www we may note that the hierarchical, twentieth century syntax of the popular press is often dumbed down to create 'user-friendly' web pages. Subtle journalistic aphorisms have increasingly tended to replaced by oppositely polarised adjectives such as 'fantastic' or 'crap'. Much of this language is traditionally associated with male values. Most of us are acquainted with the nerdish chauvinism of *Wired* magazine and *Red Herring,* just as we may accept the laddish hedonism of *Loaded* or *GQ* magazines.

Despite one or two signs of an imminent softening in the alphabetical world-view, academics still hold onto old assumptions of 'rigour' that attended the fervent quest for 'objectivity'. Remarkably, despite the general acceptance of a quantum reality, and by the epistemological revelations of Heisenberg and Gödel in the early twentieth century, the scientific and academic establishments have yet to respond by changing their methodological assumptions. This is surprising, given the extraordinary insights that have emerged from science's encounters with quantum computing, chaos theory, and connectionism. It is likely that some of the technologies that emerge from these discoveries will transform society by disabusing us of the notion that the world is profoundly atomistic and dualistic. The way that quantum computers will work is likely to remind us that miracles are possible (see Chapter 7).

Until we develop working examples of quantum clocks and computers we must work with clocks that are now, almost invariably, digital. One of the developments may reflect upon the way that a clock's digital display will jump, in theory, instantaneously from one number to the next, whether it is an hour, a minute, a second, or a part of a second. This means that we will include some reflection on number, in order to inform the more central questions about the clock, and why it might be thought to be so damaging. It will continue to assert, for example, that the 'rigour' (that is internal consistencies) within a given language will often lead to unhelpful inconsistencies.

Einstein's sceptical view of the applicability of mathematics, quoted at the beginning of this chapter, seems to disavow the Pythagorean legacy upheld by many scientists such as Galileo, who also believed that God wrote the universe in numerical form. Chapter 9 will discuss why Buckminster Fuller's term 'synergy of synergies', that he used to describe how the biosphere or universe holds itself together, is a wonderful concept that may help us to define our micro-utopian mission, and it is useful in that it embraces a sense of 'coherence', rather than 'integrity'. Here, again, this chapter seeks a wave-orientated description rather than an atomistic explanation for how a new mode of metadesign might be created, as a notion that is especially helpful in bringing our experience of time into play.

If we imagine everything in terms of 'flow', rather than 'distinction' we might be able to grasp how time was experienced before the invention of clocks with numbers. A beautiful line from the Qur'an (570–632 CE) conveys a clear sense of the numberless fluency of time.'… He coils the night upon the day and He coils the day upon the night' (a 39, verse 5). Arguably, at a phenomenological level, we may take delight in such a refreshingly non-atomistic metaphor for temporality. Indeed, we may be grateful that the Earth continues to make its smooth and uninterrupted orbit around the Sun. 'To coil' or 'to wind' is a translation of the Arabic verb 'kawwara', that describes the winding of a turban around the head. The metaphor may make us ask how sharp are the boundary edges that keep 'numbers' apart, and that we would use to measure intervals of time, or space. This contrasts with the Newtonian mathematics of flow that is essentially atomistic. As Zeno's fable of the hare and tortoise showed (c. 490 BC–c. 430 BC), this use of calculus for time and motion is deeply ironic. Whenever we use Newtonian equations of motion to visualise an object in motion we must imagine it at zero velocity. An 'algorithm' is a kind of mathematical calculus designed to respond, in advance, to certain conditions without adapting to their becoming. Unfortunately, Alan Turing's (1936) 'Halting Problem' shows that a general algorithm cannot be relied upon for a dependable decision.

Aristotle encouraged us to believe that time is linear and deterministic. It is possible that he developed his theory of time by gazing at the stars in the night sky. Because of the structure of our nervous system and the pace at which it operates, looking at a flow of stars is easier than trying to catch the movements in fire or water, because stars seem to have a fixed and eternal relationship to one another. However, in noting the obvious spatio-temporal remoteness of the heavens Aristotle overlooked their organic and relational nature. In the fifth century, St Augustine challenged the prevailing Aristotelian idea of 'astronomical time' by declaring a more 'subjective', or 'lived' time. Thus, he drew attention to the uniqueness of a temporal perspective in the way we experience events and actions. Understanding this may help us to design for 'micro-utopias'. Before Galileo introduced the idea of 'velocity' – a kind of 'de-natured' notion of speed – there had been a tacit assumption that space and time were integrated in a variegated quality of flow. Newton's intellectual authority endorsed the idea of time as a rational, autonomous, absolute, and ubiquitous entity. All of the above ideas are intermingled within the modern citizen's unconscious awareness of temporality. However, of all of the influences, from Aristotle, the Qu'ran, St Augustine, and through to Galileo and Newton, it is the Aristotelian-to-Newtonian thread that has dominated Western sensibilities. How do these sensibilities and beliefs affect the way we find an accord with the eco-system that supports us? My answer is not very encouraging.

We are so accustomed to technological innovation that recent developments such as 'International Time' now seem natural to us. As I have said, we trust machines more emphatically than our own (human) judgement. To be more precise, we tend to accept the clock's judgement as the best way to synchronise our actions with the world around us. Thus, the clock acts as a kind of ignorant superego for the body, telling it when it is the right moment to act (Wood, 1998). These tendencies are part of the intellectual assumptions that continue to inspire our folklore and everyday language. As the next chapter will show, this awareness of clock-time as a 'punctuated', linear and progress-orientated, event-based 'arrow' has helped to define the modern individual.

Today's digital clocks now function by the transmission of discrete 'pulses' or signals. Hence, the dominant (Newtonian) system of representing change as quasi-atomistic. However, if we adopt a more fluxist approach, it seems apparent that phase-relations are self-governing. In other words, events inspire one another in an emergent, emancipated way. There is therefore no 'conductor' who will ensure that the all the players in the 'orchestra' start and finish at the right time. For this reason, a unified, quasi-atomistic time scale cannot helpfully be imposed without destroying the 'natural' pace and dignity of things. This would be like putting everything in a greenhouse and emailing messages to each plant, giving the identical diary entries and outcome targets. In a sense, that is what classical science and modern technology has sought to do. Although modern scientists no longer fully accept Newton's belief in a 'Universal Time', the principle and functionality of the clock has yet to catch up with this change of view. Marx implies that, because of its austere mode of asymmetry, the clock typifies what is wrong with most machines. Indeed, the relationship between a clock and its user is highly asymmetrical. Where humans are able to adapt to an environment regulated by clock-time, the inverse is not the case. If we regard a clock and its user as a whole system we are likely to find that it works less synergistically than systems governed by externally imposed rules. Where ecosystems achieve homeostasis by self-regulation at almost every level, industry has tended to work with externally imposed plans that work in a linear way, using deadlines and targets.

So far, we have explored the alienation that curtails social synergies and that either directly, or indirectly, damages the biosphere. From a narrow managerial viewpoint, consumption is often regarded as a manageable process of linear metabolic change. All too often industry expects ecological systems to behave like mechanical systems. We therefore need to question the ecological viability of a linear, or predictable, model of change. In some ways this is a welcome shift from a purely materialistic notion of discrete 'objects' and products. Chapter 10 advocates a more 'flow-based' approach in which temporality becomes the essence of a more synergistic world (c.f. Csikszentmihalyi, 1990).

It may be relatively easy to make approximate summaries of the world by counting, but this is always abstract and reductive. The idea that numbers are everywhere is a vision that has haunted us through the centuries. It is the silent figure that saps the imagination and can never be put to death. It is the shadowy form of the Golem that the Romans would have stolen from the Jews. In the Enlightenment era we revived it and taught it how to walk. Today, it finds its shape in the romance of science, the bright lights of the Scientific Academies, and in the subterranean laboratories that conduct research into weaponry, stealthy governance and squalid algorithms designed to regulate consumption. For puritans everywhere, mathematics offers a nice, clean haven that keeps the user safe from any unguarded moments of becoming. Within the rational discourse of numbers, as distinct from the art of numerology, there is no autograph or time signature. The main heresy of number is ubiquity, and this implies that quality is only transient or fictional. This may prompt us to consider the quality of our ethical and sensual relationship with the world.

Ludwig Wittgenstein (1889–1951) was intrigued by the nature of language. He first believed, with Bertrand Russell, that he might be able to design a 'perfect' language. He had presumably been taken in by a Pythagorean belief that mathematical consistency can be mapped onto a mathematically inconsistent world. He became more aware of the emergent nature of language by attempting this task. Later in his life he noted: 'Everyday language is part of the human organism, and no less complicated than it' (Wittgenstein, 1921).

As he showed in his later work (Wittgenstein, 1961; 1967), language adapts to difference by operating within a set of mutually adaptive conditions (that is, 'language games'). This is why languages tend to lose meaning outside their use in a given context. Classical science dealt with this problem by looking for truths that would hold up outside a known context and by using unsituated languages to describe them. Perhaps it is this connotative and adaptive feature of language that gives the scientifically observed world its appearance of homogeneity. Even by adopting an atomistic approach to explore simple axioms we would believe there to be a 'combinatorial explosion' of factors.

By this point, it may be clear to the reader that this author is not being entirely 'objective' about the idea of 'objectivity'. This is not to say that he thinks the concepts of rigour and monogeneity are totally without merit. Indeed, NASA continues to show that Newtonian ballistics is indispensable for sending large objects around the heavens. Similarly, arithmetic and algebra worked most effectively for building pyramids or for managing empires. However, what I will show is that these methods were designed for the management of vast projects, but are less useful for the cultivation of convivial communities. In effect, an underlying philosophical tenet of these methods of writing and counting is the unproven assumption that the world is atomistic, rather than, say, wave-based. This may have been useful for the management of armies, weapons, ballistics and large-scale currency systems. Its deployment would therefore justify an emphasis on the role of nouns, rather than verbs. Where atomistic thought leads to divisions, dualities, distinctions, categories and facts, a wave-based world makes one more aware of analogies, compensatory systems, holistic pictures and a sense of unity. In an atomistic world it therefore makes sense to speak of certainty, because the epistemology of atomism has tended to assume that a particle must either be present or absent from a given place. This led to an enduring mystery within quantum physics that defies most (cf. Bohm, 1980) attempts to apply the self-consistent logic that has been useful for atomistic thought. Perhaps we might re-address the problem by re-designing the language of flow, and by developing new technologies that may enhance, rather than halt our experience of flow.

Our tendency to trust clocks in preference to our own sense of time emerged from a belief that machines are more precise than humans. But what does precision mean? One explanation is that clocks are observer-independent arbitrators of flow. They offer a common external reference to which our different subjective times can be related. This is because they are machines designed to be isolated from our metabolic and political temporalities. Clock time is an extremely detached and reductive referent to the idea of flow. This chapter seeks a fresh understanding of temporality that calls for 'synergy' and 'consciousness' to be regarded as desirable parameters of clock design.

Conventionally speaking, a 'well-designed' clock is thermodynamically insulated from its surroundings. In cybernetic terms it is therefore an artificial, closed-order system that entices the 'user' into following a narrow system of temporality. Despite technological refinements such as atomic counters, or radio frequency transmission, modern clocks still function as closed-order systems in which a local spatio-temporal event-horizon is used to reference the rate of change in many other events that exist in separate and different systems. When many users share the 'same' clock-time, this problem diminishes because they are all implicitly working within a shared time frame. Nevertheless, the clock remains as the primary referent for action, even though it is far more ignorant than its users. The clock regulates human anticipation in such a way that it alienates us from the very things to which we need to attune ourselves. By enabling relations between clocks and users to become more reciprocal and playful it may be possible to reduce alienation and thereby to enhance the quality of temporal experiences. However, clocks continue to add to the problem of ecological alienation because they perpetuate the myth of a single temporality (that is Newton's 'mathematical time') that is assumed to be monogeneous and one-dimensional. This is a reductionist approach in which time-space is ubiquitous yet lacking in variety. Although we still use clocks that apply the old Newtonian paradigm this is anachronistic.

In the mindset, the location of a body in motion must be considered at 'time zero' when considering its velocity. Western successors such as Galileo and Newton chose to ignore this problem. In the 20th century this fundamental problem of symbolic logic was successfully challenged (for example Wittgenstein, 1921; Sardar, 2002; Turing, 1937), but it was only with Chaos Theory (that is after 1962) that the problem was fully accepted as being more than a problem of granular precision (Gleick, 1988). Much western philosophical thought has tended to seek as much certainty and 'truth' as possible. One way to find certainty is to ignore the totality of a given question in its full context. This often makes it easier to reach clear conclusions. At first glance, simple number systems are impressive for their capacity to demonstrate unequivocal propositions. Where science long sought to demonstrate a perfect order or 'sameness' throughout the whole universe, second order cybernetics might be used to theorise a more surprising, less homogeneous world. If we can have 'second order' cybernetics in which the auto pilot 'knows' it is making a difference to things, we may conjecture that there is no upper limit to the orders of awareness and self-awareness that we can attain. Arguably, this can be found in Asian philosophies that inspired the (1999) film, *The Matrix*, and in Heisenberg's Principle of Uncertainty.

In the case of the 'smart' auto pilot, it may eventually understand that it might be making decisions that, while they conform to the flight plan, are nevertheless likely to lead to a fatal accident in which it will perish, along with the aeroplane. This obviously describes an instrument that is better than 'smart' – it is 'clever'. If it were just a bit more 'clever', then it might begin to understand that its awareness of new ideas is causing it to hesitate and that this is making the pilot nervous enough to take over, and thus, to follow the fatal flight path. This level of awareness is probably beyond 'cleverness'. At what order of cybernetic skill would we need to design it to 'wise'? How might we design such an instrument to feel 'fear' or even 'love'? In questioning human 'presence', we should confront the issue of temporality, and this is where (second order) cybernetics sought to transcend mechanistic paradigms. Nevertheless, the rise of cybernetics as we know it would have been difficult to imagine without the long history of clock making and its latent propensity for instrumental regulation and control. The 'precision' of clocks is one of the technological triumphs of the negative feedback principal that is central to the discipline of first order cybernetics. On the other hand, the apparent precision of the modern clock derives from an order of logic that upholds Newton's idea of a fundamentally extrinsic, ubiquitous and rigorous temporality. In the Newtonian mindset, time is depicted as a linear, 'closed system' and the design of clocks still upholds this illusion, long after Einstein's day.

The more that clocks have become synchronised with one another over the last few hundred years the more that subsequent developments such as GMT and World-Time sustain the Newtonian illusion of time as a universal, predestined and one-dimensional reality. By contrast, if we consider how human beings think and act, moment by moment, in pursuit of their own continuing survival, we may realise that the present must, of necessity, be multi-dimensional, provisional and contingent. When we identify the 'passing' of time from within a strict Newtonian frame we are dissuaded from including ourselves as observers. This is because Newton's approach takes a post-hoc view of 'category plus object', rather than one that is *ad hoc* to the 'verb plus subject'. It seems to confirm that 'time' is absolute, autonomous and universal. In this Newtonian order, actual events become more predictable even though they may remain translucent to experiential enquiry. In casual conversation we may speak of 'measuring' time, but we tend to co-create it, rather than 'monitor' it. Nevertheless, the popular belief in an independent temporality has had an enormous effect at the social, cultural (Virilio, 1977) and ecological levels (Wood, 1998). Although we may disapprove of Newton's epistemology as problematic, many scientists still revere him for his intellectual achievement. Some even tend to disconnect his arguments from the environmentally damaging effects that they inspired.

Micro-utopian design must work from the basis that human beings are open systems operating in worlds of considerable complexity, whose boundaries always include other participants and observers (see Table 6.1). These are worlds too complex to map in a singular time frame.

In seeking to go beyond the self-denying nature of classical scientific observation, Heinz von Foerster (1911–2002) made a helpful distinction between 'first order' and 'second order' cybernetics. First order cybernetics is characterised by the simple devices that are part of a 'self-regulation' or 'self-steering' system. Common examples are those of a radiator's thermostat, or an aircraft's auto pilot. For example, when the radiator gets hot, the thermostat notices this and sends a signal to switch off the heating supply. Conversely,

Table 6.1   Levels of temporal 'openness'

MODE of Time	DESCRIPTION
Metabolic Time	An organism's sense of its own internal processes
Environmental Time	An organism's instinctual ability to synchronise its metabolic time with changes in its surroundings
Social Reciprocal Time	The sense of a shared pace when co-operating with others (includes music, poetry and dance, and so on)
Agricultural Time	The paced management of tasks within a language that chronicles seasonal, or other natural (for example lunar) cycles
Astronomical Time	An epistemological synchronisation with changes at the scale of human epochs or histories
Clock Time	Pace of mechanical instruments designed to display regular intervals at about the scale of diurnal cycles or human actions
Newtonian Time	Newtonian epistemology of time as being independent of everything else and therefore constant, everywhere
Digital Clocks	Electronic devices that create, communicate, and record intervals too long/short for us to read in 'real time'
Globalised Time	The synchronisation of clock-times across regions or continents as a way to regularise transportation, and so on
Semi-automated, Human Reciprocal Time	The shared time of co-operation (for example where mobile phones and digital diaries are used to regulate the agreed time of meeting between travelling participants)
Networked, Machine-Assisted Reciprocal Time	The semi-automated, distributed systems of flow, using product tagging, product code readers and databases, for example with PML (Product Mark-up Language)

when the radiator cools down again, the thermostat tells the boiler to switch on again. Heinz Von Foerster describes these kinds of devices as 'observed systems', because they depend on a simple element that determines the level or state of a given parameter (such as temperature, or deviation from a chosen flight path). In von Foerster's 'second order cybernetic system' – or what he describes as the study of 'observing systems' – there are additional levels of self-consciousness that include the first level. In second order systems, the issue of self-reflexive responsibility is raised, at least, by implication. Von Foerster therefore invites the observer of systems to 'enter the domain of his own descriptions' and accept responsibility for being in the world. 'Being in the world' entails the capacity to imagine what appears to be happening and to anticipate how it might be made better. If Pythagoras and the clock-makers were correct, then the universe is a homogeneous domain of rigour. If correct, this implies that the scientist is always a neutral observer, free from ethical constraints and responsibilities. There are many arguments to refute this, including the fact that science seldom explores the genesis of a new idea, preferring to address the pathway from concept to revelation. This is unfortunate, as theories of language, chaos and psychoanalysis (Wood, 1998) are all relevant to the way that scientific observations are made.

At a more practical level, developments such as networks of enterprise, globalised consumerism and ubiquitous credit facilities ensure that we can maintain our activities at consumption levels well above what we need to make us happy. Many workers elect to buy their own personal phones and portable computers that link them to their workplaces at all hours of the day and night. In a sense, mobile phones are beginning to facilitate a more human form of consensual temporality (Wood, 1998) whereby, for example, the agreed time for a meeting is adjusted until all the travelling participants are close enough for arrival times to be synchronised. New inventions could advance this non-clock-based mode of timing, especially with satellite-based Global Position Systems and scheduling software. However, the introduction of 'smart' products (Gershenfeld, 1999), with global product-tagging systems and ubiquitous computing may mean that a viable cybernetics of human presence may become even more difficult to devise.

This chapter has sought to describe how clock-time works, and why it is less than helpful. It has hinted that the new technologies could make clocks less ignorant by linking temporality to the temporality of relative events, rather than to their own solipsistic worlds. PDAs (Portable Digital Assistants) are now capable of being more precise. When I ask my watch to tell me what the time is, I need a particular quality of answer depending on what I am seeking to do.

Instead, a clock will give me an answer without asking me why I need it. If I want to know the time because I am hoping to catch the next train to Dallas the clock would need to know where I am, how I might get to the station, the train timetable and the latest travel update. If I am asking about the time because I am meeting a friend, the clock will need to calculate our likely arrival times and how late or early each of us likely to be. In this second case, the 'time' referred to is a local consensual time, rather than a widely shared public time. Neither are 'absolute' times, although the second maybe less predictable than the first.

Returning to the challenge of how to 'dream' ourselves a little closer to a world of micro-utopias, we might see the realm of the unthinkable as exemplified by a dream state, albeit one in which our 'prime designers' are 'lucid dreamers', rather than passive sleepers. Let us assume we have the optimism and the confidence to imagine our own 'micro-utopia' in such detail that we slowly begin to see ways in which we could make it a reality. However, we are surprised to find that, before we start to build it, it emerges – almost magically – by itself. This may not be as unlikely a scenario as we might assume.

References

Ashby, W.R. (1956), *Introduction to Cybernetics* (New York: Wiley).

Benjamin, W. (1992), *Illuminations*, Zohn, H. L. (trans.) (London: Fontana Press).

Bohm, D. (1980), *Wholeness and the Implicate Order* (Boston and London: Routledge and Kegan Paul).

Boole, G. (1958), *An Investigation of the Laws of Thought on Which are Founded the Mathematical Theories of Logic and Probabilities* (New York; Dover Publications).

Csikszentmihalyi, M. (1990), *Flow: the Psychology of Optimal Experience* (New York: Harper & Row).

Derrida, J. (1978), *Writing and Difference* (Boston and London: Routledge and Kegan Paul).

Einstein, A. (1920), 'Ether and the theory of relativity' in *Sidelights on Relativity* Einstein, A. (Canada: General Publishing Company).

Feynman, R. P. (1965), *The Character of Physical Law* (Cambridge: M.I.T. Press).

Fuad-Luke, A. (2002), *Eco Design: the Sourcebook* (San Francisco, CA: Chronicle Books).

Gershenfeld, N. (1999), *When Things Start to Think* (New York: Henry Holt and Co., Inc.).

Gleick, J. (1988) *Chaos: Making a New Science* (New York: William Heinemann).

Hall, E. T. (1968), *Proxemics in Current Anthropology*, 9:2/3, pp. 83–108. [DOI: 10.1086/200975]

Halgh, J. (2000), *Taking Chances: Winning with Probability* (Oxford: Oxford University Press).

Marx, K. (1988), *Economic and Philosophic Manuscripts of 1844 in The Communist Manifesto*, Milligan, M., Marx, K., and Engels, F. (trans.) (Amherst, New York: Prometheus Books).

McCorduch, P., (1979), *Machines Who Think*, (San Francisco: Freeman).

Mumford, L. (1934), *Technics and Civilisation* (New York: Harcourt Brace and Co.).

Ong, J. W. (1982), *Orality and Literacy; The Technologising of the Word* (London and New York: Methuen).

Sardar, Z., Ravetz, J. and Van Loon, B. (2002), *Introducing Mathematics* (Royston, UK: Icon Books).

Shannon, C. E. and Weaver, W. (1963), *The Mathematical Theory of Communication*, 5th edition (Chicago: University of Illinois Press).

Spencer-Brown, G. (1969), *Laws of Form*, (New York: Dutton).

Taylor, F. W. (1911), *The Principles of Scientific Management* (New York: Harper).

Turing, A. M. (1937), 'On computable numbers, with an application to the entscheidungs problem', *Proc. London Math. Soc. Ser.*, 2:42, pp. 230-265. Reprinted in *The Undecidable*, David, M. (ed.) (Hewlett, NY: Raven Press, 1965).

Varela, F. J., Thompson, E. and Rosch, E. (1991), *The Embodied Mind: Cognitive Science and Human Experience* (Cambridge, MA: The MIT Press)

Virilio, P. (1977), *Speed and Politics: An Essay on Dromology* (New York: Semiotext(e)).

Whitehead, A. N. (1925) 'Science and the modern world, vol. 55' in *Great Books of the Western World Series*, (Cambridge: Cambridge Univeristy Press).

Wittgenstein, L. (1961), *Tractatus Logico Philosophicus*, Pears, D. F. and McGuinness, B. F. (trans.) (Boston and London: Routledge and Kegan Paul).

Wittgenstein, L. (1967), *Philosophical Investigations* (Oxford: Basil Blackwell).

Wood, J. (1998), *The Virtual Embodied; Presence, Practice, Technology* (London and New York: Routledge).

Thinking Beyond the Possible

CHAPTER

7

'The earth melts into the sea as the sea sinks into the earth'

(Heraclitus, Fragment 23)

The previous chapter criticised the language of pragmatism and expediency that sustains the current path of global capitalism. This is why the last chapter discussed the nature of numbers and their role in how we experience the world. In particular, it looked at the way that mathematics has insinuated itself into our temporal experience in order to persuade us that time is a halting process of 'stasis', rather than 'flow' (see Chapter 11). Mathematics is a profoundly unsituated language, both temporally and spatially. In this sense, it generates an ethical dilemma that is similar to that of design. Both scientists and artists ask for an ideologically 'neutral' space within which to think, yet both have to face the unforeseen consequences of their inventiveness. Classical science implies that a citizen might be able to observe 'reality' without needing to include his or her role within the account. Early in the twenty-first century, Professor Stephen Hawking was disappointed not to find a TOE (a 'Theory of Everything') and has now given up. His quest echoes the claim by Pythagoras that numbers can somehow exemplify everything that exists. For simple-minded non-cosmologists, however, it raises a number of questions about what is meant by 'everything'. This is a big word. Does it, for example, include you, who are reading this text at this very moment? Does it include what you can see around you and what you can imagine might happen in the next 5 minutes? Does it include your own 'dream' of the world? Indeed, does it include your dream of your own 'dream' of the world? This raises several more difficult questions. If the human mind is capable of observing, understanding and describing its own condition whilst taking everything else into account, why would we wish to reduce this capability?

In seeking new ways of living that compensate for the suicidal tendencies of our species, this chapter emphasises the importance of 'dreaming', or envisioning new scenarios. Although we can understand events by reading newspapers and journals, our narcissistic and solipsistic tendencies tend to blind us to important aspects of what is happening. There are many reasons for this, including an anodyne, carefully stage-managed system of representative democracy, led by highly professional politicians. This has brought about a situation in which today's citizens have become choosers, rather than dreamers. What we urgently need are more imaginative and playful ways of thinking that can be shared and enacted to create a wiser society. Certain aspects of our education and democratic systems actively discourage society from envisioning new futures. This is because the legacy of a somewhat bureaucratic and imperialistic mindset also makes it difficult to think beyond the negative discourse that characterises our disconnected behaviour as a species. What is required is a new methodology that embraces both actions and ideas. This chapter explores the feasibility of implementing a far broader and more holistic mode of design. In developing this proposal it explores the 'idea of the idea' and its influential role in the design tradition. It opens this question by outlining a positive mode of reflection that I call 'dreaming'. These arguments are used to trace out the possibility of a micro-utopian world that is far less wasteful and confused. In previous chapters, a good deal of criticism was directed at the dysfunctional nature of our society, and the attitudes, methodologies, technologies and practices that sustain it. It is easy to criticise. In fact, our readiness to adopt a negative stance is part of the problem. Within a negative mindset, bad things always confirm one's expectations. This is why 'dystopias' often seem far more real than 'utopias'. It explains why the word 'utopian' has become synonymous with the 'unattainable'.

This is a vicious circle. We get more excited by bad news than good news and we always expect the worst. The daily newspapers therefore depict the world in terms of war, hunger, plague, greed, corruption, exploitation and waste, because we expect the worst. Unfortunately, knowing more about the negative than the positive does not encourage us to improve things. Most of us probably know, for example, that the human race has consumed more resources since 1950 than in all of our previous time on Earth. We also know that this situation cannot go on for much longer. We are aware that high technologies and exploitative conditions in poorer countries are generating mountains of cheap goods that can be offered to those with money, even though they may neither want nor need them. Nevertheless, as privileged individuals we are all tempted by the chance to have more possessions, wealth and power. Meanwhile, mainstream economists warn that we must work much harder in order to compete with the poorer countries, therefore the controls on our economic system are still set for 'growth' without limit. Our debt-based money system continues to generate individual discomfort unless we earn enough to keep up the repayments. If we are workless we feel uncomfortable, because jobs win respect. Politicians feel compelled to deliver 100 per cent employment and the highest level of economic growth. Meanwhile, all around the world, the poorest people are getting poorer and the natural environment is taking a beating. All of these conditions are linked by the human tendency to avoid taking action unless we think it will bring a subsequent advantage. This is one reason why we have become cynical pragmatists, rather than optimistic dreamers. Another possible reason for our reluctance to envision a better world is the lasting influence of rationalism that reached a high point in the eighteenth century. For example, Immanuel Kant's (1724–1804) belief in a perfect God led him to conclude that it was the Christian's duty to seek a moral perfection that was perpetually out of reach. Kant's notion of ethics developed out of a strong belief in a categorical nature of truth and a consequent duty to follow strict moral codes, boundaries, duties and obligations. But if social harmony can only be upheld by the framing of laws and punishments, then any mention of 'utopia' could be painfully provocative because it reminds us of the unbridgeable gap between (God's) perfection and (our) human inadequacies. In this sense, Kantian ethics still plays a large part in perpetuating the idea of Utopia, while also rendering it unattainable.

On the other hand, in Europe, at least, society has become increasingly secular and the moral imperative is eclipsed by an increasingly expedient, consumer-based, comfort-orientated code of ethics. Kant was not the first to envision an idealistic framework for human conduct. Several thousand years before, Aristotle searched for a social state of being that, using more up-to-date language, could be described as 'Utopian'. Although the idea of 'Utopia' may be self-evident to some of us, it may not be so familiar to everyone. Indeed, some non-westerners find it a difficult idea to grasp. One reason for this is probably its peculiarly western assumption that virtue is latent in everything. Like many Enlightenment thinkers, Gottfried Leibniz (1646–1714) had faith in a rational approach, but he also had a Christian belief in the intrinsic 'goodness' of Nature. He figured that, if God is good, then we already live in the best of all logically possible worlds. This implies that design would be unnecessary in finding micro-utopias. Leibniz seems to be offering a view that some thinkers might describe as defeatist. He said, for example, '...what... must happen... will happen even if I do nothing; and if it is not to happen it will never happen, no matter what trouble I take to bring it about.'

Perhaps we might follow this kind of fatalistic approach to become more in touch with what we already have. The idea that goodness and optimism are everywhere probably stems from the traditional Christian emphasis on modesty, patience, tolerance and good intentions. In particular, it also emphasises hope. Christianity is a fusion of ideas deriving from several ancient cultures, especially the Judaic, Greek and Roman traditions. Hope is a strong idea that becomes almost palpable in the Pauline (that is Roman) side of Christianity. Many stories of Utopia are therefore anticipatory in that they contain defiant images of promise or prediction. This also helps to explain the importance of passion within the Christian belief system. Passion is both wishfully optimistic and nostalgically sorrowful. The belief in an eternal, blissful, heaven that awaits the repentant sinner is obviously a powerful idea that informs this sense of 'utopia' as holy pilgrimage. In some religious texts, for example, a kind of Utopian destination is referred to as 'heaven' or 'kingdom come'.

Since the middle of the twentieth century, political visions of well-being became reduced down to a purpose of economic growth, and – by strong implication – profligate waste (Douthwaite, 1992; Hamilton, 2003). In this respect, the growing interest in the rights and well-being of workers is still seen as a luxury in many parts of the world, for this has been secondary to the imperative of production itself. Why do we appear to sit back and do nothing positive about these urgent problems? Indeed, would we be able to make appropriate changes, even if we were concerned about these issues? Perhaps we are just too confused by the speed and complexity of modern life. In preparing to make things better, we must begin to understand why things work the way they do, and then adapt to them in a more positive and optimistic way. This is because it is essential to believe that change is feasible, otherwise we may not proceed with the appropriate level of urgency. Logically speaking, however low the probability of a given scenario, its existence is affected by our frame of reference and our mental and emotional outlook. The more we assume something to be possible, the more likely we are to be lucky.

This approach is an inverted mode of scepticism. It is diametrically opposite, for example, to Karl Popper's famous scientific method, which looks for evidence that that will falsify a given hypothesis. Using this approach, we are left only with the irrefutable evidence. Within the Popperian approach, a hypothesis is only good enough if it can survive strenuous attempts to discredit it. This type of science therefore eschews 'passion' and 'faith', choosing, instead, to confine itself to the search for rational evidence from the material world.

How might we join up visions to make an inclusive and viable world? What is connectable and what is not? These are practical questions that will need to be addressed if we are to work more collaboratively, towards a better world.

This means exchanging values and principles. We might risk generalising some of the main differences that need to be integrated. On the other hand, many aspects of contemporary science and mathematics seem extremely playful and open to the 'unthinkable'. Where artists and designers are often fascinated by the act of invention, scientists maybe more interested in the process by which it can be proved to be correct. The proclaimed task of science is to observe and to make claims to truth, rather than to design for a better world, or to indulge the scientist's personal ideologies or predilections.

In the 'developed' world of the twenty-first century we have never had more access to more information or technology. Our institutions of learning have never worked harder in finding better solutions to more problems, and our collective knowledge has never been more extensive. This suggests that we are already living in a perennially imperfect Utopia, so why doesn't it feel like that? The good news is that, in an open society we can all write to the newspapers and make our objections known. The bad news is that, as citizens, we don't really believe we can change anything. In a turbulent culture of blame and 'spin' we depend on politicians to have good ideas, but we are cynical and therefore don't really expect them to. We behave as though the voter's job is merely to criticise by choosing a colour, every 5 years or so. Arguably, the unthinking acceptance of this system is what stops us from visualising Utopia. For us, the politics of 'blame' is more familiar than the politics of resistance, and the politics of resistance is easier than the politics of the collective imagination. Ironically, there are changes that, in private, politicians will admit are needed, but which would prove highly unpopular to address. We are desperately in need of new visions, but the more professional our politicians become, the less space is left for the private imagination. In a prosperous society of comfort and speed the perceived need for dreaming may seem to be distant. This puts us in a dangerous predicament. In order to move beyond cynicism and pessimism, we must therefore learn to dream. If we lose the art of dreaming for ourselves we will eventually become unable to change anything. For this reason, envisioning and exchanging dreams of better possible futures should be seen as a civic duty that is far more important than voting or paying taxes. By 'dreaming' I do not mean choosing the most exotic, outrageous, or selfish lifestyles from a repertoire of holiday or retirement fantasies.

The kind of dreams that a holarchic (cf. Koestler, 1969) society would need are likely to be broad, rather than deep. Positive dreams need to be inclusive, heterogeneous and connectable. This means that each dreamer should, ideally, be sensitive to adjacent dreams, and capable of dovetailing in with them, or complementing them in some way. We already have many familiar genres of science and science fiction that tease, frighten and alienate us. These should not be discouraged, but we also need new genres that will simply encourage us to ask how we would really, really, really like to live with one another. Arguably, humans do not usually feel happy for long when they act in a duplicitous or self-centred way. The task of dreaming should therefore be an invitation to be exceedingly honest with oneself. Perhaps this technique can be taught in schools and colleges. The work of the Attainable Utopias Network has shown that 'dreams' like this can be elicited through a simple interview and questionnaire format. This rather clumsy approach is merely the starting point. It may not be necessary once we all learn how to 'dream', but can be, for many, a helpful starting point. It is important that each citizen should eventually feel willing to offer a coherent vision that reflects how she or he feels. We do not really need our citizens to invent highly advanced technologies, or to envision strange utopias in the style of *Star-Trek*, or *Star Wars*. However, we do need to ask each other what makes us happy. We need to share practices and visions that help to make us feel 'at home' with ourselves, and with our earthly surroundings. This is where the practices of dreaming can be politically transformative. It is very likely that dreams will need to be interpreted and exchanged across the boundaries of age, gender, wealth, language, culture and class.

It is important to establish a depth of meaning for 'dreaming'. Several thousand years ago the Taoist master Chuang Tzu (369–286 BCE) is said to have dreamed he was a butterfly. When he awoke it occurred to him that he could not be sure whether he was a man who had just dreamed of being a butterfly, or whether he was a butterfly dreaming he was a man. This may suggest that wise dreams are probably contingent, self-reflexive and open to interpretation by others. By contrast, Descartes' questions seem to show a less subtle understanding of this idea (Veitch, 1907). By reducing the question of his own existence to a single decision, 'how can I know that I am really here?', Descartes achieved lasting notoriety for reflecting on a doubtful mode of self-confidence. He wrote in his Meditations: 'Indeed! As if I did not remember other occasions when I have been tricked by exactly similar thoughts while asleep! As I think about it more carefully, I see plainly that there are never any sure signs by means of which being awake can be distinguished from being asleep'. Compared with the Taoist master's enquiry, Descartes' version seems to lack imagination.

Not surprisingly, the word 'idealism' is connected to the word 'idea' and, in the last few thousand years, Western thought has tended to emphasise its importance as a way of moving toward action. Most of us use it so often that we may never question what we mean by it. Loosely speaking, an 'ideal' is a paradigmatic version of an imagined scenario. For extreme pragmatists, ideals are not very helpful, unless we can imagine, discuss and realise them. The word 'idea' derives from the ancient Greek word ('eidos') that refers to a 'bed'. In Plato's day, it referred to the form of the bed, which was first modelled in his divine workshop by God, copied by the human model maker and finally, perhaps, even less perfectly copied for manufacture in many different factories. Today, manufacturers are aware that markets follow trends, and that beneath these trends there is often a basic concept or premise upon which they are founded. In the west we have become used to looking for this founding concept, or 'idea', often in preference to assimilating the vastly complex and unnameable flow of experiences. This way of thinking emerged over the last three and a half thousand years. Broadly speaking, virtually all of the formative thinkers before Socrates (the so-called 'Pre-Socratics') were hoping to find a single, unifying metaphysical theme that would serve to summarise everything in and about the world. The Hindus had already postulated a uniform but imperceptible stuff generating the phenomenal world – the stuff often compared with clay, copper, or iron, out of which all manner of things are made. Hence, different philosophers believed the world to consist of a particular element such as 'air', 'water', 'rock', or 'fire'. This way of seeing things may also have been inspired by a growing manufacturing industry in which certain raw materials were refined and used to develop product types that could be replicated in batches.

We know, for example, that a successful international ceramics industry had evolved in places like Corinth and Athens by Plato's day. This would have meant that the thinkers of the day would almost certainly have been familiar with what we, today, call 'mass production'. This helps to explain why the concept of 'form' became so important, and why it became associated with the notion of the 'idea'. In a product-centred mass market, the shape or appearance of one particular product is often what makes it more attractive and therefore more saleable than another. John Onians (1991) shows how this may have inspired Plato's theory of a pure realm of perfect form that we might imagine to be latent or implicit within the actual world of less than perfect objects emerging from, say, a potter's wheel. Perhaps surprisingly, the Greeks held trade exhibitions, rather like the ones we have today. As a way to initiate orders for products, they showed samples called 'deigma'. This word was derived from 'deiknumi', literally meaning 'I show', and used to describe a sample product picked out from the others on account of its high standard of perfection. This informs our modern word 'paradigm', which derives from a 'paradeigma', or production prototype that would have been stored well away from the risky world of actual use, because it embodied the very highest standards of 'perfection'.

Plato particularly valued the qualities of 'paradeigma', which he saw as being eternal and fixed rather than flexible and organic. He ascribed this scenario to the structural basis of Creation, that is, the 'Idea' of the universe, arguing that beauty only derives from things that endure by virtue of their precedent. In this influential scenario God is portrayed as the master craftsman who provides the 'paradeigmata' for all subsequent ideas and products. The idea of the idea has become a genre, in which claims to perfection are probably best enshrined in words, rather than in more revealing media such as images or forms. In some respects the 'idea of the idea' has not changed so much in the modern era. Perhaps the greatest transformation has taken place in respect to how we understand the role of the human mind in the universe as a whole. Where Plato saw all 'ideas' as having, of necessity, originated from God, John Locke (1689) proposed that an 'idea' could emerge from the individual mind of a mortal human being. This represents a truly momentous change in the Western belief system.

The deeply ingrained 'idea of the idea' is probably what enabled biologist Richard Semon, in 1921 (c.f. Schachter, 2001) to conceive of the idea of the 'meme' as the smallest unit of evolution within society. Much of Semon's original interest in what we now call 'memetics' was sociological. Today many people are more familiar with the term 'meme', after Richard Dawkins popularised it within the context of biological evolution (Dawkins, 1976). It is tempting to interpret the word 'meme' as meaning anything that seems to replicate itself, whether it is biological, physical, an object, a fashion, style or organism. Interestingly, compared with the sociological and biological realm, less attention has been paid to the memetics of designs and how they interact with their individual 'users'. I have suggested that we might be able to design successful 'memes' by ensuring that the following four key parameters are present at appropriate times throughout the expected life of a transformative idea (Wood, 2004):

1.   A sufficient level of desirability

2.   A sufficient level of attainability

3.   A sufficient level of reproducibility

4.   A sufficient level of maintainability

We can clarify these conditions by saying that, by speaking of 'desirability' the idea in question must be clearly identifiable, or recognisable as a desirable entity. One person may have an idea that would be highly attractive, yet may be unknown, invisible, meaningless, or unclear to others. In the second condition, it is not enough for an idea to be attainable. Unless citizens believe that it is feasible they will be very unlikely to reach out for it. This underlines the importance of 'thinking beyond the possible'. The notion of 'attainability' reflects an important aspect of the way the human mind works. If we want something we are likely to try to reach out for it. However, if we adamantly believe it be unreachable we will probably ignore it. If we can prove to ourselves that something is desirable and attainable we may try to sustain the experience. In the third condition, the idea of reproducibility really means that the concept in question can be successfully copied and, if required, adapted to suit a new context. Finally, the notion of 'maintainability' means that the functionality or effectiveness of the idea can be prolonged. This means that it can easily be improved or adapted to suit new or emerging conditions.

In the natural world, living organisms evolve, sometimes by finding new patterns of behaviour that are noticeable and attractive and replicable. Homo sapiens seems to do this with particular pleasure and wit. With our indomitable habits of trading, exchanging, designing and making, it is likely that all of the four conditions above would be recognisable in all societies. Richard Dawkins' idea of the meme has been adapted and adopted as a metaphor in the creative industries. For example, we may find it implied in the notion of 'viral marketing' that is intended to inspire a 'zeitgeist' that pervades the whole system. According to Dawkins, genes behave as invisible, self-serving agents of change. In this scenario, the living organism is cast as a mere host to be colonised and manipulated by the gene. The 'meme' is not easily categorised as either 'material object' or 'active process'. However, it may be helpful in advancing the idea of the 'idea', and how it can work.

Some new ideas certainly seem to change the way we see the world, and they therefore affect the way we live our lives. The way this happens is therefore important to anyone seeking to design micro-utopias. It is useful to know why some ideas seem 'of the moment', where others take a long time to 'catch on'. Part of this process is in the way that mammals and the more complex creatures connote the meaning and possible purpose of an event, entity or predicament that is unexpected. The mathematician, Charles Peirce coined the term 'abduction' in 1899 to account for the ingenious logic of pragmatic actions in an uncertain world (Peirce, 1958). Abduction is a mode of anticipatory interpolation in which the thinker conjectures possible explanatory schema from outside the problem space in order to account for a surprising event. The abductive process is akin to the mathematical idea of factoring, in which two unknown numbers have been multiplied together to produce a factor. The task is to decide which numbers might have produced the known factor. Bateson (1973) suggests that this mode of logic is ubiquitous within the natural order. Without abductive reasoning, he argues, there could be no evolutionary change and adaptation in the ecosystem. Abductive reasoning is a convincing way to explain how we cope with the highly complex and ambiguous information that we encounter in any situation where predators and prey are seeking to hide from or to find one another. Where bureaucratic thinking starts with written facts or imperatives ('A' and 'B') and looks for a factor ('C') that follows from this, abductive reasoning is often more immediately situated and imaginative. In the industrial world, Taylorism and bureaucracy usually dictate the terms of reference by which a problem must be solved. Often, this means that prices and regulations set the conditions for clear decision-making. In abductive reasoning we must always look beyond the given situation for our answer. The designer's task is usually a tangle of 'wicked problems' (Rittel, 1973) rather than a series of linear, finite questions (see Chapter 8, page 152). In dealing with 'wicked problems', it is usually necessary to think 'in stereo' rather than 'in mono' – that is by making many interconnected abductive inferences at the same time. I call this 'parallel abductive reasoning', but it is akin to dreaming. Hence, a surprising fact may imply a very complex situation that might be coded as a co-creative set of conditions (A, B, C… n). The answer could be visualised as a four-dimensional picture resembling a real event rather than a 2D movie.

At the design level this might, for example, offer a single, unified answer to several, simultaneous problems. Parallel abductive reasoning might therefore include the integration of smaller and familiar projects, such as local, renewable energy production, far better standards of house insulation, sophisticated heat-exchange systems, diversified and non-intensive farming, local and aerobic sewage treatment systems, micro-currency systems tailored to local needs and human energy-generation systems that add value and meaning to all of our needs. These are no longer new, or radical ideas. Many have been known for decades, or even centuries. Indeed, luminaries such as Richard Buckminster Fuller and Victor Papanek were designing and writing about them in the early nineteen sixties and seventies. In those days, most of us assumed that the problem was fundamentally technological. Clearly, this underestimated the task. Although society may have the right technological fix it often does not know how to implement it in the right way, or at the right time. The reasons for this are complex, but they are not always insuperable.

In what he called a 'eudemonic' ethics, Aristotle reconciled several different levels of action. Here, 'eudemonia' derives from the idea of a good, or virtuous spirit. Today, we might describe it as the 'feel-good factor'. It therefore describes a kind of situated and benignly meditative mode of being that enables us to flourish. This would be a very different approach from a deontological (that is rule-based) ethics in which we are simply bound by prevailing codes of morality. Where the legal system designs rules in order to keep society in order, eudemonic systems call upon our willingness to be self-reflexive and to share our good feelings with others around us. In this sense it is both an emotional and a rational capability. Arguably, it could be regarded – literally – as a spiritual state in which beneficial ideas, practices, and 'things' speak to one another in a kind of sublime philosophical space. To the busy professional this may sound suspiciously like 'dreaming'. However, it also implie the need for action. By transcending the dualism of 'reality' and 'fantasy', designers may be able to get closer to an idea of eudemonic ethics. Because Aristotelian notions of the 'Good' could also be characterised by 'forms' we may conveniently find a connection to the idea of design. Indeed, Aristotle's seminal idea of 'design' emerged from an ethical project that already associate the idea of 'Form' with the social 'Good'. This is an important idea for the twenty-first century. Arguably, what is lacking in today's 'full-speed-ahead' growth economy is a sense of balance. This is something that designers of 'forms' can teach orthodox economists. The notion of 'form' as the 'Good' is a quality, not a quantity.

All of these philosophical arguments may be regarded as 'academic', or 'otherworldly'. For one thing, Aristotle was snobbish about business. His fondness for the philosophical life therefore makes his vision seem nebulous and 'unrealistic' by today's standards. This is another reason why, within the current scheme of things, the idea of 'design for Utopia' appears to be a rather lofty, spurious or unattainable project. The emphasis on materiality, and the frustration that came with organised religion has made us less alert to new possibilities. In short it has eroded our capacity to dream. Many Utopian narratives are exemplified and heightened by recounting the stages in an epic journey. They manifest a yearning for happiness or good fortune at a final destination. In a somewhat more secular and pragmatic way, the idea of 'design' also conveys an exhilarating sense of faith or, at least, a strong belief in the future. It is interesting to note that the word 'perfection' was simply a term used in the workshop that meant 'finished', or 'completed'. Paradoxically, it may also remind us that the act of designing is always an incomplete activity, because it is a process that precedes the necessary stages that enable us to implement, monitor and evaluate its effectiveness in a given context. In a world that has become so rational, purposive, and instrumentalist, we have tended to follow Galileo's method of scientific observation in which we ignore the surrounding detail and go straight for what we believe to be the 'essential' ingredients. Scientific methodology meant that observable phenomena in nature were only acceptable if they could be explained without reference to a supernatural realm. 'Materiality' was increasingly assumed to encompass 'reality', so it seemed logical to assume that our well-being would emerge out of materialism.

What is the connection between dreaming, optimism, and the design of miracles? The answer may depend on how sceptical, pessimistic or cynical you are. Max Weber's belief in a modern 'disenchantment of the world' (Weber, 1958) reflected his view that capitalism has robbed us of our belief in magic and the supernatural. This seems understandable within a technological era in which new solutions and extraordinary accomplishments occur an almost daily basis. Within such a context it seems more reasonable to place one's faith in the rational, rather than the irrational. Hence, if you mistrust anything unless it is backed up by scientific evidence, common sense logic or material proof you may be suspicious of 'miracles'. In our sceptical, cynical world it has become almost self-evident that miracles are unthinkable, impossible or both. This masks a logical confusion between the unthinkable and the impossible. Some things are said to be 'unthinkable' because they are too complex or counterintuitive to be understood (for example quantum physics). Others are 'unthinkable' because we fear or dislike them (for example, military annihilation of the human race). Nevertheless, you may agree that both are possible. If you believe that 'unthinkable' means 'impossible' you are probably a cynic or a pessimist. What pessimists see around them tends to confirm their worst suspicions, so pessimism is self-perpetuating. One version of this is the idea that partial solutions are pointless (for example 'why should I use energy-saving light-bulbs when not all nations signed up to the Kyoto agreement?'). If pessimists are cynical about positive outcomes they may discourage themselves and others from working altruistically. This makes it harder for society to recognise the connection between small acts of generosity and their net outcome. Pessimism is contagious. Luckily, a positive spirit of optimism is also contagious. Does this mean that we can create miracles simply by dreaming optimistically? This idea may be hard to swallow in a pragmatic world in which bureaucratic procedure is valued more highly than creative vision. Dreaming optimistically simply means envisioning possibilities that others may not have noticed. It's the first step to creating a better world.

As I said at the start of the chapter, as consumers and voters we are obliged to choose but seldom invited to dream. Dreaming of what we really want for society may feel strange, so we may have to talk ourselves into it. In a rational, sceptical, cynical world, dreaming of miracles without a clear plan or purpose is frivolous and futile. On the other hand, dreaming is quick, easy, painless and legal. Unless you are a helicopter rescue pilot or a brain surgeon it is safe to do it anytime, any place, anywhere. Importantly, dreaming will not stop you being practical. It may even help. The first step is to allow yourself to imagine something that is wonderful but impossible. Stage magicians do this to get ideas for new tricks, in effect, transforming the unthinkable into the thinkable. A miracle may be around the corner, but it is important to clarify what I mean by this. The empirical philosopher David Hume (1711–76) refuted the existence of miracles, which he saw as 'a transgression of a law of nature by a particular volition of the Deity, or by the interposition of some invisible agent.' By contrast, Littlewood's Law describes miracles within a purely statistical context, rather than seeing it them as supernatural events. This is an interpretation of the Law of Truly Large Numbers (Bollobás, 1986), which shows that a big enough sample size will include extraordinary conditions. E. J. Littlewood (1885–1977) defined a miracle as an exceptional event of special significance. If we define this merely as a 'one in a million' chance, it follows that we can expect a miracle every 35 days, although we may not notice it. What we need to do is to find a way to attune ourselves to the auspiciousness of the world around us. What we also need is a method of sharing and therefore of multiplying good fortune. Optimistically speaking, if we can do this, miracles may become more thinkable. Mostly they go unnoticed because they are too trivial to notice. What is missing in the rational, technological world is a lasting sense of 'wonderment' or charm. If the mathematics is correct latent miracles are hidden all around us, waiting to be realised by optimistic dreamers. The role of creative alertness is vital. If someone is convinced that a miracle will not happen, it is more than likely they will be proved right (cf. Sheldrake, 1981). What we regard as miracles is pretty subjective. Surviving a fall from a plane without a parachute may be seen as a miracle. On the other hand, winning the lottery may be seen merely as luck – even if the odds are equal. Our scientific understanding of 'luck' has helped us to become more optimistic in the last few years. Research has shown that not only are some individuals 'luckier' than others, but also that anyone can increase their luck by following certain simple procedures. As Tennessee Williams once said, 'Luck is believing you are lucky' (Wiseman, 2003).

Many dystopic situations can be thought of as 'vicious circles' because they replicate their own complex, negative conditions. The poverty trap is a simple example. One challenge for Attainable Utopias is how to convert 'vicious circles' into 'virtuous circles'. Perhaps quantum computers can help. Where digital computers use strings of numbers to perform deductive tasks, quantum computers are able to work in a far more abductive way. They will be able to crack numerical codes that only decades ago were regarded to all intents and purposes as impossible. Unlike conventional computers, a strange thing about quantum computers is their ability to 'imagine' extreme contradictions. We might therefore see them as optimistic machines because they ignore the pessimism (narrowness) of the rational world. Perhaps quantum computers will teach us how to 'surf' around on tiny waves of utopian bliss. Maybe they will help us to design 'beneficial memes' ('catchy' ideas) that will replicate themselves everywhere. One of these will become the first 'miracle meme'.

References

Bateson, G. (1973), *Steps to an Ecology of Mind* (London: Paladin Books, Granada Publishing).

Bollobás, B. (1986), *Littlewood's Miscellany* (Cambridge: Cambridge University Press).

Dawkins, R. (1976), *The Selfish Gene* (New York: Oxford University Press).

Douthwaite, R. (1992), *The Growth Illusion* (Hartland: Green Books in association with Lilliput Press, Totnes).

Hamilton, C. (2003), *Growth Fetish* (Crows Nest, NSW: Allen & Unwin).

Onians, J. (1991), 'Idea and product: potter and philosopher in classical Athens' *Journal of Design History*, 4:2, pp. 65–73.

Peirce, C. S. (1958), *Collected Papers of Charles Sanders Peirce, Vols. 1–6*, Charles Hartshorne, C. and Weiss, P. (eds.); Vols. 7–8, Burks, A. W. (Ed.), (Cambridge, MA: Harvard University Press).

Rittel, H., and Webber, M. (1973), 'Dilemmas in a general theory of planning' *Policy Sciences*, Vol. 4, pp 155–169 (Amsterdam: Elsevier Scientific Publishing Company, Inc.).

Schacter, D. (2001), *Forgotten Ideas, Neglected Pioneers: Richard Semon and the Story of Memory* (Philadelphia: Psychology Press).

Sheldrake, R. (1981), *A New Science of Life: The Hypothesis of Formative Causation* (Los Angeles: Jeremy P. Tarcher).

Veitch, J. (1907), *The Method, Meditations, and Selections from the Principles of Descartes* (Edinburgh: Blackwood).

Weber, M. (1958), *The Protestant Ethic and the Spirit of Capitalism*, Parsons, T. (trans.) (New York: Scribner's).

Wiseman, R. (2003), *The Luck Factor* (London: Century).

Wood, J. (2004), 'Could Synergies of Relations in Design Become the Basis for Professional Standards of Eudaemonia?', refereed paper given at the European Academy of Design's 'FutureGround' Conference, Melbourne, Australia.

Synergy

'...synergy is of central importance in virtually every scientific discipline, though it very often travels incognito under various aliases (mutualism, cooperativity, symbiosis, win-win, emergent effect, a critical mass, coevolution, interaction, threshold effects, even non-zerosumness).'

(Corning, 1998)

Charles Handy's view that the main role of the corporations is to be of service to society (Handy, 1998) probably sounds rather idealistic. Some would even regard it as an impossible dream. However, logically speaking, it is a reasonable point that is hard to refute (cf. Arthur, 1996; Moore, 1997). One might want to push it further by arguing that a profoundly effective business culture would have little choice but to embrace symbiotic and altruistic principles within its primary agenda. Where once this might have sounded hopelessly idealistic it now makes more sense, largely because altruism and symbiosis are now seen as integral to how the biosphere works. Until recently popular mythology had it that the self-seeking and predatory behaviour of large corporations was a sign of their ultimate efficiency. The economic establishment has asked citizens to believe that ruthlessness in business was a 'natural' practice that needs to be tolerated, humoured, or even handsomely rewarded. This largely stemmed from Adam Smith's extraordinarily influential idea of 1776, namely that self-interest leads to collective benefit (Smith, 1904). This idea influenced Darwin's theory of evolution, which, in turn, gave credibility to the economics of the far right. The received Darwinian model emphasises the importance of violent struggle in nature's selection of the 'fittest' genes in a given species. However, what this model overlooked is the important role of interdependency within eco-systems. This interdependency means that the majority of organisms are able to work together to conserve precious (calorific) energy within a given region.

Another way to refer to this process is by describing it as 'synergistic'. Literally speaking, the notion of synergy simply means several things working together. Its simplicity, however, is a double-edged sword. On the one hand it means that everyone can understand it. On the other hand, it is so universal that it often means little beyond the most generic definition. It is safe to say that few things in modern society are anywhere near as synergistic as natural systems but it is difficult to be more specific. This means that some quite radical political and economic adjustments would be required before this became even thinkable. For example, there might need to be clear incentives for those in corporate life, who see the world only as an opportunity for local, short-term advantage, rather than for long-term, collective benefit. There would also need to be new and additional benefits for those who can develop shareable visions that promote and enhance the deep collective purpose of being alive. Hence life-threatening, combative competition tends to be far more common in creatures near the top of the food chain, where surplus resources are more abundant. This does not represent the majority of species. Lower down the system, it happens less frequently, where decisive selection without bloodshed seems to be the only viable alternative. Modern humanity has managed to ignore this principle by creating technologies that require continuous and abundant sources of energy. So far it has achieved this without committing mass suicide.

At one time most people were food gatherers or producers; now those are only a small fraction of the total population. The good news is that, in the wealthy nations, automation enables us to produce far more than we need for basic survival. Unfortunately, this is creating environmental damage on a large scale. Second, politicians and economists in the rich world do not know how to reduce their economic advantage by sharing it with the poorer peoples of the world. Instead of addressing these two problems directly, poorer countries are also learning how to produce more than is good for their, and our, collective wellbeing. Unfortunately, what can be produced is not universally available and we are beginning to see the likelihood of further protracted wars over dwindling strategic resources. This would be an unnecessary and painful step for us to take. In seeking to avoid it we may find inspiration from nature. In the last 50 years or so, certain scientists (for example Margulis, 1991) have realised the evolutionary importance of symbiotic behaviour, crucial because it offers a greater shared benefit to all concerned. This is good news, as it is now being interpreted in the context of innovative business methods, such as 'co-opetition', that describes 'cooperative competition' (Brandenburger and Nalebuff, 1996). The Darwinian logic of competition was harsh, but it seemed to complement the universally accepted 'Law of Diminishing Returns'. Possibly the best known of all economic laws, this reflects the assumption that business operates according to the logic of mining, in which we extract exhaustible resources from the ground until they are gone. This is rather a gloomy theory, so it is comforting to find that the ecosystem is a synergistic system rather than a finite stock of materials (Fuller, 1975). As a living organism (Lovelock, 2006) the earth actively resists the physical process of 'winding down'. In other words, it has the capacity to work against the law of entropy. In the second half of the 20th century several thinkers increasingly began to realise that we had overlooked the presence of a Law of 'Increasing Returns' (Romer, 1986; Arthur, 1996) that seems to promise enduring benefits for everyone. At present we can foresee no finite upper limit to the extent of this potential bounty, and it is gratifying to find that our current economic system is slowly waking up to this truth. Indeed, it is heartening that some of the new digital technologies of the 21st century have shown how radical, large-scale, consensual change has never been more possible. The more that consumers become aware of their true power, the more likely it will be for symbiosis and therefore for the benefits of altruism, to bring collective benefits to business and society. This marks an important distinction that separates a competitive, hierarchical society from one that can realise its full potential. The more corporations maintain a clear sense of their purpose and role in the community and eco-system at large, the more chance they will have of surviving in the market place. Ultimately, corporations are sustained by the goodwill of their customers and stakeholders. It is fortunate that we now have these emergent models of business as a portent of how things could be in future.

Both of these ideas are very important for the cultivation of what Buckminster Fuller described as a 'synergy-of-synergies' (Fuller, 1975). It seems likely that creating a lattice of mutually enhancing synergies would be more effective than appeals to 'sustainable development', especially if it can be explained clearly to world governments, corporations and end-users alike. This raises a number of questions. How can we recognise synergy when we see it? Moreover, what is it? In colloquial terms, the idea of synergy is understood to describe situations or conditions where the whole exceeds the sum of its parts. It would be useful, therefore, to be able to define the notion of 'synergy' in terms of design and ecology. This might help designers to work more explicitly with the complex relations between things. Simple synergies are reasonably well understood. Their uses are documented in traditional studies of metallurgy (Fuller, 1975), chemistry (Polanyi and Grene, 1969) and engineering (Jones, 2005). However, applying the same principles to a new order in society is unlikely to be straightforward because social, cultural, ecological, or aesthetic synergies are less quantifiable and predictable than their mechanical counterparts.

It is worth remembering that the rather abstract nature of these modern definitions reflects a growing familiarity with 'systems thinking' that emerged through cybernetics (for example Wiener, 1948) and General Systems Theory (Bertalanffy, 1968). This is a helpful development. It enables us all, for example, to compare machines with living creatures, or ecologies of species. This may prove useful to designers who may in future work at higher organisational levels, say, for the creation of benign cities, currency systems or communities. The word 'synergy' derives from two ancient Greek words meaning, roughly, 'with' and 'work'. This may suggest a rather modest definition – that is merely the act of (people) working together in order to obtain some advantage. If we attempt to define synergy in too bland or generic a way it may not help us much. Indeed, it is hard to think of any reasonably complex system that does not satisfy the popular definition: 'where the whole is greater than the sum of its parts'. It is therefore less than helpful to designers who may need to understand, and who may need to intervene in, systems of enormous complexity. Richard Buckminster Fuller's version (1975) is a little better, but not much: '[the] ...behaviour of whole systems [is] unpredicted by the behaviour of their parts taken separately.'

This idea is confirmed by Peter Corning (1998), who itemised a number of synergistic states, from those that display relatively predictable 'linear effects' to far more complex ones with complementarities of many types. Many synergies can be seen as systems that are not just more complex ('greater') than the sum of their parts, they are also quite different – often surprisingly so. Although the old platonic idea of a 'division of labour' can provide new potential for coherence at subordinate levels within the whole system, it follows that complexity leads to new conditions that are seldom predictable from the conditions that produced it.

The idea of synergistic emergence is often associated with relatively simple and potentially precise examples such as the creation of new alloys from a mixture of metals. A more complex and 'messy' example is that of a dinner party in which we invite a small group of dinner guests and set up a conversational theme for the evening. No matter how carefully we choose them, and how well we know their views, we would not be able to predict exactly where the conversation might go. Just as a host may be wary of inviting too many guests to dinner, so designers should be wary of 'designing' complex systems unless they consider their responsibilities very carefully. Also, they should always expect the unexpected to emerge. In the case of the dinner party, we may like to visualise the most effective balance of complementary interests and experiences that our dinner guests would have. One type of emergence in such a system might be that, say, of unforeseen facilitation or moderating skills that were latent but masked by other aspects of the whole group. Here, new 'wholes' may emerge from the existing 'whole' of the group. For example, some of the guests may choose to launch a new company after their dinner party meeting. It is quite likely that the success of this process will also depend on the collective skill of the group in inhibiting or encouraging appropriate individuals to take the lead at an optimum time. In the professional context this is commonly known as 'teamwork' and is a helpful example of 'synergy'. This raises the issue of hierarchies and how they could, or should, be 'designed' or 'cultivated' within complex systems.

The whole field of synergy resembles a constellation of many different cuisines that are each known by a particular region, era or chef. Working with synergy is therefore similar to the process of cooking, whose many possible 'flavours' will range from 'simple' to 'complex'. Few of the outcomes of good cooking are likely to follow a really simple, linear or predictable path. Even the apparently simple process of boiling an egg has attracted many styles and preferred variations in cooking time, changes in water temperature and ways to present, prepare or eat the final outcome. Most cooking methods are far more complex. Many involve the lengthy preparation of a huge variety of ingredients over a long period. Synergistic systems encompass a comparable range of complexities. Some synergies within metallurgy, for example, can be described as simple physical processes. The creation of an alloy such as stainless steel produces a material that is stronger than any of its constituent ingredients. However, some new metals deriving from industrial processes at the nano-scale defy previous understanding. Toyota's 'gum metal' is a good example (Ranganathan, 2003). Synergies that occur in the chemical realm are likely to be more complex than at the physical level. Similarly, biological systems are even more complex, and then we come to ecological complexities, and then complexities at the social level. What synergies can be more complex than those that occur at the social level? Perhaps they would be events in the spiritual realm.

The fact that nature's synergies are manifold provides a fine inspiration for how we might design micro-utopias. The chemists Polanyi and Grene (1969) speak of a 'hierarchy of levels' that operate within more or less inclusive boundaries. Each level works under principles that are irreducible to the principles that operate at levels lower down. In other words, hierarchical systems may demonstrate a number of different, 'level-specific' characteristics. As physicist Philip Anderson (1972) put it, 'At each level of complexity entirely new properties appear.' This is both exciting and daunting because we would need to be able to manage the arrival of the unexpected as each design stage evolves out of the last. Here, biologists Eldrege and Salthe (1984) offered a helpful differentiation between 'genealogical' and 'ecological' hierarchies in nature. This distinction can be adapted to reflect upon successive versions of a given design and its relation to already existing products of a comparable type. We may note, for example, that the order of events that produces a better design usually sets up a (temporal) hierarchy of knowledge or meaning; but it does not necessarily mean that the original will always remain subsidiary to its successor. This explains why, although the bicycle can be seen as an exemplar (that is ancestor) to the motorcycle, it may nevertheless be functionally superior to it in some circumstances.

So far, this addresses some ideas that relate to notions of efficacy and complexity. But how can it be applied to practical designing? Although some synergistic systems may seem reasonably straightforward this might be deceptive. The notion of what Corning (1998) calls 'bioeconomic' efficiencies may inspire designers to explore cooperative behaviours of different types. He quotes the example of Emperor penguins who reduce their loss of bodily warmth to the Antarctic cold by huddling together in very large groups. Although the physical principle is very simple, the process relies on the mutual co-operation of some highly sophisticated living creatures before a critical self-organising mass can be attained. Designers can extrapolate this simple principle to many other situations in which there is joint environmental conditioning, cost and/or risk sharing, or information sharing, for example. In this sense, many synergies represent an intelligent form of sharing. If synergy can be established and observed in one form, it can simultaneously be enhanced elsewhere. In theory, inefficient power stations could share their energy expenditure with nearby housing estates. More swimming baths could be passively solar heated at relatively little expense, in the long term. Passive solar heating systems, rather than silicon photovoltaic panels, are not so good at generating very hot water. However, even in temperate northern climates, they are excellent at heating large volumes of water to a medium or moderately high temperature. Laundries, bakeries and restaurants need not share only their energy management systems; they can also work together to optimise business opportunities. If they did, visitors could have their clothes laundered while they went swimming. More customers would be attracted to a shared resource in which to enjoy a 'work out' in an electricity-generating gymnasium. While they charge their own mobile phone batteries they are washing or spinning their washing in human-powered washing machines.

These examples serve to illustrate the practical potential of more integrated forms of business, but they represent a relatively wasteful approach when compared with smaller and longer established societies. Many have an 'ecological footprint' (cf. Wackernagel and Rees, 1996) that is tiny by comparison. Drucker (1978), for example, described a people called the Igorot, who lived in the mountainous regions of the Philippines. Over several centuries, and using only simple tools, they maintained a complex network of dams, canals and terraces. With this, they managed to evolve a complex, irrigated rice cultivation system. The particular cyanobacteria in their ponds had nitrogen-fixing properties that were symbiotically adapted to the rice. This enabled their whole food system to be highly productive. Indeed, 1 hectare of land enabled them to grow almost enough food to maintain a family of five. Not surprisingly, their intensive work habits were highly co-operative. Their social and cultural order also helped them to coordinate and to regulate their way of life. In effect, this represents the synergising of many simultaneous levels of synergy.

It is hard to think of comparable levels of ecological efficacy within the commercial, legal, or public service area. Chapter 3 provides some reasons as to why this is the case. Within the current political system it is hard to envisage how our gas-guzzling societies will meet synergy targets that get anywhere near those of the Igorot people, but there are ways in which we may, at least, set the criteria for significant improvement. As I stated in the discussion on 'dreaming' (Chapter 7), the first task is to identify a desirable state of being. Here, there is good reason to be optimistic. Compared to technological systems, synergy levels are extremely high in all living creatures, so 21st century designers can learn a great deal from eco-systems, however local they may be. It is comforting to know that a well-tended domestic garden probably has greater biodiversity than the so-called 'natural' regions such as rainforests or savannah. This is a good example of Fuller's notion of a 'synergy of synergies'.

Synergy refers not only to the accord that exists between individual parts of the whole, but also to the accord between those individual parts and their separate relations to the whole. It therefore supports a heterogeneity that enables systems to become more adaptively self-aware. The idea of 'synergy' is a suitable starting point. It is not too technical an idea for non-experts to grasp, and it has been routinely used within the business and management communities for many years. One problem is that there is no scientifically accepted definition for it. Buckminster Fuller's (1975) development of what he called 'Synergetics' was a pioneering approach, yet he developed it more at the theoretical level (cf. 'dynamic geometry'), rather than the practical level. It is well known that the idea of synergy accommodates a range of types, each with its own distinctive qualities and parameters. The fact that synergy is more interesting within complex systems than within simple ones is part of the problem. Ultimately, if – as Fuller's definition shows – synergy is often unpredictable and emergent, then we cannot design with it in the same way we design for 'performance' or 'efficacy' in discrete products and services.

Classical science is of little use at this level of thinking, because it tends to offer closed theories based on a number of invariant, atomistic distinctions. What is needed is a model that embraces the idea of 'subjective distinction', or 'variable distinction' (cf. Heylighen, 1989). This is needed in order to accommodate the changing nature of local synergy. It is highly likely that the ecological sophistication of the Igorot represents a complex network of adjacent synergies that we would need to orchestrate before they will support a general equilibrium. Orthodox Western managerial approaches are unlikely to be adequate, because we are unaccustomed to synergising so many simultaneous synergies at the physical, chemical, biological, ecological, social, cultural and spiritual levels. In our specialist society, most of these fields are explored by experts who work in relative isolation from those of other disciplines. Up to now, some researchers (cf. Corning, 1998) have defined synergy at the physical, chemical, biological and ecological levels. In theory, many of these synergies would be integrated in a manifold form. In practice, however, it is necessary, for reasons of expediency, to identify separate clusters of synergy types, and then to see how they might be made to synergize with one another. Although mindful of the dangers of splitting synergy modes ineffectively, the author offers four provisional orders of synergy that represent work in progress (Table 8.1. See also http://attainable-utopias.org/m21).

In reflecting on the potential for designers to repair some of the environmental damage caused by the human species, von Nieuwenhuijze (2007) argues that design be regarded as a form of healing. This is an interesting metaphor that needs some careful thought. How might we develop a more synergistic design discourse that would encourage designers to work as systemic 'healers'? Arguably, a 'healthy' organism has a very large number of simultaneous and interdependent factors that operate within a whole system. This may pose difficulties for those of us without training as doctors, systems analysts, or statisticians. One primitive way to explore this is by mapping the number of independent factors in a given system and by counting the theoretical number of interconnections that it implies. Figure 8.1 shows how, even at the smallest and simplest level, the number of possible combinations rises exponentially.

Table 8.1   Four orders of synergy

First Order Synergy

Synergies that emerge from the sharing of data. These would include smart materials, nano-scale metallurgy, as developed by Toyota (cf. 'gum metal'), large-scale projects that bring surprising results, such as Buckminster Fuller's floating geodesic city.

Second Order Synergy

Synergies that emerge from the sharing of information. These would include synergies that emerge from smart systems or (for example the thermostat), or biological systems, such as Emperor Penguins huddling together to keep warm.

Third Order Synergy

Synergies that emerge from the sharing of knowledge (for example flying geese, or collaboration systems, such as cooperation using tag-based web media).

Fourth Order Synergy

Synergies that emerge from the sharing of wisdom (for example (for example James Lovelock's *Gaia* hypothesis (Lovelock, 1995), or what Buckminster Fuller called Nature's synergy-of-synergies).).

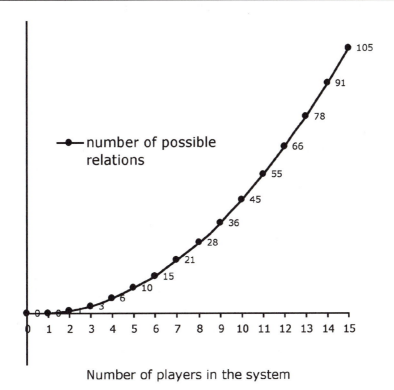

Number of players in the system

Figure 8.1   The rise in relations relative to the number of active agents

This means that any attempt to deal consciously with each and every relation established between all of the agents soon becomes practically impossible. This is because humans are not very adept at grasping more than four or five interrelated issues in a conscious or explicit way.

This is not to say that humans cannot deal with complexity at an unconscious or implicit level of thinking. Indeed, many designers cope happily with the non-linear nature of single design tasks because they can be processed in the imagination. As highlighted earlier, complex design tasks are described as 'wicked problems' (Rittel, 1973), not only because their ingredient factors are complex, but also because the salient factors became entangled with one another. When this is the case, the designer needs to think in a more intuitive, inventive way. When there are many defining factors in a complex situation it is quite likely that, to some extent, each determines the state of the others. This means that the designer's decisions cannot be based entirely on existing data, because there is insufficient evidence to guide an obvious course of action. Designers are very good at thinking in a provisional and contingent way. They know that every arbitrary decision may lead to a new situation in which a secondary decision can follow more deductively. However, as professionals, they are trained to work within narrow, local boundaries of possibility. In this sense, designers are entrepreneurs, albeit without a license to practise, that is, beyond their training as specialist designers.

If it is true then the larger and more complex a system becomes, the greater the opportunity for new synergies to emerge. This also implies that complex systems might easily become sub-optimal or even self-defeating (Fuller, 1975; Corning, 1998). When they sustain their own state in a harmonious way they can be said to be synergistic; but the presence of a high level of synergy does not guarantee that there will be a pleasant or beneficial outcome for human societies. Arguably, the Mafia is a synergistic organism that works with minimal managerial overheads. If it were to behave more like a large corporation, it would become more visible to the law enforcement agencies, because of its bureaucratic footprint. Because of their complexity, many systems can operate together to enable stability to emerge. Despite the theoretical difficulties of maintaining a complex synergistic system, social organisations have a high potential for self-management, because humans are very alert and clever. If we can maintain elaborate gardens or captain large wind-powered galleons on the high seas, perhaps we can develop and manage massive synergistic enterprises.

Part of the process of synergy maintenance involves all of the levels so far described, such as physical, chemical, biological or ecological synergies. However, humans are also emotional beings that undergo complex problems of self-doubt, disagreement, uncertainty and lack of the ability to share a particular vision. This means that many important levels of synergy will remain elusive and intangible. Some systems hover on the edge of chaos because they are affected by marginal or barely perceptible events. At this level, one of the important factors affecting the success of a given venture is the participant's state of mind. This raises new practical, political and philosophical questions for the cultivation of synergy. For example, the optimism and positive spirit that exists within a given process of 'co-design' may influence the boundary conditions for its success. This is a virtuous circle that is sustained by positive feedback. For example, some people are able to generate an affirmative spirit that is, in effect, contagious. Richard Wiseman (2003) has explored the way that certain people appear, statistically, to attract 'luck' because of an innate belief that they will be lucky. Similarly, others feel too unhappy to commit themselves to work towards success, even though this success would make them feel able to work. Mihaly Cziksentmihalyi has discovered that people feel happiest when they experience a sense of 'flow' (Cziksentmihalyi, 1990). In order to propagate a shared sense of flow, a self-seeded process of persuasion is desirable. Hence, exemplars of success will become increasingly important to the cultivation of synergy. Designers can begin the process by conceiving and launching attractive ideas ('beneficial memes' – see Wood, 2004) that replicate themselves in the same way that a joke or story is passed from one person to the next.

Where Figure 8.2 reminds us that each relationship implies two 'viewpoints', Figure 8.3 represents an (intuitive) graph of how combinatorial possibilities rise with complexity. It also shows that there is an optimum intersection between that rising complexity and the fall-off in our capacity to grasp it consciously. This suggests that it may be difficult to sustain an explicit grasp of many more than four interdependent elements.

Although it may not be possible to manage the complexity associated with synergy at the rational, conscious level this may not be an insuperable problem. Much of what creative designers traditionally do is often more intuitive than explicit. Although we tend to assume that useful knowledge is normally rational and declarative this is only partially true. In discussing tacit knowledge (that is loosely, procedural, rather than declarative knowledge) Michael Polanyi suggests that all knowledge is tacit if it rests on our subsidiary awareness of particulars in terms of a comprehensive unity. Tacit knowledge

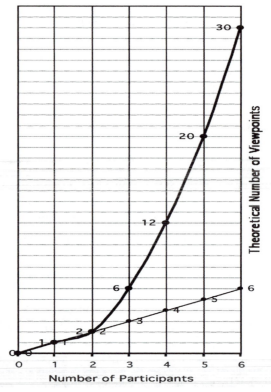

Figure 8.2   The rise in 'viewpoints' relative to the number of players

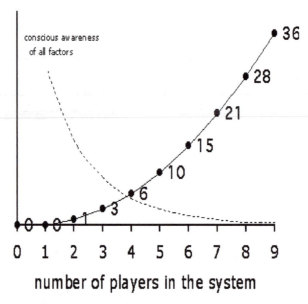

Figure 8.3   Possible relationship between consciousness and complexity

is therefore deeper than we know. We cannot grasp it fully, or discuss it in a conscious and explicit way. This can be illustrated by the way that doctors deal with a complex condition like an illness. Polanyi and Grene (1969) describe a doctor's skill in diagnosing disease by its 'physiognomy'. This has always remained an intuitive process that is virtually impossible to replicate by machine. In explaining the ancient art of diagnosis Immanuel Kant coined the term 'unformalizable powers' and described 'an art hidden in the depth of the human soul'. It would appear that (western) medicine still relies largely on the expert experience (that is, informed intuitive judgement) of doctors, aided by a very small set of discrete indicators such as temperature, fever, breathing difficulties and so on. Arguably, a holistic approach should be able to map not only a full range of significant 'players', but also the relations that pertain among them. Dr Vadim Kvitash has developed a method called 'relonics' which maps whole conditions within a given (medical) context (1983; 2002). An important feature of this work is that it can read aspects of data that are normally discarded under standard clinical methods. In one application he uses his system to map twelve chemical constituents of the blood. Although doctors routinely use machines to monitor all of these chemicals within the blood each one is identified independently for any abnormal levels. By contrast, Dr Kvitash's methods explicitly explore all of the relations among all of the data deemed to be relevant.

In registering complex and subtle patterns of interdependency, Kvitash uses his system to forecast diseases before conventional symptoms show up. Because of the unusual nature of this approach, a new language of measurement was needed in order to represent relonics precisely enough for diagnosis. In any complex system, measurement must be suitable for what is being measured. In highly complex systems it is usually important to express many dimensions simultaneously. This may be difficult using discrete number systems. Indeed, patterns can display relationships better than standard statistical formulations in numbers. This not only reveals a surprisingly high quality of data about the health of the patient, but it also gives a dependable prognosis. In effect, compared with the use of single indicators or small sets of discrete indicators to diagnose an illness, Dr Kvitash's approach is akin to amplifying the data without filtering them. This is because of the additional properties that can emerge from within adjoining parameters. The presence of what we might call 'imbalance' among these relations is used to make this explicit. Using this approach, relationships emerge as quasi-entities in themselves. His neologism 'relons' reflects this fact. He coined the term because it describes phenomena that are similar to, but not synonymous with, more familiar terms such as 'balance', 'equilibrium' and 'symmetry'. In order to find reliable conclusions it is essential to find commonalities. These are derived from clinical cases observed over time.

The process developed is a systemic one that may be applicable to any complex organism. The primary parameters are derived from a simple scale of levels that registers the upper and lower limits within which the system in question is likely to survive. This would normally be calibrated using any arbitrary scale (for example 0–100 per cent). In this way, potentially dissimilar measurements and values can be normalised. Standard statistical methods do not represent relationships effectively. They may misrepresent pertinent values because they impose a scalar arithmetical logic of 'averages' on systems that apply a logic of manifold relations. In some cases, the identification of 'relons' (that is, a kind of balance between two specific items) can be shown to act as part of a compensatory aspect of relons between other items. There are three ways in which a system adapts to its own internal and external conditions:

1.   by control

2.   by regulation

3.   by coordination

When the natural regulatory pathways begin to lose their effectiveness, a higher level of coordination may compensate for it. Hence, within the system's 'control' process it will show that there is both a sub-system of 'regulation' and another sub-system of 'co-ordination'. Importantly, neither is independent of the other, although one may take over, or overshadow the effects of the other. These methods enable predictions about the health of certain patients. For example, Kvitash can predict, with 95 per cent accuracy, whether the effects of a heart operation will be fatal or otherwise within 3 years of the operation. Typically: a set of (usually incommensurate) features within a given system (for example chemicals commonly monitored in laboratory blood tests) are mapped onto a circular chart so that every item's relation to every other item can be shown (see Figure 8.4). Simply by noting and representing zones of 'balance' and 'imbalance' in comparison with previous observations, the metadesigner would be able to draw surprising conclusions about the present (and future) well being of the system. The systems explored so far show that 'balance' and 'symmetry' may be different.

Another way to explain this would be in reference to the reductionist convention of seeing information as discrete 'channels' (cf. Aristotle, Locke, Shannon & Weaver). By seeing information only within separate channels it is

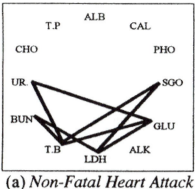 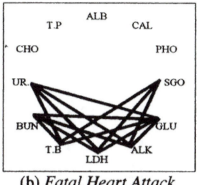

(a) *Non-Fatal Heart Attack*   (b) *Fatal Heart Attack*

Figure 8.4   Relonics used to map the relations among blood chemicals

possible to ignore or misread some emergent data as 'cross-channel interference' when it may be an inalienable feature of a coherent, but complex whole.

The Combinatorial Explosion

As Kant implies (cf. MacCorduch, 1979) although the complexity of nature exceeds the finite boundaries of number, humans need to work with sets of clear data, such as binary distinctions, in order to grasp some aspect of a complex reality. Dr Kvitash's system of relonics does this in its use of topologies that are organised into sets (that is 'orders') with one, two or three dimensions. This belief is heavily inspired by the Pythagorean faith in numbers as the defining and primordial essence of the world. Marvin Minsky once argued that consciousness is merely a 'low-grade system for keeping records' (Minsky, 1994). Using this crude assumption I realised that we might be able to map the richness of 'consciousness' (in Minsky's terms) in a network by evaluating the level of adjacency between nodes that may need to communicate with one another. Koestler described a similar hypothesis that he called the 'paradox of the centipede' (1964), whereby most of the nodes in this creature's nervous system appear to be dedicated to the local task of walking, rather than addressing the task at a higher strategic level.

As creative practitioners often prefer to think with images, rather than plain text, I will map out the above proposition in the form of a 3D model. Some sociologists exploring network theory have used the topological

Players and Their Relationships	Features	Some Implications
	2 players 1 relation	Two players and their one relationship.
	4 players 3 direct relations	As a chain gets longer, player-relations become less direct.
	4 players 4 direct relations 2nd figure	Team misunderstandings may build up if some collaborators only deal indirectly with some others. 'Looping' A chain raises the average number of direct relationships. In this case, looping increased 'directness' significantly. In much longer chains the looping process this is less effective, relatively speaking.
	5 players 4 direct relations	A 'fan' format implies a hierarchy. When we create long chains of command we risk introducing alienation. A hierarchical management system is therefore unlikely to be highly synergistic. To achieve synergy we may need to de-centralise.
	4 players 6 direct relations (This is the only 3D figure in our examples.)	By its nature, each of the vertices in a tetrahedron is a close 'neighbour' of all the others. When used to model relations, it can therefore exemplify a leaderless, peer-to-peer system, that is it illustrates the optimal values of a non-hierarchical team of four.

Table 8.2   Line and node system for mapping relational criteria and structures

Number of Players	Possible Relations	Convenience/ease of Comprehension	Additional Implications
1	0	not applicable	Perfect conditions for solipsism
2	1	very high	Minimum collective potential
3	3	High	A mnemonically trivial number, but its potential is relatively limited
4	6	Largest number of possible peer-to-peer relations in a 3D form	Mnemonically, useful. Can be mapped either consciously or intuitively
5	10	Exceeds the scale of exclusively peer-to-peer relationships	Going beyond the average person's conscious grasp
6	15	Richer, but difficult to manage	Would probably require 'chunking' of the factors involved
7	21	Increasingly dependent on intuitive modes	Relies increasingly heavily on experience, and/or intuitive skills and insights
8	28	Increasingly dependent on intuitive modes	Relies increasingly heavily on experience, and/or intuitive skills and insights
9	36	Increasingly dependent on intuitive modes	Relies increasingly heavily on experience, and/or intuitive skills and insights
10	45	Increasingly dependent on intuitive modes	Relies increasingly heavily on experience, and/or intuitive skills and insights

Table 8.3   Examples of player-relations, mapped using Euler's notation

conventions of Leonhard Euler (1707–83), who devised a mapping of nets and polygons using dots (vertices) and lines (edges). Tables 8.2 and 8.3 show how the language of lines and nodes can map some simple relational criteria.

This may be a helpful way to introduce the system of nodes and links that has been adopted by Vadim Kvitash. If these elements represent 'players' and 'relations' the minimum number of players for any relationship is two. This can be represented as a single unbroken line with a node at either end (see Figure 8.5). Larger versions can only attach themselves as additional nodes to produce an unattached 'chain'. Communication in a chain is obviously limited by the logic and scale of its sequential links.

What the model shows is that there is always one less 'relation' than the number of nodes in a given chain. Also, no node can have direct contact with more than 2 others, although it may be indirectly 'aware' of all of them. This fulfils our notion of synergy in that we need to ensure that a given node is reasonably conscious of the whole system. In a eulerian map of this type, the synergy is relatively low, because a high proportion of information leading to this awareness must, of necessity, be derived indirectly via the 2 adjacent nodes. Both of these adjacent nodes will then have to deal with their neighbours who are further away, and so on. Hence, the chain's 'immediacy of awareness' will be in inverse arithmetical relation to its length (that is number of nodes).

Kvitash's second configuration is the fan (see Figure 8.6) comprising a minimum number of 4 'players'. Here, the potential for 'primitive consciousness' is greater, even though – as with the 'chain' – there is always one less 'relation' than the number of nodes in a given fan. However, in a simple fan, no node can have direct contact with more than one other node, unless it happens to be at the fan's centre, in which case it will be in contact with all of them. Thus, the fan establishes a kind of fixed hierarchy of elements that may be advantageous under the right circumstances.

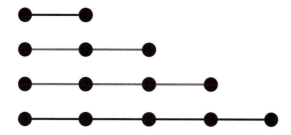

Figure 8.5   **'Chains' (min. involvement of 2 parameters and 1 relation)**

Figure 8.6   'Fans' (minimum involvement of 4 parameters and 3 relations)

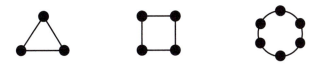

Figure 8.7   'Loops' (minimum involvement of 3 parameters and 3 relations)

In what Kvitash calls 'loops' (see Figure 8.7) there is a minimum association of at least 3 players or parameters. Notably, within this class of form, the 'smallest' loop (3 nodes) has unique properties in that it offers equal and immediate contact between, or among all of its nodes. In this triangular loop each node is in indirect connection with 100 per cent of its 'internal world'. The frequency of direct contacts reduces progressively as the number of nodes increases. Each node in a 4-node loop is only one link away from its 2 adjacent partners; therefore 66.6 per cent of all the nodes in its 'world' are accessible directly. In a 5-node loop, 50 per cent of the other nodes are out of direct reach. The rate of descent slows down and by the fourteenth node we are down to just over 15 per cent (see Figure 8.8).

Webs have a minimum association of 4 players or parameters. Although this is not guaranteed in every case, it is possible to ensure direct contact between/among every node and every other node, irrespective of their total number. Using this mapping method, if the direct connections between nodes represent peer-to-peer relations it can be shown which configurations are optimal. The example of a tetrahedron (that is a triangular pyramid) is particularly auspicious. It has 4 faces, 4 vertices (corners), and 6 edges. Euler's famous theorem of 1751 showed that, out of all known polygons the tetrahedron has the maximum edge-to-face ratio and the maximum edge-to-vertex ratio. Possibly for this reason, it has an optimally memorable number of components (four). It can be visualised as the meeting of four equal-sized spheres, whose centres are joined up to create the tetrahedron. Four is the largest number of spheres that will touch one another simultaneously, therefore four players is an auspicious number for several reasons. This means that each node can 'see' each of the other nodes directly, without anything getting in its way. Fuller

Figure 8.8   Additional possible configurations

(1975) argued that, by representing 4 complementary entities as a tetrahedral whole, we emulate an aspect of the human mind, and how it works.

Unfortunately, while the number four may be convenient or optimal, actual situations usually include a vast array of interdependent factors. Indeed, practical projects commonly fail for any number of small, subtle and interconnected reasons, rather than because of a handful of causes. While the human mind is able to remember a small number of co-dependent elements, it also needs to work with more complex processes that defy clear description. In trying to balance these needs it is possible to map larger clusters using matrices of elements. However, this is less easy to visualise than Vadim Kvitash's circle plotting approach.

Chapter 9 describes the UK's BedZed zero-energy housing project, conceived and managed by architect Bill Dunster. We developed several mapping methods that facilitate close enquiry into such a question. In one example (Figure 8.9), the early difficulties in gaining acceptance for a novel scheme can be grasped by monitoring the actions of four 'players' and the six relations that co-sustain them.

While useful, this is inadequate way to represent the vast number of tiny but significant factors that are reciprocally self-creating. In short, it may not contain enough information to be effective. Complexity must therefore be apprehended as a simplified entity.

In this case, for example, BedZed needed to gain the support of a cluster of interested parties, each of whom may have a different 'vested interest'. The support of a given individual is usually, also, influenced by the perceived views and likely actions of others within the cluster. Figure 8.10 shows all of the above 8 players (the dots on the diagram) linked together (by lines) in a minimum set of 28 links. If we are to represent all of the possible relations within the system, it would be wise to explore each link in turn, using a positively creative, opportunistic, and open-minded approach. This may mean that the 28 links can also be represented as 56 relational viewpoints. By using this map opportunistically and creatively it is possible to design points of critical intervention, and to devise new solutions to this kind of complex problem.

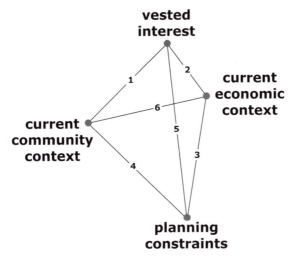

Figure 8.9   Simplified (four-fold) model of the challenges in housing
              innovation

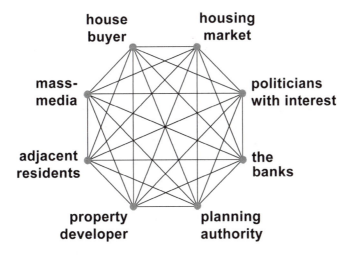

Figure 8.10   The 28 possible relationships in an 8-player map of vested
              interest

We believe that this mapping system can enable complex 'vicious circles' to
become transformable into more 'virtuous circles'. As such, it is a useful tool
for metadesigners.

   Although BedZed was the first successful venture of its kind in the UK,
it should have happened many decades earlier. Moreover, despite popular
assumptions, its success does not rely on new, sophisticated or expensive

technology. Why there were no equivalent successful schemes before, or indeed after BedZed is a fascinating question. This type of collective failure is called a 'vicious circle'. We can analyse any lack of synergy by mapping all the interested parties within a single cluster and exploring their relations, one by one (see Figure 8.10). Each of the parties cited represents a vested interest that is eccentric to the project itself. Nonetheless, their perceived interests will influence the plans and possible contributions of others within the cluster. In cases such as BedZed, the list of players is likely to include:

- The Bank/s

- The Developer

- The Planning Authorities

- Potential customers for the final building

- The client who commissions the design

- Residents who live near the intended site

- The mass media and other leaders of opinion

- Politicians who may take an interest (either for or against)

Figure 8.10 shows all of the above 8 players (the dots on the diagram) linked together (by lines) in a minimum set of 28 links. If we are to represent all of the possible relations within the system, it would be wise to explore each link in turn, using a positively creative, opportunistic, and open-minded approach. This may mean that the 28 links can also be represented as 56 relational viewpoints. By using this map opportunistically and creatively it is possible to design points of critical intervention and to devise new solutions to this kind of complex problem. By breaking complex systems into their component parts it may be possible to identify high levels of synergy that need to be sustained. The next challenge would be to see whether different types of synergy could synergize with one another. In order to develop this within an effective management system it will probably be necessary to establish a new set of professional practices that work at a higher organisation level than that of the current design specialisms. Although it is difficult to prove that this can be done in any practical way, it is, nevertheless, the underlying purpose behind Chapter 9 and its discussion of 'metadesign'.

References

Anderson, P. W. (1972), 'More is different', *Science*, 177, pp. 393–396.

Arthur, B. (1996), 'Increasing returns and the new world of business', *Harvard Business Review*, July–August, p. 100.

Brandenburger, A. and Nalebuff, B. (1996), *Co-opetition* (New York; London: Doubleday Books).

Corning, P. A. (1998), *The Synergism Hypothesis: On the Concept of Synergy and it's Role in the Evolution of Complex Systems*. Available at: www.complexsystems.org/publications/synhypo.html

Csikszentmihalyi, M. (1990) *Flow: The Psychology of Optimal Experience* (New York: Harper & Row).

Drucker, B. (1978), *The Price of Progress in the Philippines* (Portola, CA: Sierra Books).

Eldredge, M., and Salthe, S. (1984), 'Hierarchy and evolution', *Oxford Survey in Evolutionary Biology*, 1, pp. 184–208.

Fuller, R. B. (1975), *Synergetics: Explorations in the Geometry of Thinking* (New York: Macmillan Publishing, Inc.).

Handy, C. B. (1998), *The Hungry Spirit: Beyond Capitalism – A Quest for Purpose in the Modern World* (New York: Broadway Books).

Heylighen F. (1989), 'Building a Science of Complexity', proceedings of the 1988 Annual Conference of the Cybernetics Society, London.

Jones, P. (2005), 'Data-Sharing Synergies in Buildings Science', a talk given to the M21 team at Goldsmiths, University of London. Available at: http://attainable-utopias.org/tiki/tiki-index.php?page=PhilJonesDataSharing

Lovelock, J. (2006), *The Revenge of Gaia: Why the Earth is Fighting Back – and how We can still Save Humanity* (Santa Barbara, CA: Allen Lane).

Lovelock, J. (1995), *Ages of Gaia* (Oxford: Oxford University Press).

Margulis, L. and Fester, R. (Eds.) (1991), *Symbiosis as a Source of Evolutionary Innovation: Speciation and Morphogenesis* (Cambridge, MA: The MIT Press).

McCorduch, P. (1979), *Machines Who Think* (San Francisco, CA: Freeman).

Minsky, M. (1994), 'Can science explain consciousness?', *Scientific American*, July, pp. 88–94.

Moore, J. (1997), *The Death of Competition, Leadership and Strategy in the Age of Business Ecosystems* (New York: Harper Business).

Polanyi, M. and Grene, M. G. (1969), *Knowing and Being; Essays* (Chicago: University of Chicago Press).

Ranganathan, S. (2003), 'Alloyed pleasures: multimetallic cocktails', *Current Science*, 85:5, pp. 1404–1406.

Rittel, H. and Webber, M. (1973), 'Dilemmas in a general theory of planning', *Policy Sciences*, 4, pp 155–169 (Amsterdam: Elsevier Scientific Publishing Company, Inc.).

Romer, P. M. (1986), 'Increasing returns and long-run growth', *Journal of Political Economy*, 94:5, pp. 1002–1037.

Smith, A. (1904), *An Inquiry into the Nature and Causes of the Wealth of Nations*, Cannan, E. (ed.) (London: Methuen and Co., Ltd.).

van Nieuwenhuijze, O. (2007), 'Can Design become a Form of Healing?' presented at The Idea of Metadesign Conference, Goldsmiths College, University of London. Video available at: http://attainable-utopias.org/tiki/tiki-index.php?page=Metadesign28-6-7

Von Bertalanffy, L. (1968), *General System Theory: Foundations, Development, Applications* (New York: George Braziller).

Wiener, N. (1948), *Cybernetics, or Control and Communication in the Animal and the Machine* (Cambridge, MA: MIT Press).

Wiseman, R. (2003), *The Luck Factor* (London, Century).

Wood, J. (2004), 'Could Synergies of Relations in Design become the basis for Professional Standards of Eudaemonia?', paper presented at the European Academy of Design's 'FutureGround' Conference, Melbourne, Australia.

Wackernagel, M. and Rees, W. E. (1996), *Our Ecological Footprint: Reducing Human Impact on the Earth* (Philadelphia: New Society Publishers).

Metadesign

*'We combine the art and logic of design to help organizations compete.
Welcome to Meta Design.'*

(From the website of the design company 'Metadesign')

So far, the book has sought to map out some terms of reference by which our economy might be re-united with the eco-system upon which it depends. It began by criticising the disconnected, bureaucratic, over-specialist and egoistic nature of our society. In offering an alternative approach the last chapter suggested that 'synergy' could be used as a combined social and industrial performance indicator. While some synergies can deliver practical, material outcomes, others must work to attract participants and engage them, say, at the phenomenological level. This raises the question as to how the performance of metadesign projects might be evaluated, which may not be easy, as an entirely new mode of qualitative benchmarking may be required. It would be helpful to devise a unified calibration system that identifies different modes of synergy at different levels and cross-references them to give a single index. One of the questions this raises is how society might be able to synergise its many levels of synergy. This chapter answers the question by calling for the development of a more sophisticated and coherent culture of organisation. In seeking to adopt a more positive, optimistic standpoint, previous chapters described the need to create new words and grammars in order to bring about an eco-centred society. In his influential theory of a 'hierarchy of needs' Maslow (1987) argues that human beings must satisfy what he calls 'basic' needs, such as hunger and sex before the so-called 'higher' needs. This is sometimes interpreted as a justification for economic growth. In other words, it is taken to mean that citizens must reach a certain level of financial prosperity before they will feel inclined to reduce their level of consumption. While this assumption may be hard to disprove in our own historical terms, we need to assume it is wrong. In short we have little alternative but to take a positive stance, and redesign the way it works. While I am not suggesting that we try to change human nature, it is important to remember that all human activities take place within a linguistic and cultural framework that moderates and guides the way we behave (see Chapter 5). It is at the deep level of values, beliefs and acquired reflexes that we may re-design our world. Designers in the advertising industry probably understand this better than almost all other professionals. By inviting individuals to contribute more actively to the language, they may feel more inclined to see themselves as co-creators of a shared socio-ecological domain.

One way to achieve this would be to develop a more extensive, holistic, consensual, ethical, eco-mimetic practice of design that I will call 'metadesign'. Despite the increasingly bureaucratic and instrumentalist discourse of modern life, it is clear to many of us today that the world cannot usefully be defined in terms of simple, discrete factors. Designers will therefore need to work in cross-disciplinary collaboration with other designers (Jones, 1980) or to work with other specialists (Archer, 1971). These approaches underpin Marzano's (1999) idea of 'high design', which introduces new design skills to deal with the complexity of new products and markets. In developing desirable, ecologically sympathetic living styles, we will need to transcend the conventional problem-orientated approach because we need to develop an auspicious culture of serendipity that will help us to cultivate new micro-utopias. Over the last few hundred years design has become a presumptuous and predictive mechanism of control. In future, it should be seen less as a remedy to short-term, local problems and more as a way to share the envisioning of our full potential. This will mean optimising many levels of a complexity in order to bring the many specialist design practices within a coherent whole. This would work at the broadest operational levels, and at the most subjective epistemological levels. In order to achieve this we require common terms of reference.

The use of this term 'metadesign' has nothing to do with any existing commercial organisation, font style, or the hybridisation of two or three types of specialist practice. What I am proposing is the setting up of a government-sponsored metadesign profession that synergises national governance, local communities and corporate enterprise. This does not mean that any individual could train to become a 'metadesigner'; because the tasks involved would be too onerous and complex for any one individual to address, it is also unlikely that hierarchical management would be the appropriate way to manage them. In the past, design has been associated with discrete items like products or images. This remains a noble and positive tradition because the individual designer can take, and share, pride in the development of a single, identifiable 'thing' that is directly and immediately accessible to him or her. Metadesign teams would probably invite traditional designers to work alongside experts from many other disciplines. The whole process would be organised using design paradigms in preference to bureaucratic protocols of decision-making. Metadesign therefore incorporates a unification of many far-reaching and existing strands of social, cultural, managerial and design practices. This would work by designing for lifestyle, rather than by delivering discrete products or services purely for economic expediency. A given metadesign team's task would be to orchestrate many simultaneous ideas and processes and to make them accessible to and shareable by all. For this reason, it would need to work within a certain scale of operation. When the metadesign process becomes effective it will need to be perceived as a primary source of wellbeing and fun. As such, it must attract goodwill support, active approval and creative engagement. It would help society to live more as a network of joined-up heterarchies, rather than as monolithic hierarchies. At the logistical level, metadesign might create the conditions necessary to encourage more food production in urban areas, or foster the emergence of highly complex, interdependent live-work communities. In this way it would reduce the average person's perceived need for transportation. New business incentives would therefore need to encourage a greater variety of interdependent enterprises that offer synergies at more levels.

In order to achieve these aims we would need to augment the existing economic system with a network of inter-reliant, bespoke currencies that would discourage growth beyond a certain scale and encourage local renewal and enhancement. While it would be designed to discourage a GDP-based growth economy it would more than compensate for this process by adding considerable value to more systems at more levels. For example, by matching a new money system to the specific character and aspirations of a given region, and by putting an appropriate upper limit on its circulation, the face value of a given coinage system would be adaptable to the actual practices of real local people. When the scale of a given currency outgrows the scale of a viable size of local community it may continue to work well as a surrogate for quantity (Simmel, 1990) but will fail to adapt to the additional needs of the new users. However, when a local currency system is designed well it can adapt to the styles and qualities within which the currency's users wish to trade (Douthwaite, 1992). In addition to offering financial remuneration, a greater proportion of social enterprise and industrial initiative or endeavour would be rewarded with limited, licensed access to appropriate resources, social privilege and marks of respect. All legal and educational processes would be predicated on a generic, four-fold logic that integrates the respective parties in a continuum of rights and responsibilities. This can be illustrated using the tetrahedral diagram, as in Figure 9.1. In such a situation, a minimum grammar of relations would pertain:

A.   The agent (for example, citizen, professional individual, and so on) contextualised by nodes B-D

B.   The significant action or proposition in question (for example, idea, task, action, and so on)

C.   The recipient (for example, trading partner, victim of the action, beneficiary, and so on)

D.   The full local and global context of A–C (for example, social and ecological conditions)

This four-fold system can be visualised as a tetrahedral form that would be understandable by virtually everyone. By dint of its formal qualities (see also Chapter 5) it reveals a minimum set of six simultaneous relations that pertain to a given situation. Alternatively, it can be used to map the total of twelve standpoints from which all the parties might perceive their predicament and try to empathise with the other eleven players. As a template for a system of jurisprudence this system goes beyond orthodox modes of ethics such as rights-based, eudemonic, or deontological forms of morality. Where many aspects of education and the law are bureaucratic and, therefore, one or two-dimensional, this system is three-dimensional. In the sense that it implies a minimum set of active agents that operate interdependently in real time, it is a four-dimensional model. This system would also serve as a template for the minimum conditions within which individuals are educated. The above proposals would also require a new type of politics that is based less on representation and more on direct, shareable, local actions. It would therefore offer individual citizens the freedom to dream, rather than to choose. Citizens would have additional responsibilities that derive directly from their role as dreamers. Importantly, they would be asked to help those around them to

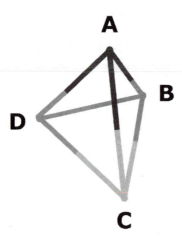

Figure 9.1   A tetrahedron depicting a minimum grammar of ethical relations

optimise their full potential (Fairclough, 2007) and to initiate positive actions at the local and collective level. While this scheme contains a number of novel, and therefore untested, propositions it is intended as the basic model from which better systems might evolve. It is designed so that more people would become more deeply enfranchised and emotionally satisfied, and therefore less prone to the addiction to resource-intensive substances, products, toys or other treats.

In a number of different ways the previous chapters have sought to emphasise that the ecological domain can never be under humanity's full control. Nevertheless, it is the assertive and predictive nature of design that is proving increasingly interesting to the commercial world. To recap, we have all helped to create what Anthony Giddens (2000) called a 'runaway world' of profligate consumption and waste. Designers have played a special role in this process but, to be fair, they are not free agents. To a great extent they are managed and educated within a framework of values that are part of the problem, rather than the solution. Society needs to change very soon. It will not be good enough just to teach designers the honourable specialised subjects of design. While they should not be lost, at some level they will also need to be integrated within a much larger, single discipline that is taught over a longer period, perhaps even longer than that of architecture or medicine. In this regard, metadesign would become a creative link between agriculture, medicine, architecture and urban planning. Moreover, although some designers will remain as specialists, they will need to learn how to augment their current activities with a broader range of managerial, philosophical and communication skills.

Here it is important to distinguish between the self-perception of designers and that of urban planners and other professionals. One major difference is the fact that designers are trained to see facts as opportunities for innovation, rather than as a 'reality' that requires a suitable response. For example, where scientists and public servants may assume that a rise in energy consumption must be met by appropriate increases in supply, designers and inventors are trained to challenge the *status quo*. In any case, what we take to be an inalienable public or consumer 'demand' was probably shaped by the decisions and actions of previous planners, economists, bankers, managers, advertisers and designers. We need to build new types of design team in order to transcend the respectable, or even to think beyond the feasible limits of design as it is now. While designers already play a decisive role in reducing the potential damage of products and services (Thackara, 2005) in general they lack the confidence to seize the initiative. By virtue of its relatively recent evolution, design is what Schön (1985) has called a 'minor' profession. This not only affects how designers are perceived, but also how they see themselves. For example, Whitely (1993) and Bevers (2005) have noted that many designers still see their work more as an aspect of business than as a fully fledged established professional role. Where the medical and legal professions spend a good deal of their time debating ethical issues, in design there is a perennial emphasis on 'skills' and 'economic competition' (for example UK Design Council, 2007) rather than 'education' and 'responsibilities'. This is symptomatic of an obedient, old fashioned, service-orientated mentality. It illustrates why, in the last few decades, although many designers may have dreamed – privately – of a holistic world order, few have seen much alternative to offering their skills in support of market forces. While much of design education is extraordinarily useful in many ways, its founding principles have evolved from a platonic emphasis on 'form', rather than 'flow', as the essential nature of reality. This is partly why designers learn how to gaze at objects in a way that overlooks their full context, purpose and potential. This has suited the corporations quite well, especially if they merely want designers to modify the shape, colour, or texture of an existing product. It is rare for designers to be asked to re-think the whole political, ideological, technical and economic context that conditions these issues. Metadesign would need to augment this narrow remit by inspiring a broader, more transdisciplinary level of understanding. It would help to overcome the narrowness of the average designer's repertoire and to strengthen his or her sense of ecological responsibility.

Arguably, professional designers reinvent the world by intervening beyond the level of its appearance, functionality and significance. As others have used the word 'metadesign' in a variety of ways it is important to declare how an ecological version will work. Perhaps one of its primary aims with the minimum expenditure of resources, should be to put people more happily in touch with the rest of the natural world. This would therefore entail the cultivation of a more entrepreneurial-entredonneurial approach that is far more socially and ecologically responsible. Excellent progress has already been made by a small army of pioneers in 'green design', 'eco-design' and 'design for sustainability'. However, despite these vital initiatives, we have failed to avert the disastrous and destructive course of industrialised, consumer-centred capitalism. This failure reflects the scale of need, rather than any shortage of vision or passion. The book asserts the need to take these tried and tested agendas onto a new and more imaginative level. Designers and advertisers will be a key part of this quest. They know how to bring many factors together in a way that is desirable and graspable. They have a repertoire of abilities that complement those of the politician, economist, or planner. For example, they know how to utilise 'affordances' (Gibson, 1979) and 'design affordance' (Norman, 1988). These are terms that define the conditions under which a given form or situation encourages other things to happen (see Chapter 5). As Norman said, 'Affordances provide strong clues to the operations of things. Plates are for pushing. Knobs are for turning. Slots are for inserting things into. Balls are for throwing or bouncing. When affordances are taken advantage of, the user knows what to do just by looking: no picture, label, or instruction needed' (Norman, 1988). Together, we must integrate energy production with a network of specially designed currencies. These need to be designed to help promote local communities that are more autonomous. This cannot simply be organised in a mechanistic way, because an effective metadesign would need to work with hearts, minds, systems and technologies. Many of the tasks we undertake are a combination of conscious strategies requiring planned actions combined with skilled sub-tasks. Many of these are 'tacit', or unconscious, because they become enacted within an acquired repertoire of other actions. At the personal level, we may consider this as a kind of 'design shamanism'.

These developments coincide, however, with changes that have also accelerated de-forestation, species depletion, pollution of air and waterways, and the exhaustion of natural resources. They have made the threat of human annihilation a foreseeable probability. The task needs to be seen as the design of a whole and the design of suitable parts that will make up the whole. Designers operate at an interface between many agencies. This is a crucially important position from which to make changes. It requires a reconciliation of creative, analytical, integrative and receptive thinking. It also requires the ability to shift one's understanding from issues of 'living styles' to technological models and to a broad grasp of cultural trends and philosophies. This is what designers would be uniquely good at, provided they are given the right education. A troubling feature of capitalism and, indeed, Taylorism in the twenty-first century is the market's tendency to measure up the whole world as an arbitrary stockpile of resources – valued by price and demand – rather than by seeing it as a complex environment that will afford mutual, or reciprocal benefits at a local, long-term level. This loss of meaning is a significant aspect of efficiency, because the development and sharing of meaning is essential to a healthy society. If a society is unable to co-create meaning its inhabitants will be less able to communicate and support one another. It will also be unable to build trust within relationships. This has implications for the cost of maintaining law and order, because a low-trust society has high overheads. One of the reasons we need a metadesign approach is because, as in any complex system, there is always the risk of sub-optimisation. This is the process whereby a small improvement in a larger process can lead, often unexpectedly, to a net reduction in performance. For example, by producing smaller cars with lower toxic emissions and better fuel-efficiency we have made them more desirable and affordable. The net result is that, in total, we are consuming more fuel than ever before.

Similarly, if we were to insist that all new houses must meet the most stringent ecologically benign building standards, with zero-carbon emissions, locally sourced materials, autonomous services such as water, gas or electricity it seems likely that our world would improve. If, however, we continue to drive long distances to work each day and to fly further and further for our holidays, we may still fail to meet agreed international targets for reducing the total carbon throughput. Designers must to do more integrative thinking at the large scale. It is likely that government and supra-government agencies will need to be involved, perhaps in conjunction with the corporations. Hence, where an individual product may seem, intrinsically, to be environmentally benign this may still cause significant harm to the environment. As Chapter 8 explained, no part should be seen in isolation from the whole system. Specialist designers have very little control, if any, over the broadest context of their work. However, that could change if we were to develop a system within which the economic conditions were made to be part of the whole business context. This would mean integrating banking, healthcare, town planning, energy and food production with the design of communication systems, services and products.

In theory, if metadesign can attend to many subtle matters in a complex way it might be able to turn vicious circles into virtuous circles. The ability to do this reliably may take some time to perfect. If we were to develop an ecological mode of metadesign we would need to augment the good efforts of more specialist approaches, such as 'green design', 'eco-design' and 'design for sustainability' and integrate them into a synergistic operation. The early pioneers of these more ecological modes of design devoted a lot of thought to the best way to choose the most suitable materials for a given product. Too many goods are manufactured with materials that break down too rapidly, or that outlive their purpose. Fry (1999) has shown how, in the last decade or so, many consumer products are deliberately designed to lose their attraction after a short time, so that we will be ready to dispose of them when the next model becomes available. He calls this practice 'de-futuring'. At the other end of the scale, other products and methods are equally unwelcome, because they are too synthetic or toxic to find a benign place in the food chain; but often, waste would appear to be more closely tied into 'desirability' than most of us had realised. Design theorists such as Ed van Hinte (1997) and Jonathan Chapman (2005) have reminded us that, in a sense, we only throw products away when we have lost our affection for them. It may be obvious that what we usually call 'sustainability', then, is closely related to our assumptions about the 'maintainability' of our affections and our perceived capabilities. Although improving the design of products is a vital task, compared with the total effects of a given 'living style', or 'lifestyle', product enhancement is likely to be of only contributory importance. Fortunately, designers now create less tangible goods, such as brand identities, experiences, values and services. In this regard, they must work within more complex systems that are intended for regulating flow, rather than for improving individual products for sales purposes (Wood, 2003).

The term 'design' is increasingly applied to a variety of approaches that range from the highly ordered (for example managerial) to what may appear to be more formative at the ideational level (for example 'creative'). Design may therefore be described in many categories, such as technological functionality, rhetorical form giving, tactical scheduling, human relations, economic strategising, and so on. This does not mean that designers consciously control what they do. Indeed, much of their work leads to unforeseen consequences that emerge from the richness and complexity of their metadesigns. Again, it is important to keep in mind the strongly wilful nature of Western discourse that is embedded within the language that designers adopt, share, replicate and disseminate to others. Popular usage of the traditional idea of 'design' carries powerful overtones, partly because it conveys a confidently predictive sense that derives from the ancient Greek sense of teleology (from *telos*). In a culture in which the 'consumer is king' it also conveys a peculiarly Western sense of 'individualism'. Where our concept of 'telos' relies on a fatalistic, mutable vision of what is yet to come, individualism depends for its meaning on the perceived differences between individuals; their particular predispositions, imaginations and capabilities. Just as 'telos' reminds us that the Aristotelian idea of 'design' means little without a strongly predictive sense of 'future', so the idea of individuality has served to engender social respect for the designer as a 'celebrity'. If we are to transcend these conditions we must, therefore, envisage design as a more holistic, dynamic and sensitively adaptive process. Metadesign would therefore need to emerge from a continuously consensual view of what is happening. This cannot be achieved unilaterally and it is unlike what we normally think of as 'design'. Eric von Hippel (2006) has observed the tendency for innovation to become democratised because of industry's ability to innovate in the appropriate way. In his scenario, individual users need not develop everything on their own. They would also be able to benefit from innovations developed and freely shared by others.

On the other hand, the idea that designers could work at the highest level of planning or healthcare is a promising one. The way that designers think is often different from, say, bureaucrats or politicians (Schön, 1985; Lawson, 1994). It therefore represents untapped potential if applied at a higher level. One way that designers may be helpful is by working across boundaries (creativity) to reframe purposes such as health, or happiness. In the 18th century, Carolus Linnaeus (1707–78) categorised species by making judgements based on their shared physical characteristics. This is an appropriate metaphor for the way that designers are still regarded as superficial 'form-givers' and 'taste-makers'. However, in science, the original Linnaean approach has been revised to fit into the Darwinian principle of common descent. Instead of working from the appearance of things, 'molecular systematics' uses DNA sequences as a way to find patterns that may be invisible to botanists and zoologists. A similar step is needed within the way designers are employed within society. Where the discourse of legislation, planning and politics often needs to operate in a categorical domain of thinking, good design must work more contingently and holistically, often within a conceptual 3D, or 4D space that is more specific.

John Thackara (2005) claims that 80 per cent of the environmental impact of today's products, services and infrastructures is determined at the design stage. In regard to the above problems, designers therefore have a huge collective potential, but have so far been unable to fulfil it. Attempts to inform designers about the 'best practices' of Eco-design (for example Datschefski, 2001; Fuad-Luke, 2002) are always helpful, but they have not been robust enough to halt the growth of a global economic system that has become immensely powerful. Despite the heroic efforts by the pioneers of 'eco-design', 'design for sustainability', and so on, global carbon emissions are rising steadily, and bio-diversity continue to fall. Since the 1950s, many professional designers had sought to create a 'sustainable' world by 'reforming the environment' (Fuller, 1969), reducing the scale of enterprise (Schumacher, 1987), or creating biodegradable, longer lasting products. However, by the 1980s, many designers had become resigned to market forces while seeking to emulate nature (Benyus, 1997), 'de-materialise' their products (Diani, 1992) or make them leaner (Stahel, 2006), or cleaner, slower, service-based (Manzini, 2001). Although we now have a better understanding of our effect on the eco-system (for example 'Ecological Footprint', Wackernagel and Rees (1996)) this message has failed to transform the way most designers practice. Indeed, some designers might even regard the pursuit of 'Eco-Design' as worthy, but economically risky or even futile.

Annoyingly, some 'green' products have even fostered new markets and thus contributed to a net rise in consumption. Metadesigners would need to challenge the imperative at a more serious level. This is why I have sought to frame design as a profoundly entrepreneurial activity. Arguably, 'social enterprise' is intrinsic to the way designers think. In a sense, this would mean reversing the directionality between employer and employee, and this is clearly problematic. However, by starting with the proposition that designers are entrepreneurs, it is relatively easy to see how new businesses, concepts, visions and practices may emerge. A number of imaginative thinkers have begun to identify the whole production-consumption cycle as a panoply of opportunities for sustainable business (Hawken, Lovins and Lovins, 2000). In 1995, Ernst Ulrich von Weizsäcker, working with Amory and Hunter Lovins put forward what they called the 'Factor Four' argument, suggesting that we can double the wealth while halving the resources used. Another way that metadesigners might wish to conceive of this approach is to identify iterative use and re-use as a 'zero-waste' process (Murray, 2002) that operates throughout a ceaseless 'cradle-to-cradle' cycle of exchange (McDonough, 2002).

Again, Richard Buckminster Fuller anticipated this idea. He was reluctant to see any chemical as a 'pollutant', because this may confuse its identity with its use. He saw that society may need to encourage commercial enterprise to flourish in the right way. As he once dryly observed, 'the people who let the sulphur go into the air are not in the sulphur business'. The shift of view this scale of thinking represents is beyond what we currently recognise as within the remit of any known practice of design. If metadesign is to be more extensive and comprehensive than orthodox design it would need to transcend specialist boundaries such as 'product design', interior design, graphic design, and so on. This means that designers would orchestrate different types of knowledge within a common professional framework.

In the nineteenth century, William Morris (1834–96) did not want to see a hierarchy emerging within the different arts professions. A more current perspective might add that specialism can lead to competitive struggle, which in turn may limit the designer's possible sphere of influence at the highest level. By evolving in separate 'silos', such as illustration, advertising design, landscape design, graphic design and product design, different worldviews and, therefore, conflicts emerged. For example, where engineering designers feel inclined to criticise product designers for merely 'tarting-up' something that already 'works', so product designers may feel that it is they who deserve most credit for turning dull machines into more desirable, collectible, or even useable products. In the world of the hammer, everything looks like a nail. Hence, in the battle lines between specialist designers it is easy to see ethics as an optional extra, or to see the task of designing for an ecological society as the domain of the politician or legislator, rather than the enterprising designer. This tendency has been exacerbated by the growing success of the design profession over the last decade or so. In the development of a strenuous consumer-orientated culture, specialist designers have become indispensable as the 'fixers' who ensure that a given high-investment venture will work. They are the new pragmatists who manipulate society's habits and dreams in order to ensure that a never-ending flow of sexy, new products will continue to pile up in the consumer's shopping basket – on time and within budget.

What is the long-term potential of the design tradition as a whole, to make a radical contribution at the practical, collective, organisational level? One thing is clear, unless we work at a sufficiently high level of intervention, none of the above measures are likely to tame an economic system designed for limitless growth. This intervention would need to ensure that designers are highly responsible professionals. They would need, therefore, to be highly adaptive and responsible. It will not be enough to train designers as entrepreneurs and develop an ecologically responsible designer. Where business seems inclined to regard environmentalism as a meaningless moral obligation that poses an additional burden or workload, metadesigners remind society of the highly creative and opportunistic nature of Nature. Such a plan would certainly represent a bold and ambitious step, not least for the many specialist designers who may require re-training for working within 'metadesign' teams.

In his 1991 book *Designing Designing* (Jones, 1991), John Chris Jones called for designing to become the process of devising, 'not individual products but whole systems or environments such as airports, transportation, hypermarkets, educational curricula, broadcasting schedules, welfare schemes, banking systems, computer networks'. In this agenda, he acknowledged the important need for design to become more publicly participative, and he mooted the idea of 'designing without a product, as a process or way of living in itself'.

Jones's concept is very helpful for establishing some terms of reference for establishing a 'metadesign' profession. It is an exceptionally bold and insightful vision. The first step is to imagine the solution before deciding whether it is possible or otherwise. In effect, this means a considerable broadening of the remit of 'eco-design' and 'design for sustainability' in order to make it operate beyond and above the limitations of global capitalism as we know it. This represents a massive undertaking, but one that is needed in order address the real scale of the problem.

In 1967, Belbin investigated the effectiveness of management teams (Belbin, 1993). What he found was that the more complementary their contributions or roles, the better the teams performed. He also found that teams selected solely on the basis of high mental ability or intro/extroversion performed significantly less well than other teams. What was more significant in predicting the success of teams was the presence of a number of team roles. These were additional to the functional role individual members had been assigned. Belbin defined team role as a tendency to behave, contribute and inter-relate with others in a team in certain distinctive ways. He identified nine team roles:

1.   coordinator

2. team worker

3. plant

4. monitor-evaluator

5. implementer

6. completer-finisher

7. shaper

8. resource-investigator

9. specialist

A monitor evaluator with a capacity for careful analysis and objectivity may not be the best person to inspire others. Enthusiasm would interfere with assessment. A completer-finisher may be poor at delegating. A need to make sure things are done properly does not fit easily with giving someone else the job to do. Attempting to correct allowable weaknesses may undermine the strength of that team role. It is important, however, to manage the weakness in case it tends towards unacceptable behaviour. For example: a resource investigator may lose enthusiasm once the initial excitement has passed but it is not acceptable to let clients down by neglecting to make follow-up arrangements. Shapers may be prone to frustration and irritation but this becomes unacceptable when they are unable to recover a situation with good humour or an apology.

Successful Teams

Belbin identified certain factors that seemed to be critical in determining the success or failure of a team:

- a similarity between the personal qualities of the person leading the team and the typical characteristics of the coordinator team role

- the presence of one strong plant

- a reasonable spread of mental abilities

- wide coverage of all team roles

- a good match between functional role and team role characteristics

- awareness by team members of the various team roles

Ross Ashby's famous 'law of requisite variety' (Ashby, 1956) states that, in effect: 'only variety can control variety'. This implies that externally imposed 'improvements' may fail to achieve a designer's purpose if he or she is not part of (that is, not sufficiently in touch with) the working complexities of the system itself. In systemic terms, many large, successful entities display qualities of self-organisation and self-balance that are similar to that of a living organism. This means that they may appear to be self-aware and intelligently adaptive, often in a way that is difficult for humans to grasp at the conscious level. This obviously raises deep questions about the way we comprehend things above a certain scale of complexity, subtlety or magnitude. Moreover, it also challenges the idea that designers might be able easily to 'design' complex systems in any effective and sustained way.

Within the context of the electronic arts, metadesign was mooted as a new practice in which 'design as planning' was replaced with 'design as a seeding process' (Ascott, 1994). It therefore placed the 'metadesigner' in the role of 'systems integrator' (Galloway and Rabinowitz, 1983) that, according to Giaccardi, entails a shift from normative planning ('how things ought to be') to the humanistic enterprise of seeding ('how things might be'). As such, metadesign is a higher order design in which participation and emergence are critical components to nourish and evolve the initial conditions set by the metadesigner(s). Metadesigners would therefore need to work more consensually, cooperatively and entrepreneurially than conventional designers. They may need to incorporate elements of self-organisation and opportunism within their remit. This might include the questioning of the way that projects are conventionally resourced. It may therefore offer novel (for example non-linear) forms of organisation that would impinge on questions of resourcing, transaction and/or currency creation.

Fortunately, this is already happening in some of the more de-centralised design movements such as Copy-Left, Open Source, Share-Alike, Creative Commons, Group Thinking, pledge-based activism and other social enterprises. Some of this work can be informed by heterarchic industrial practices (cf. Semler, 2001) such as 'worker autonomy' (Fairclough, 2005).

Combinatorial terms such as 'co-design', 'co-evolution' and 'co-authorship' have taken a long time to become familiar, even though they refer to practices that seem characteristically human. This is because they tend to be under-estimated within a culture that still valorises the cardinal role of the individual in private and public life. Since the era of Socrates, western thought has tended to intensify and extend its understanding of the individual psyche, rather than develop a culture in which wisdom is seen as a shared and emergent process. The terms 'enterprise' and 'entrepreneurship' therefore suggest a peculiarly western mindset. This is famously exemplified in Adam Smith's theory (1776) that collective benefits will emerge when individuals focus upon, and actively attend to, their own interests. Arguably, this idea remains enormously attractive because it is framed as an implicit 'win-win' scenario, in which individuals can feel good about 'taking', knowing that their selfishness will contribute benefits for all. Previous research has shown that many consumers still find terms such as 'sustainable consumption' (UNEP, 2007) confusing, inconsequential or counterproductive (Wood, 1997). 'Sustainability' arguments are popularly perceived (that is in subjective cost-benefit terms) as a 'lose-win' scenario (Wood, 2007), in that they invite citizens to be less selfish in order to give more to future generations. The term 'win-win' is familiar and attractive to most people. It can be depicted as two players connected by a single, synergistic relation (cf. Margulis, 1991). By connecting it to two other players we can accommodate more 'winners' within the same configuration. The tetrahedral model shows (Figure 9.2) that, 'Win-Win-Win-Win' can be six times more advantageous than 'Win-Win' (Figure 9.3).

For all the above reasons we have identified our basic building block of synergy as a 'win-win-win-win' scenario (Wood, 2007) because it is optimally mnemonic (Fuller, 1975), unique (Euler, 1752, cited in Weisstein, 2007) and non-hierarchical (Fairclough, 2005; van Nieuwenhuijze, 2005) when mapped using a tetrahedron (see Figure 9.2). If each of its four nodes is used to represent a 'winning' player, it is clear that there are six peer-to-peer relations. Whereas 'win-win' refers to a mutually beneficial partnership, our notion of 'win-win-win-win' can be applied to the mutually beneficial relationships among a metadesign team, in addition to possible benefits to the surrounding context within which they are working.

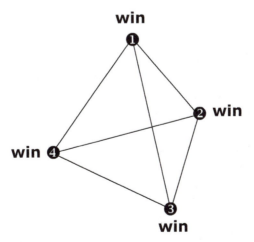

Figure 9.2   A tetrahedral set of 'winners'

Figure 9.3   A single 'win-win' axis

As the difference between a line (Figure 9.3) and a tetrahedron (Figure 9.2) illustrates, simply by doubling the number of 'winning' nodes (that is from two to four) we can obtain six times the number of working relations. We can use tetrahedral filtering to explore types, or 'chunks' of data that we encounter within companies and institutions. As we have found it so helpful in facilitating creative (design) judgement we also use it as a non-hierarchical, non-linear method of managing shared data.

In the system we developed we assigned each researcher to one of four organisational groups. These range from the highly intuitive, spontaneous and somatic to the analytical, critical and deliberate – that is: 1) pushing & doing, 2) languaging, 3) envisioning, 4) new knowing. Each operates as a 'cognitive filter' that complements the other three. The system also reflects four levels of complexity that are embodied within their characteristic roles (see Table 9.1).

If we interpret this idea in terms of existing value systems we may therefore fail to understand its full potential. Within a highly corporate and consumer-orientated vision this would probably mean customers paying for their lifestyle benefits in more ways, in more places and at more frequent intervals, which would mean devising a system that is de-centralised, but comprehensive. This is because a less centralised alternative offers more opportunities for increasing the level of synergies within and across the social, political, cultural and industrial domains. It would also facilitate a range of new and surprising benefits, both tangible and intangible, to be shared across a more heterarchic community in which production and consumption, enterprise and altruism become increasingly interdependent. It may mean persuading producers to accept rewards that place less emphasis on income, and more on an enhanced quality of life.

John Ruskin's famous description of the craftsman's pride in his work affords benefits at four locations (that is natural environment, client, craftsman and society). A tetrahedral map of this schema reminds us that it implies six simultaneous opportunities for gains that can be factored into similar design scenarios.

Table 9.1   The four groups and their roles

Complexity	Role/Group	Approach / Mode of enquiry
HIGHER	NEW KNOWING	Intuitive / spontaneous / anticipatory
	ENVISIONING	imaginative / critical / self-reflexive / tactical
	LANGUAGING	discursive / interpretive / adaptive / facilitating
LOWER	PUSHING/DOING	Hands-on / decisive / resourceful / managerial

References

Archer, L. B. (1971), *Technological Innovation: A Methodology* (Frimley, Surrey: Inforlink).

Ashby, W. R. (1956), *Introduction to Cybernetics* (New York: Wiley).

Ascott, R., (1994) in Giaccardi, E., 'Metadesign as an emergent design culture', *Leonardo*, 38:4, August 2005, pp. 342–349 (Cambridge, MA: The MIT Press).

Belbin, R.M. (1993), *Team Roles at Work* (Oxford: Butterworth-Heinemann).

Benyus, J. (1997), *Innovation Inspired by Nature: Biomimicry* (New York: William Morrow & Co.).

Bevers, R. (2005), Paper written to the Australian Graphic Design Association. Available at: www.agda.com.au/dm/observations/Develo.html

Chapman, J. (2005), *Emotionally Durable Design: Objects, Experiences and Empathy* (London: Earthscan Publications).

Datschefski, E. (2001), *The Total Beauty of Sustainable Products* (Switzerland: Roto Vision SA).

Design Council (2007), *Skills Inititative*. Available at: www.design-council.org.uk/en/Design-Council/3/Press/Skills-plan-calls-for-UK-design

Diani, M. (1992), *The Immaterial Society: Design, Culture, and Technology in the Post-Modern World* (New Jersey: Prentice Hall).

Douthwaite, R. (1992), *The Growth Illusion* (Hartland: Green Books in association with Lilliput Press, Totnes).

Fairclough, K. (2007), 'How can Metadesign become more Eco-mimetic?' presented at The Idea of Metadesign Conference, Goldsmiths College, University of London. Video available at: http://attainable-utopias.org/tiki/tiki-index.php?page=Metadesign28-6-7-PM

Fairclough, K., (2005), 'Using the Tetrahedron in Organization', from a lecture given on 22nd June, 2005 at Goldsmiths College, University of London.

Fry, T. (1999), *A New Design Philosophy: An Introduction to De-Futuring* (New South Wales, Australia: NSWU Press).

Fuad-Luke, A. (2002), *The Eco-design Handbook: A Complete Sourcebook for the Home and Office* (San Francisco, CA: Chronicle Books).

Fuller, R. B. (1969), *Operating Manual for Spaceship Earth* (Carbondale, IL: Southern Illinois University Press).

Fuller, R. B. (1975), *Synergetics: Explorations in the Geometry of Thinking* (New York: Macmillan Publishing, Inc.).

Galloway, K. and Rabinowitz, S. (1983), *Online manifesto*. Available at: http://telematic.walkerart.org/timeline/timeline_ecafe.html

Gibson, J. J. (1979), *The Ecological Approach to Visual Perception* (Boston: Houghton Mifflin).

Giddens, A. (2000), *Runaway World: How Globalization is Reshaping our Lives* (New York: Routledge).

Hawken, P., Lovins A. B. and Lovins, H. L. (2000), *Natural Capitalism: The Next Industrial Revolution* (London: Earthscan Press).

Jones, J. C. (1980), *Design Methods* (Chichester: John Wiley & Sons).

Jones, J. C. (1991), *Designing Designing* (London: Architecture Design and Technology Press).

Lawson, B. and Roberts, S. (1994), 'Modes and features: the organisation of data in CAD supporting the early phases of design', *Design Studies*, 12:2, pp. 102–108.

Manzini, E. (2001), *From Products to Services. Leapfrog: Short-Term Strategies for Sustainability, Metaphors for Change: Partnerships, Tools and Civic Action for Sustainability,* Allen, P. (ed.) and Gee, D. (Sheffield: Greenleaf Publishing).

Margulis, L. and Fester, R. (1991), *Symbiosis as a Source of Evolutionary Innovation: Speciation and Morphogenesis* (Cambridge, MA: The MIT Press).

Marzano, S. (1999), *Creating Value by Design – Thoughts* (London: Lund Humphries).

Maslow, A. H. (1987), *Motivation and Personality* (New York: Harper and Row).

McDonough, W. and Braungart, M. (2002), *Cradle to Cradle: Remaking the Way We Make Things* (New York: North Point Press)

Murray, R. (2002), *Zero Waste* (London: Greenpeace Environmental Trust).

Norman, D. (1988), *The Psychology of Everyday Things* (New York: Basic Books).

Schön, D. (1985), *The Design* (London: Studio, RIBA Publications Ltd.).

Schumacher, E. F. (1987), *Small is Beautiful: A Study of Economics as if People Mattered* (London: Abacus Penguin Books).

Semler, R. (2001), *Maverick* (New York: Arrow Books).

Simmel, G., Frisby, D. (1990), *The Philosophy of Money* (London: Routledge).

Stahel, W. R. (2006), *The Performance Economy* (Basingstoke, Hampshire: Palgrave Macmillan).

Thackara, J. (2005), *In the Bubble: Designing in a Complex World* (Cambridge, MA: The MIT Press).

United Nations Environment Programme (UNEP) (2007), *Application of the Term 'Sustainable Consumption'.* Available at: www.uneptie.org/pc/sustain

van Hinte, E., Bonekamp, L., Muis, H., and Odding, A. (1997), *Eternally Yours. Visions on Product Endurance* (Rotterdam: 010 Publishers) PDF available at: www.eternally-yours.org

van Nieuwenhuijze, O. (2005), 'Using the Tetrahedron in Design', from a lecture given on 22nd June, 2005 at Goldsmiths College, University of London.

von Hippel, E. (2006), *Democratizing Innovation* (Cambridge, MA: MIT Press).

Weisstein, E. W. (2007), 'Polyhedral formula', from MathWorld, Wolfram Web Resource. Available at: http://mathworld.wolfram.com/PolyhedralFormula.html

Whiteley, N. (1993), *Design for Society* (London: Reaktion Books Ltd.).

Wood, J. (1997), 'Situated criticism and the experiential present', in the Special 'Criticism' Edition, Whitely, N. (ed.) of the *Journal of Design Issues*, 3:2, pp. 5–15.

Wood, J. (2003), 'The Wisdom of Nature = The Nature of Wisdom', paper given at the 5th Conference of the European Academy of Design, "Techné: Design Wisdom", University of Barcelona, 28–30 April. Available at: http://attainable-utopias.org/tiki/AcademicPapers.

Wood, J. (2007), 'Win-Win-Win-Win: synergy tools for metadesigners', in *Designing for the 21st Century*, Inns, T. (ed.), (Aldershot: Gower Publishing).

Towards an Ethics of Flow

CHAPTER

10

> *'The speed of action, the intricacy of trails, the detail of mental pictures,*
> *is awe-inspiring beyond all else in nature'.*
>
> (Vannevar Bush, 1945)

This chapter continues its reframing of the existing discourse of 'environmental sustainability', asking whether designers should become the facilitators of flow (Wood, 2000), rather than the originators of maintainable 'things' such as discrete products or images. The previous chapter's discussion of metadesign acts as a pretext for this enquiry. Chapter 8 argued that, in order to design effectively at the level of 'living styles' designers would need to create a 'synergy of synergies' (Fuller, 1975). This would call for us to understand more deeply how things change. It is especially poignant for western discourse, which has frequently been associated with an emphasis on materiality and durability, rather than 'flow' (cf. Capra, 1975). In addition to the chapter's philosophical challenge to the popular notion of 'sustainability' there is also a practical purpose. In 1987, the Brundtland Report's term 'sustainable development' was defined as development that meets the needs of the present without compromising the ability of future generations to meet their own needs (Brundtland, 1987). Since then, a proliferation of conflicting definitions has emerged around the world. Some researchers have counted at least 70 different uses for the term 'sustainability'. This chapter argues that, since 1987, subsequent terms such as 'sustainable business' and 'sustainable consumption' appear to emphasise certainty and permanence, rather than ecological cohesion. At the practical level this has strained the credibility of 'sustainability' as a useful generic term. So why is it still the touchstone of environmentalism?

The nature of our western belief system and language is strongly humanistic, individualistic and rhetorical. In this sense, it makes the assumption that we can expect to predict, influence, or control everything around us, at every level. In some political theory it is common to speak of the need to 'reclaim' certain things. Perhaps we need to 'reclaim Nature', albeit in a more selfless, practicable, and meaningful way? 'Nature' cannot be 'reclaimed', because we do not 'own' it. Many might argue that Nature owns us, rather than the other way round.

On reflection, perhaps we may consider adopting the idea of 'attunement', rather than the more clumsy, nebulous idea of 'ownership'. 'Attunement' can be interpreted as a feeling of being 'at home'. This is also a convenient starting point. Modern evolutionary theory shows that we are exquisitely adapted to the Earth's complex variety of conditions. In this sense, 'Nature' co-exists with us in the present tense. This means that what is 'real' to us is always a blend of our experience and the language system that frames it. In this sense Nature is always latent within us, and therefore we should be able to feel enfranchised to our world whenever we 'tune-in'. Many religions and sects have used devotional or contemplative practices to infuse a magical sense of flow or 'well being' into the immediate present. In this sense, micro-utopias might invoke a heightened experience of the 'here and now'. We do not necessarily need to visit the East African savannah in order to regain this nostalgic feeling of 'home', but it may help. The poet and artist, William Blake was a celebrated critic of industrial alienation. However, his poetic descriptions of South London in the nineteenth century also indicate a heightened, blissful sense of reality. This suggests that we have the ability to define, as well as to inhabit, our own micro-utopias. He is an interesting example, as his work carries values and feelings that are characteristically Christian.

While Nature is characterised by emergence and flow, traditional Western thought tends to value materiality. From within this mindset, the idea of 'sustainability' may appear as a quest to conserve 'finite resources'. This also reflects a profoundly atomistic logic that upholds the importance of 'laws', numbers, facts, and material properties. Within this belief system, what we currently mean by 'resources' can usually be defined by quantity; that is, they are measurable by volume or weight, or trackable by absolute location, and so on. In theorising, the chapter argues that the human experience of flow defies the logic of categories.

While some aspects of the sustainability agenda relate to the nature of flow, designers are trained to live in a world of individual objects and images. The dictionary offers two distinct senses in which we commonly use the verb 'to sustain'. Where one emphasises coherence the other speaks of duration. Where the first describes the basic idea of supporting, or holding something together, the second and more common usage emphasises the longevity of so doing. These ideas are related because the endurance of something is usually a testament to its viability. When we see it as a temporal mission we are blinded to the subtlety of how it holds together in the non-temporal sense. Sometimes, when we look into the future we forget what we are doing and fall over. In the mid-1990s, eco-design pioneers noticed that cherishable products will resist early disposal if their perceived value remains high (van Hinte, 1997; Chapman, 2005). Ultimately, the 'Eternally Yours' concept invited designers to plan for eternity. It is interesting to note that, while this was an important practical way to reduce over-consumption, it is not the way that eco-systems do it. Nonetheless the idea of conserving possessions probably seems natural to western readers, because our intellectual tradition is inclined to focus on individual objects, or on the categories of things, rather than on the coherence and flow of whole systems (cf. Tarnas, 1991). Where non-western cultures might embrace the idea of eternity as an auspicious space of endless becoming, western beliefs are more inclined to interpret it in terms of clock-time or calendar-time. For example, mainstream western science has remained sceptical of certain traditional non-western theories of flow (for example Feng Shui), presumably because they are not based on 'hard' evidence and 'objective' forms of empiricism. This is why this book explores and challenges strongly atomistic concepts such as 'academic rigour' (Chapter 5), 'transferable skills' and 'sustainability' (Chapter 9). Chapter 5 also stressed the importance of language in determining how we as citizens and consumers experience the world, and thereby the way we behave in it. Ancient Hindu texts (*The Upanishads*) tell us that the ontological domain is without name or form (see Chapter 6). Nonetheless, we like boundaries because they are semantically convenient.

In today's world of litigation, digital software and political spin, unscrupulous people can manipulate the boundaries of meaning in order to gain competitive advantage, or to evade responsibility. As Chapters 3, 4 and 6 pointed out, some of the above problems can be attributed to the fixing of metaphysical ideas – that is substance, quantity, quality, relation, place, time, situation, condition, action, and passion. Where human experience reveals a world in transition that is complex and fuzzy, Aristotle invented the idea of the 'excluded middle' in order to ensure that each category can be distinguished readily from its neighbours. Chapter 6 explained how Immanuel Kant developed this method, and how this led to the invention of binary logic, the digital computer (McCorduch, 1979), and the database. However, there are several problems stemming from what is known as the 'logic of category'. The first is that, no matter how much care we may take in creating it, any given category will often seem arbitrary when viewed from within a different context. Secondly, like numbers, categories are designed to make unequivocal distinctions. By guiding the act of description, categories encourage us to ignore, or to overlook, the character or 'slope' of the boundaries that separate the types, classes, or attributes described. Using this logic, for example, how would one account for the dynamic quality of transition between 'this' and 'that', or the gradient and profile of transition between 'stop' and 'go'? This is a source of confusion that, for designers, is useful to understand.

Importantly, while metadesigners must learn to understand very large, complex, emergent systems, categorical logic is only consistent in situations in which there is little or no change. This is because many of the names and attributes that define a given category do not hold true for long. It is hard to scrutinise objects in motion because we do not educate ourselves to do so. This is probably because our perception is no longer sensitised by the need to hunt, or to gather food on a daily basis. Rather, it is more influenced by the kind of verbal reasoning that is necessary to sustain bureaucratic hierarchies and teams. The main problem with this way of thinking is that everything that flows tends to resist categorisation over a sufficient time scale, and categories are comforting to us.

Several hundred years before Aristotle (384 BC–322 BC) created his theory of categories, Heraclitus (535–475 BC) came to the conclusion that what seem like opposite terms in language are simply compresent aspects of the same thing. He pointed out that, for example, 'the same thing is living and dead, and what is awake and what sleeps, and young and old... for these, having changed about are those, having changed about are these' (cf. Barnes, 1979). This is an important idea for anyone wishing to reveal possible micro-utopias. In order to open oneself to meaningful sensations as they happen, it is necessary to adapt to very subtle changes. The world around us is always changing, even though the names of things tell us otherwise. Living attentively within the moment is hard to achieve without ignoring categories, and this can be difficult. For one reason, unlike the turbulent world around us, facts, categories, and boundaries offer freedom from doubt. Like theories and laws they can be tested and agreed, then stored in encyclopaedias or databases for general usage. The more educators teach children to work with existing categories of 'factual' meaning, and to emphasise the epistemological, rather than the ontological, the more ecologically alienated our society may become. This is an experiential, not just a conceptual issue. Chapter 5 described the tendency in some countries to exaggerate casual descriptions of the weather by confining descriptions to oppositional adjectives, such as 'fantastic' or 'awful'. While this may have the effect of dramatising everyday conversation, it also discourages us from experiencing more subtle changes or patterns of experience. In order to ignore categories it may be necessary to undergo shamanistic training that would enable metadesigners to become attuned to the undifferentiated logic of flow.

As suggested above, Aristotle's logic of category is appealing because it sustains certainty, and certainty promises power. At the height of classical science, Pierre Laplace (1749–1827) was so impressed by Newton's laws of motion that he saw them as the key to absolute knowledge. He declared that 'nothing need be uncertain: past, present, or future' (Laplace, 1819, cited in Rubino, 2002).

However, by the middle of the 20th century this confidence had been placed in serious doubt by arguments from other scientists including Heisenberg in 1927, Gödel in 1931, and Lorenz in 1963. At face value, Laplace's proposition would have demanded an omniscient and omnipresent apparatus of discovery. His argument was an extrapolation of Newton's atomistic theory of the linear flow of time. However, if one can accept the view of Heraclitus, then the flow of things is not incremental. As such, it can never satisfactorily be quantified (Lorenz, 1963, cited in Gleick, 1987). Heraclitus is quoted as saying, 'everything flows, everything always flows, and everything always flows in all respects'. It is easy to overlook the fact that 'everything' here refers to events both at the epistemological and ontological level. One reason why it is hard to grasp the logic of this flow is tha, as 21st century citizens we are continually bombarded by the rhetoric of our digital culture. As this remains such a strong influence on the way we see the world it is useful to reflect further upon some of its assumptions, especially where they relate to flow. In Newton's Laws of Motion, as in virtually all mainstream scientific description of flow since Zeno (490 BC until around 425 BC), the moment of observation is assumed to be virtually instantaneous. While this fundamentally numerical approach continues to be of practical use it is philosophically self-contradictory. This renders it dubious as the basis for informing a better experiential understanding of flow.

As classical scientists, Galileo and Newton would have been less interested in their own phenomenological presence than in charting the 'laws' of Nature. Nevertheless, they must have resorted to a kind of retrospectively imagined thought-experiment, because direct observation was only a partial feasibility. If so, they are likely to have ignored their own relational flow, as co-creators of the events they described. In devising equations of motion Newton must have sought to 'observe' moving bodies by halting their flow, albeit in the mind's eye. In order to equate this technique with observational experience one might say that the temporal width of observation is required to be zero (that is $'t = 0'$). In effect, this means that the observer must focus his or her full attention onto an infinitesimal region in space, for an infinitesimal time. In other words, cognitive intervention must take place at infinite speed. The impossibility of this action is probably what prompted *Parmenides* (approximately 515 BC until 450 BC) to make the persuasive argument that the human senses are untrustworthy. For example, it is only since the advent of high-speed cameras that we may be sure in which order a horse places each foot on the ground when galloping. However, this should not deter us from seeking to understand flow in a way that is meaningful to the whole human mind-body. Societies need to develop a greater sensitivity to flow that will enable them to become less dependent upon technological gadgets and more attuned to the rhythms of life. Designing for micro-utopian realities may require us to develop our bodily senses to a far greater extent, even if we accept that they may not always agree with laboratory instruments. Another way to explain this problem of observation is by considering it as a ubiquitous form of entanglement that always takes place between phenomenon, observer, and description. This is where it is vital to face up to what I call the 'Z' paradox, that is Zeno and his method of 'Zero-ing' time. If we are to believe that past, present, and future can all be said to equal '0' at the same time we would find ourselves believing that the world is solid, and therefore that flow is impossible. Here, to understand what is wrong with this argument we need to acknowledge the synergistic relationship between manifold points of co-creation. In order to do so, we would have to explore simultaneous, multiple temporalities, instead of adhering to Newtonian time (see Chapter 6). This would help us to grasp the interdependent nature of events in flux.

Western thought has tended to make people aware of causality and agency more as single entities, rather than whole systems that are co-created. One of the limitations of the term 'sustainability', therefore, is that it does not make clear exactly what sustains what, or for how long. Nor does it distinguish between transitive and intransitive actions of sustainment. For this reason, I have suggested that we might use the term 'co-sustainment' in place of 'sustainability' (Wood, 2002). One advantage of the idea of 'co-sustainment' is that it, unlike 'sustainability', it emphasises the dynamic and reciprocal nature of 'being-in-the-world'. In non-western religions such as Buddhism or Sufism, ideas of emptiness and transience have a positive meaning. For example, the Chinese Book of Changes (or 'I Ching') reminds its readers that nothing is sustainable, hence everything comes to pass. This suggests that everything unfolds, emerges, and evolves, rather than remaining as a dependable fixture. Consequently, the elation of success will invariably be followed by relative disappointment at some point. Conversely, a despondency or anxiety is likely to give way to a less painful state. How might such an emphasis on 'flow' and transience inform a quest for micro-utopian values and wellbeing? At the level of personal experience, the preciousness of life is a key factor that brings special significance to everything around us. Heidegger (1889–1976) believed that it is the fact that we will die that defines the special nature of our humanity. He called this awareness our 'being-towards-death', arguing that this awareness of mortality is what ultimately limits and shapes the boundaries of our world of meaning. However, he also warns that it is because most people deny, or forget, their radical finitude that we have become dangerously nihilistic. Our anxiety, and our refusal to acknowledge our existential plight is what makes us want to build a world in which humans would become the omniscient and eternal rulers of Nature. An emphasis on the fugitive nature of our existence is an old idea that is retold in many cultures. One story can be found in different versions by Jewish, Hindu, and Persian commentators. It concerns a King who mischievously sent one of his ministers in search of a magic appliance that would make a sad person happy and a happy person sad. After roaming the earth for a long time the minister eventually finds a gold ring upon which is inscribed 'even this shall pass'.

Although it was probably intended as a morality tale, the above story can also be interpreted as a challenge to atomism. If we believe that the world exists as a single, unified wave then we may choose to live in an actative, performative, or even shamanistic way (Wood and Taiwo, 1997). If, on the other hand we believe the world to consist of atoms then we are likely to value facts, and written rules, rather than the more relational world of the spoken. By placing our trust in the sanctity and certainty of individual 'things' we may find ourselves disappointed when they turn out to be perishable. This is unfortunate because it tends to diminish the possibility that eternal products might enable us to sustain the world. While this is not intended as a criticism of the 'Eternally Yours' movement it nevertheless suggests that other, less 'sustainment-oriented' perspectives are also important. Part of this issue is informed by the question of freedom that was explored by the psychologist Erich Fromm (1900–80). Today, while average citizens experience less certainty of belief, they are given far more personal freedom than their grandparents or their parents. According to Fromm (1976), many modern citizens deal with the psychological burden this creates by identifying with owning things, rather than by experiencing them. While 'being' and 'becoming' may sound easy or unproblematic they are strongly informed by today's economic system. As Chapter 2 suggests, the notion of the modern citizen as a sovereign, self-owning individual (MacPherson, 1975) is a highly influential idea from the seventeenth century or before. It became a key component of today's consumerism. As Chapter 1 argues, the American Dream became a prototype for the act of consumption. In order to sustain a ceaseless flow of economic transactions it is the unwritten duty of every consumer to explore and then to satisfy his or her cravings in a conspicuous way. As Chapter 1 pointed out, this is an extravagant system that places an unacceptable burden upon the natural environment.

Using design to find a better balance has so far proved elusive. In order to 'act co-sustainably' one must exercise a degree of self-restraint. Abraham Maslow's (1908–70) 'hierarchy of human needs' (Maslow, 1987) is often cited in this regard. It is usually depicted as a 5-tiered pyramid that assigns primary instincts and values to lower sections and the more spiritual, contemplative pursuits to the upper sections. Maslow suggests that human beings have no choice but to satisfy the 'lower' primitive urges such as survival, hunger, and sex before they can attend to 'higher' interests such as morality, or the exercise of creative play. The flow of this type of behaviour is likely to be characterised more by opportunism than by careful planning and righteous behaviour. Maslow's idea of 'self-actualisation' refers to the successful attainment of higher values at the apex of the pyramid. Unfortunately, in an economic system that is based predominantly on the quantified exchange of material things, there is the residual possibility that every 'self-actualiser', however well-intentioned, will compromise the experience by fetishising her/his body, or the experience of wellbeing. In a burgeoning world of individualised consumption we are all encouraged to manage our individual identities by choosing just the right healthcare products, cosmetic surgery, fashion accoutrements, and entertainment accessories to create the image that will make us feel right. This is principally an economic problem, brought into the social sphere by skilful designers and advertisers who are able to show performance as movies, often with music and text. Finding a new way to attune oneself to the immediate present is therefore a difficult and important issue for educators. It is especially important in sport, drama, music, and live discussion. The ethics of flow is an under-explored issue, partly because our language is not well-suited to describing it. It is far more complex to theorise when more than one individual travels near to others. As it is strongly involved with the way living beings negotiate their relations with one another it is affected by how players see themselves, and how they see the other players. Humberto Maturana and Francisco Varela's (1980) theory of living systems is particularly helpful in theorising this process (see Chapter 5). Here, a 'living system' may be defined as many possible entities, from a single cellular life-form to a complex international organisation.

A living system engages and adapts to its context or habitat by managing the information it receives via, and within, its nervous system. All its dealings with the world take place within its own characteristic limits. These may be thought of as its self-identity. According to the theory, maintaining this self-identity in terms that are viable within its external context, are its only means of survival. Maturana and Varela refer to the individual organism's process of self-creation, self-stabilisation and self-sustainment as 'autopoiesis'. This derives the living system's powers of adapation from its surroundings. A dynamic process is required because living systems are dissipative structures that only remain stable if they can successfully manage the different levels of matter and energy that are constantly flowing through them. The fact that the biosphere consists of a multitude of co-existing living systems means that the idea of 'sustainability' is inadequate for describing how things work. This is why more consensual terms such as 'co-sustainent' (Wood, 2000) or 'sympoiesis' (van Nieuwenhuijze and

Wood, 2006) may be preferable. One of the important ideas that can be surmised from the theory of 'autopoiesis' is that involvement is a necessary superset of communication. As Maturana and Varela note, 'everything said is said by an observer' (cited in Maturana and Varela, 1998). Where many of the most popular communication theories seem to ignore the prior conditions or ecological context that facilitates an exchange of information, autopoietic theories address this as a crucial issue. The state that is prior to communication is referred to as 'structural coupling'. It is a vital process which enables the 'structural congruence between two (or more) systems' (Maturana and Varela, 1980). In effect, structural coupling is what enables living systems to establish a rapport and to co-evolve.

When a pedestrian walks swiftly into the likely path of another on a busy sidewalk both need to establish an appropriate level of structural coupling that will enable both to achieve what they want. This is a complex, multi-layered task that calls upon each to manage and negotiate many things simultaneously. In an actual situation each participant would seek to manage many co-dependent things, including its self-identity, and the other's likely perception of this identity. The above example is highly complex because there are so many more opportunities for negotiating the level within which structural coupling and communication can take place. Many of these possibilities are contingent on others; hence there is a great deal of entanglement. Freud cited the example of two people who are nervous and indecisive when trying to pass one another in a narrow corridor, suggesting that it may be a kind of sexual flirtation. As this is complex, an easier example may be useful. A pedestrian is walking slowly up a hill and is surprised to see a large tractor tyre hurtling directly towards him. This is simpler because, unlike the pedestrian, the tyre has a very rudimentary sense of its self-identity and no ability to steer a different course. Nevertheless, the pedestrian soon grasps the threat to his integrity as a living system. He fears that his identity may be seriously, even fatally compromised by a possible collision. As a result, with little hesitation he steps aside to allow the tyre to follow its fateful path. The type of structural coupling that occurs between a rolling tyre and a pedestrian is reasonably simple to describe because it is up to the human to make all the decisions. The ethics of this example is informative, because it begins to describe a possible ethics of flow between a moving car and a walking pedestrian. Here, the reader is invited to conduct an experiment (devised by my son, Sam). Try walking moderately fast in a crowded street and notice how much effort it takes to avoid a collision. Now, continue at the same pace, while appearing to have your eyes closed. If you are lucky, an unobstructed path will open up for you. When you are seen to be less attentive, others tend to assume you may behave like an animate object. They therefore do not bother to negotiate with you. This is a fascinating game that can also be played by pedestrians or drivers. Importantly, it can change the logic of flow that normally pertains in a given situation. (It is worthwhile remembering that this experiment can be life-threatening.)

How might we begin to use the idea of flow to help twenty-first century metadesigners and citizens to become more sensitively attuned to the natural world? Francisco Varela (1946–2001) offers some self-help techniques that derive from theories of autopoiesis. He suggests that, by suspending our habit of objectifying or particularising our experiences we can learn to become more acutely and sensitively in touch with the actual world around us. Secondly, he proposes that we broaden our focus in order to perceive the whole, rather than the separate parts. Finally, he suggests that we should try to relinquish our strong tendency to analyse, interpret, think about meaning and of our own perspective, so we instead 'see' what is happening from inside it, rather than from our traditional position as 'objective' viewer. Compared with a way of life that is characterised by Maslow's primitive urges, Varela's technique seems to be that of living rewardingly in the present. However, what we call 'the present' is not a constant. It is open to many interpretations, depending on the situation and context. Science has sought to quantify it in an absolute way but, in the search for precision this led to its temporal width being declared as infinitesimal. It is always construed from contingent probabilities that may be a combination of anticipatory and backwardly referred tenses. Long before alphabetical writing and clocks became so important to the networked world economy, there was probably only one temporal state. Today we would describe it as the local, or immediate 'future' tense that related to imminent dangers, and the collective tactics that could be mustered to deal with them. Part of this tense is now called the 'present'. It is a mode of anticipation that promises two simultaneous temporal states:

1. An attention to events that continue to directly emerge from the situated present. This includes the surprising ideas, plans, and images that may form themselves in the mind of the designer.

2. An anticipatory present (or 'presence'). This includes possible conditional actions that are outside the immediate horizon of current tasks and conditions of the designer.

What may be recognised as a modern equivalent, is probably the 'experiential present'. This is a composite temporality that hovers between a remembered past and a contingent future. We encounter it when we savour an auspicious moment, at a time of peace and wellbeing. As with many types of temporality, the experiential present tense is difficult to conceptualise without also thinking about the 'space' that it implies. In design terms this relates well to the idea of 'metadesign'. For example, the Toyota car company has developed a cluster of design attributes that seek to synergize many of the user's experiences in a single whole. It uses the Japanese term 'Jinba Ittai', which refers to a great sense of pleasure that the rider feels when 'at one' with the horse. It is interesting to compare the way a 21st century craftsperson is encouraged to work with the more traditional approach of his or her 18th or 19th century counterpart. In this context, the popular idea of the present is also construed from an anticipated sense of pride that will come from the future state of satisfaction when the work is completed.

At this point it is helpful to return to the claim made at the very start of this chapter; that the logic of flow defies the logic of categories. Over the last few hundred years the factory system evolved out of a faith in simple mechanical principles and a somewhat teleological (that is Newtonian) notion of 'mathematical time'. By contrast, in the nineteenth century the Arts and Crafts Movement sought to enrich the making process by espousing simplicity, an honest use of materials, and a resistance to historicism. Before the advent of mass-production, designers were only needed to take responsibility for the completion of one or more batch-produced products. After Fordism, designers were increasingly called upon to design systems of flow. Marx coined the term 'alienation' (Marx, 1988) to describe the way that workers were put in such a position that they lost touch both with their own value as employees, and with the fruits of their labour. Part of this process can also be described in terms of flow. Alienation within office or factory life can also be defined in temporal terms where the worker is engaged in activities whose work shifts are badly 'out of sync' with their own metabolic pace (Wood, 1998). This is especially true in shift work, or in the relentless practice of working without stopping, to meet an employer's deadline. Chapter 7 complained that the way we live has become regimented by the number systems of calendars and clocks. In bureaucratic systems, these tend to translate the worker's experience of the world into arbitrary, or de-contextualised judgements such as 'early' and 'late', 'success' and 'failure'. This is why temporal alienation can be characterised by boredom; that is, a painful or numbing awareness of the present. It might seem, therefore, that working to achieve an old fashioned 'pride in the job' is a straightforward example of living, being self-reflexively aware of our role in the present. However, what we consider to be the present is almost always a complex issue. In this case it is construed, to a significant extent, from a post-hoc sense of satisfaction with what has already been achieved. In this regard it is defined by the memory of what has taken place.

Here, it is convenient to describe this process by using the example of moving cars and pedestrians. In theory, the rights of every citizen are equal, whether standing, walking or driving, but in practice, pedestrians can easily be intimidated by a large, fast vehicle, rather than something small, lightweight, and slow-moving. This ethical question is governed to a large extent by a strong culture of (car) ownership. It is determined by a large number of interdependent factors, including by-laws, police enforcement regimes, penalty arrangements, attitudes to life, attitudes to business, social status, and so on, where although fixed boundaries may, in theory favour the pedestrian who reaches a given position in the road before a fast-moving vehicle does, this does not work in situations of flow. For example, if we apply static, or categorical logic in a consequential way, any pedestrian who is on a pedestrian crossing when hit by a car could be argued to have the legal right-of-way. However, the way that rights and responsibilities are negotiated in 'real-time' works entirely differently from this process. In the case of the road traffic, it is only after an accident, when police inspect the skid marks and make chalk notations on the road, that legal experts can begin to analyse the witness statements and expert interpretations. On the other hand, within the active moment of flow, individuals often behave in a way that is at odds with the legal right-of-way. The ethics of flow are less dependent on where each traveller is at a given instant (that is, where $t = 0$) and more on a contingent interpretation of the other traveller's speed, anticipated pathway, and determination. In his later work, Wittgenstein was aware that meanings can change, depending on whether or not they are offered into the flow of discourse, 'Conversation flows on, the application and interpretation of words, and only in its course do words have their meaning' (Wittgenstein, 1981). This idea has relevance on many levels of actuality.

Donald Schön explored the characteristic way that designers think without halting what they are doing. In terms of western logic it is interesting to consider that what he called this 'reflection-in-action' (1983) would probably have been regarded, by Aristotle's standards, as an incomplete mode of reasoning. Davidson's idea of 'passing theories' (1986) is similar, in that it cannot be scrutinised in the way that we might analyse all the separate parts of a written theory or assertion. In some situations, when we observe things at a slower pace, we are likely to become bound by the techne of category, rather than by the poiesis of flow. At this point it is helpful to return to the claim made at the very start of this chapter, that systems of flow defy the logic of categories. I was once in a stationary taxi, and watching the driver of an articulated lorry trying to steer his way out of a congested narrow road. Suddenly, he slowed down, stopped, and then lost his nerve. The taxi driver commented, 'He shouldn't have stopped. It's much harder to get your bearings when you're standing still.… if he had kept moving he would have had no problem'. This syndrome can be explained, in part, by the way that humans recognise signs and interpret them. How quickly we react is vital to the effectiveness of the logic we adopt. Let us assume that you are driving along the road and you approach a traffic light that is green. According to Wittgenstein, humans perceive only 'aspects' of a situation, rather than their totality (c.f. Mulhall, 1990). Another of his theories is that humans are able to see one thing, but 'regard-it-as' another. These are useful observations in explaining the logic of flow. Within the static logic of categories, red is red and not green. The two colours were chosen because they are so easily distinguishable from one another, for there must be virtually no ambiguity between the commands 'stop' and 'go'. However, once a driver becomes accustomed to the routine of obeying the signals, when she sees a green light she soon learns to 'regard-it-as' the sign to go, rather than as a green light. Soon, she may even not be conscious of seeing the green light as such, but will begin to travel forward on the appropriate signal.

Within normal conditions this system behaves according to the familiar logic of categories. However, when this action takes place at higher speeds categorical logic begins to break down. When the speeding driver sees the green light from a long distance away, she must decide whether to 'regard-it-as' a 'go' sign, or whether to anticipate that it will soon change to red. For drivers of high-speed police cars, or fire engines, it is quite often necessary to regard 'red-as-meaning-go' or 'green-as-meaning-stop', because the decisions taken to stop or go must be taken at a different phase-angle from those taken at slower speeds. In order to be safe, when a driver approaches traffic lights as they begin to change, he or she must take into account the speed at which the car is travelling, estimating how quickly it is possible to stop, before being able to safely decide whether to accelerate or brake. Ultimate decisions like this must always be made as a matter of situated judgement, rather than as an *a priori* categorical decision. In absorbing tasks such as driving, when situated judgements like this are successfully being made, without too many stressful interruptions, the individual may experience a feeling of satisfaction or pleasure. According to Mihaly Csikszentmihaly this ability to feel 'at one' with the present is the key to happiness and wellbeing. In his book entitled 'Flow' (Csikszentmihalyi, 1990) he defines the term in a more phenomenological way than the way I have so far used it. In exploring the positive experiences described by interviewees from many different backgrounds he found similar descriptions of their experience of 'flow'. Many spoke of 'joy', 'deep concentration', 'emotional buoyancy', a 'heightened sense of mastery', a 'lack of self-consciousness', and a feeling of 'self-transcendence'. Csikszentmihalyi also presents his findings as a technique for exploring, and regulating, the subjective flow of our daily lives. This entails merging our personal quest for optimum satisfaction with a common purpose.

In prosperous, industrialised economies the shopping environment is designed to give consumers a feeling of flow (using Cziksentmihalyi's sense of the word). By contrast, the traditional role of the designer is to develop discrete products that, when presented in the midst of many other goods, will bring the shopper's gaze to a halt. Again, after the exhilaration of the 'chase', the shopper's attention falls upon the materiality of the product, rather than upon the full range of actions and processes that brought about its acquisition. Many products seem to be designed almost exclusively for the moment they are captured by the hunter. They are the alluring fruits whose identities are contrived for the moment they are unpeeled, rather than for the nutritional sustenance they offer. A good example of this process is when a store buys in cheap products especially to make them seem like genuine reductions, for their winter sales. The busy shopper gains pleasure by eliding many tasks and dreams into a euphoric sense of quickness and anticipation. During the sale season many transactions occur within a short period of time. The flow of desire and acquisition for a quick sale then becomes substituted for the legal ownership of a material product. After this, the consumer may or may not substitute ownership for usage. If little or no usage takes place, then a bond of attachment is unlikely to occur. Finally, if there is insufficient emotional or purposeful attachment, then a great deal of effort, energy, and other material resources will have been expended for a trivial outcome (van Hinte, 1997; Chapman, 2005). In seeking to move closer to a 'fluent', rather than a static understanding of the natural world it will be necessary to redesign many meanings of words. This would help to alter the likely experiences of all those who engage with and use these words. The idea of 'flow' is important, whether it is used to mean a mechanical, atomistic description of change, or whether it describes a pleasurable sensation that attends a continuing and satisfying involvement in an ongoing task (Cziksentmihalyi, 1990).

In the west we have developed a self-justifying language of the 'I', but are less able to comprehend the 'we'. Indeed, Jean-Luc Nancy has described the modern western concept of society as the notion of 'pluralised egos'. Maintaining a quest for personal happiness is important, but it will also be vital to develop an active ethics of eudemonia that enshrines self-actualisation within situated altruism. At the immediate level of experience, this would bring responsibility for managing a shared, or mutual type of epicureanism. In translating this into a possible direction for metadesign, designing would become more enterprising. This calls for skills of situated action that are both opportunistic and conciliatory. Whereas some aspects of the received, or idealised practice of design may appear to be timeless, a more entrepreneurial type of design requires judicious timing. This mode of metadesign may produce creative teams who can perform many magical tasks simultaneously, to combine a new sense of flow within society. Their work may, therefore, overlap with the work of healers, bankers, builders, clowns, chefs, or lifestyle counsellors. In order to understand this new approach it will be crucial to develop a more effective discourse of metadesign, based on a shared cycle of 'self-respect' and 'client user empathy'.

References

Barnes, J. (1979), *The Pre-Socratic Philosophers, Vol. 1* (London: Routledge and Kegan Paul).

Brundtland Commission Report (1987), *Our Common Future*. Available at: www.anped.org/media/brundtland-pdf.pdf by courtesy of ANPED (Oxford: Oxford University Press).

Bush, V. (1945), 'As we may think', *Atlantic Monthly*, July 1945. Available at: www.theatlantic.com/doc/194507/bush

Capra, F. (1975), *The Tao of Physics* (Boston: Shambala).

Chapman, J. (2005), *Emotionally Durable Design: Objects, Experiences and Empathy* (UK: Earthscan Publishers).

Csikszentmihalyi, M. (1990), *Flow: The Psychology of Optimal Experience* (New York: Harper & Row).

Davidson, D. (1986), 'A nice derangement of epitaphs', in *Truth and Interpretation: Perspectives on the Philosophy of Donald Davidson*, LePore, E., (ed.), (Oxford: Basil Blackwell).

Fromm, E. (1976), *To Have or To Be* (London: Abacus).

Fuller, R. B. (1975), *Synergetics: Explorations in the Geometry of Thinking*, (New York: Macmillan Publishing, Inc.).

Gleick, J. (1987), *Chaos: Making a New Science* (New York: Penguin Books).

Macpherson, C. B. (1975), *The Political Theory of Possessive Individualism: Hobbes to Locke* (London; New York: Oxford University Press).

Marx, K. (1988), *Economic and Philosophic Manuscripts of 1844 in the Communist Manifesto*, Milligan, M., Marx, K. and Engels, F. (trans.) (Amherst, New York: Prometheus Books).

Maslow, A. H. (1987), *Motivation and Personality* (New York: Harper and Row)

Maturana, H. and Varela, F. G. (1980), 'Autopoiesis and cognition: the realization of the living' in *Boston Studies in Philosophy of Science*, (Dordrecht, Holland: Kluwer Academic Publishers).

Maturana, H. and Varela, F. G. (1998), *The Tree of Knowledge* (Boston; London: Shambhala).

McCorduch, P. (1979), *Machines Who Think* (San Francisco: Freeman).

Mulhall, M. (1990), *On Being in the World: Wittgenstein and Heidegger on Seeing Aspects* (New York; London: Routledge).

Rubino, C. (2002), 'The consolations of uncertainty: time, change, and complexity', *Emergence*, 4:1 and 2, pp. 200–206, (Hillsdale, New Jersey: Lawrence Erlbaum Associates, Inc.)

Tarnas, R. (1991), *The Passion of the Western Mind* (London: Pimlico).

van Hinte, E., Bonekamp, L., Muis, H. and Odding, A. (1997), *Eternally Yours. Visions on Product Endurance*. Available at: www.eternally-yours.org (Rotterdam: 010 Publishers).

van Nieuwenhuijze, O., and Wood, J. (2006), 'Synergy and sympoiesis in the writing of joint papers: anticipation within imagination', *International Journal of Computing Anticipatory Systems*, Dubois, D. M. (ed.), 10, pp. 87–102, ISSN 1373-541 (Liège, Belgium: Centre for Hyperincursive Anticipation in Ordered Systems).

Wittgenstein, L. (1981), *Zettel*, Anscombe, G. E. M. and Wright, G. H. V. (eds.) (Oxford: Blackwell).

Wood, J. and Taiwo, O. (1997), 'Some proprioceptive observations of "being-with"', paper given at the Problems of Action and Observation Conference (Amsterdam: University of Amsterdam).

Wood, J. (1998), *The Virtual Embodied: Presence, Practice, Technology* (London and New York: Routledge).

Wood, J. (2000), 'Towards an ethics of flow: design as an anticipatory system', paper published in *the International Journal of Computing Anticipatory Systems* by the Centre for HyperIncursive Anticipation in Ordered Systems, Liège, Belgium, Daniel, M. D. (ed.), 10: , pp. 87–102. ISSN: 1373–541.

Wood, J. (2002), 'Un-managing the butterfly: co-sustainment and the grammar of self', *International Review of Sociology* (Revue Internationale de Sociologie), 12:2, pp. 295–307, ISSN 0390-6701. (London and New York: Routledge, Taylor & Francis).

Index

References to illustrations are in **bold**

A
A-to-Z Cartesian grid 84
abduction, concept 137
abductive reasoning 137-8
academic rigour
    critique of 68-70, 75-6, 81
    exemplification 80-1
    meaning 69
    persistence of 116
    vs ecological attunement 94
    see also rigour
Action Network (BBC) 5
Adams, James Truslow, *The Epic of
    America* 20
affordances
    design of 98, 172-3
    meaning 97
agribusiness 23
agriculture, practices 19-20
alienation 34
Ambrose, Bishop of Milan 34
America, consumption 20-2
American Declaration of Independence
    (1776) 7, 21
American Dream 20-1, 22, 56, 191
    manifestations of 40-1
    see also consumption
Aristotle
    categories 60, 113, 189, 190
    on time 117
Armstrong, Karen 69
art, and individualism 36
art students
    Coldstream Report 95
    dyslexia 95
artists, extravagance 43

Ashby, Ross, Law of Requisite Variety 55,
    180
atomism 111, 120, 191
Attainable Utopias 12, 141
    Network 134
Augustine, St 34
    on time 117
aura concept, Benjamin 85-6
autopoiesis 194-5

B
Babbage, Charles 113-14, 115
Barlow, Perry 74
Bataille, George 8
Baudrillard, Jean 59
BedZed housing project 162, 163, 164
    model **163**
    relationships **163**, 164
Benjamin, Walter, aura concept 85-6
Bentham, Jeremy 52, 56
Bergson, Henri 18
Berkeley, George, on self-reference 45
Big Brother (reality show) 35
binary
    logic 112, 187
    system 115
Blake, William 188
Bohm, David 77
book production, and rigour 79
Boole, George 112, 115
Brazil (film) 11
Brummel, Beau 38
Brundtland Report (1987) 22, 187
Buckminster Fuller, Richard 25, 102, 117,
    138, 145, 177
building standards 25
bureaucracy
    examples 51

and feedback 52
origins 51, 53
and writing 59
Byron, Lord 39

C
capitalism, and individualism 33
car design 24-5
car ownership, costs 24
carbon credit system 10
carbon reduction 174
Carroll, Lewis, *Alice in Wonderland* 57
cars, energy consumption 28
categories
Aristotle 60, 113, 189, 190
and certainty 191
and change 190
disadvantages of 190-1
logic of
in driving situations 199
vs logic of flow 197-8, 199
and thinking 60
Celebration Village, Disney Corporation
56
celebrity 35, 39, 43
celebrity examples, power images 44
change, and categories 190
chaos theory 77, 115, 121
Chapman, Jake & Dino 43
Chapman, Jonathan 174
children, diseases 27-8
Chuang Tzu 134
Clement of Alexandria 59
climate change 2, 8, 33
Clivus Multrum system 26
clock time 92, 109, 120, 124-5
clocks 11, 53
as closed systems 120-1
digital 118
and solipsism 110
synchronisation 122
vs flow 120
'co-sustainment', vs sustainability 192,
195
cognition, distinction as 112
Coldstream Report, art students 95
Coleridge, Samuel Taylor 37, 39
collaboration, vs individualism 82
commuting, costs 24
complexity, illustration of **154**

computers
analogue 114
digital 114
quantum 141-2
consciousness, mapping 157
consilience 70
consumer products, obsolescence 174
consumer rights 41
consumption 8, 11, 18-19, 27
America 20-2
as duty 39
and individualism 33-4
psychology of 30
contentment, and economic growth 3
Corning, Peter 146
credit 9
criteria, relational, mapping 157-60
Csikszentmihalyi, Mihaly 63, 153
on flow 199-200
cybernetics 46, 84, 101, 122
first order 123-4
second order 124
cynicism 29-30, 44

D
'Dandyism' 38, 39
Darwin, Charles, evolution theory 7
data management, tetrahedral filtering
182
Dawkins, Richard 136, 137
de Bono, Edward 73
decisions
optimal 81
top-down, vs bottom-up 4
Defoe, Daniel, *Robinson Crusoe* 37
Derrida, Jacques 112-13
Descartes, René 37, 42, 134
A-to-Z grid 84
the *cogito* 45
scepticism 81-2
design
of affordances 98
categories 175
non-linearity 81
and Platonic forms 53
as process 139
profession, status 171-2
vs flow 63
see also metadesign
designers 73

constraints on 96
as entrepreneurs 177
role 200
self-perceptions 172
specialist 177-8
Diderot, Denis 74
Disney Corporation, Celebration Village 56
distinction
as cognition 112
as expediency 113
vs flow 117
DNA evidence, fallibility of 112
Donne, John 35
dreaming, need for 133-4, 140-1
Dunster, Bill 162
Dymaxion Car 25
dyslexia
art students 95
as gift 95

E
eco-solipsism 35
ecological footprint 176
London 22
ecology, and metadesign 172, 174
economic growth 9, 132
and contentment 3
ecosystems, interdependency 143
education
purpose 67
vs training 111
Einstein, Albert 76-7, 85
energy production 26
energy use, extravagance 26-7
'entredonneurs' 100
entrepreneurs, designers as 177
epistemology, ontology, distinction 58, 113
Erasmus, Desiderius 36, 37
ethics
deontological 138-9
eudaemonic 138, 139
eudaemonia 138, 201
Euler, Leonhard 157
Euler's theorem, tetrahedron 161
extravagance, artists 43

F
Factor Four argument 177
facts, vs flow 63
fashion, Wilde on 33
feedback 46
and bureaucracy 52
positive/negative 47
Feynman, Richard 114
flow
Csikszentmihalyi on 199-200
ethics of 194-5, 198
and happiness 153
Heraclitus on 191
logic of, vs logic of categories 197-8, 199
need to understand 192
in shopping environment 200
vs clocks 120
vs design 63
vs distinction 117
vs facts 63
vs rigour 71
Foerster, Heinz von 46-7, 123-4
Ford, Henry 55
Fordism 114
forms, Platonic, and design 53
France, cuisine 40
freedom, burden of 193
French Revolution (1789) 7, 9
and individualism 40
Friedmann, Alexander 77
Friedrich, Caspar David, The Wanderer Above the Mists 42
Fromm, Erich 193

G
Galileo 79
garden, as synergy-of-synergies 149
Gates, Bill 10
GDP, components of 23
General Systems Theory 146
genocide, origins of term 99-100
Gibson, James J. 97
Giddens, Anthony 171
glass manufacture 26
global capitalism 10
Gödel's theorem 78
Goody, Jack 59
grammar, as metalanguage 57

H
Handy, Charles 143
happiness, and flow 153
Hardin, Garrett 29
Hawking, Stephen 70, 77, 129
Heidegger, Martin 42, 102, 192-3
    Being and Time 18
Heisenberg, Werner 78
Heraclitus 58, 59, 78, 111
    on flow 189
    Fragment 50 86-7, 101, 104-5
heterarchy, vs hierarchy 4
Hippel, Eric von 175
Hirst, Damien, *Hymn* 43
Hobbes, Thomas 7
Hoover, Herbert 55-6
Houdini, Harry 72
housing design 24-5
    see also BedZed housing project
Hubbert Peak 8
human rights, concept 39
Hume, David 141
hypertext 74

I
idea
    etymology 135
    of the idea 136
idealism 134-5
'identity of indiscernibles', Leibniz 61,
    112
Igorot people 149, 150
individual
    concept 36, 181
    living alone 34
    and society 35
individualism 9, 18
    and art 36
    and capitalism 33
    and collective wisdom 181
    and consumption 33-4
    etymology 36
    examples 38
    and the French Revolution 40
    literary expression of 37
    and Protestantism 36
    vs collaboration 82
    see also public selfishness; social
        individuation
information 73, 74

intertextuality 100-1
irony, as selling tool 44-5

J
Jarry, Alfred 57
Jones, John Chris, *Designing Designing* 178
journalism, tabloid 116
jurisprudence, as metadesign 63

K
Kant, Immanuel 42, 131, 155, 189
Klee, Paul 43
knowledge
    model 69
    tacit
        diagnosis example 153, 155
        nature of 153
        vs factual 74
    task-based 69
    task-guiding 75
    text-based 69
    truth-oriented 75
Kuhn, Thomas, paradigm shifts 77-8
Kvitash, Dr Vadim 155, 160, 162

L
language
    oppositional words 100
    and reframing thought 98-9
    and thought 91-2
    Wittgenstein on 119
'languaging' 94
Laplace, Pierre 191
Law of Diminishing Returns 144
Law of Increasing Returns 145
Law of Requisite Variety 55, 180
Law of Truly Large Numbers 141
Laws of Motion 191
Leibniz, Gottfried Wilhelm
    fatalism 131
    'identity of indiscernibles' 61, 112
    monadic self 45
Littlewood, E.J. 141
Locke, John 42, 136
London, ecological footprint 22
Lorenz, Edward 114, 115
Lovelace, Lady Ada 115
Lovelock, James 100
    Gaia Theory 47

Loyola, St Ignatius 69
luck, nature of 141, 153
Luhmann, Niklas 112

M
Macchiavelli, Niccolò, *The Prince* 93
McCulloch, Warren 115
management teams
    roles 179
    success factors 178-80
Mandeville, Bernard de, *The Fable of the Bees* 7
Marx, Karl 11
Maslow, Abraham 167, 194
materialism 139-40
The Matrix (film) 121
Maturana, Humberto 17, 92, 194, 195
meat consumption 20
Melissus 76
memes
    beneficial 142, 153
    design of 136-7
metadesign 17, 201
    ecological mode 172, 174
    jurisprudence as 63
    movements, examples 180
    need for 96, 168
    profession, establishing 178
    as seeding process 180
    teams 168-9
    use 171
    see also design
metalanguage, grammar as 57
metaphors 98
micro-utopias
    design 4, 22, 123
    map of **12**, 13
    obstacles to 13
    see also Attainable Utopias; Utopia
mind, dualistic 42, 81
Minsky, Marvin 157
miracles
    designing 13
    nature of 5, 141
mobile phones 124
Modern Times (film) 11
monadic self, Leibniz 45
More, Thomas, *Utopia* 1, 2-3
Morris, William 177

N
Naess, Arne 42
Nancy, Jean-Luc 200-1
Narcissus myth 35
nature
    attunement to 186
    and numbers 114
needs, hierarchy of 167, 194
Nelson, Ted 74
New Economics Foundation 23
Newton, Isaac, Laws of Motion 189
Nietzsche, Friedrich 58
NLP (neuro-linguistic programming) 98
numbers
    and nature 114
    rationality of 110
    ubiquity 119

O
observation, theory of 42
Ockham's Razor 61, 111
Ong, Walter 113
Onians, John 135
ontology, epistemology, distinction 58, 113
'Open Source' design 5
organism, identity maintenance 93-4

P
Panofsky, Erwin 80, 81
Papanek, Victor 138
paradeigma 135-6
paradigm shifts 77-8
Parmenides 76, 111, 191
Pascal, Blaise 110
Pask, Gordon 47
'passing theories' 198-9
Peirce, Charles 137
personal growth 43
Petrarch 42-3
Pitts, Walter 115
Plato 59
    Atlantis 3
Pledgebank website (BBC) 5
Polanyi, Michael 153
Pollock, Jackson 43
Popper, Karl 132
positive feedback, role 4
Poundbury village (UK) 56

power images, celebrity examples 44
power structures, and rigour 77
pragmatism, political 6, 12
Protestantism, and individualism 36
proxemics 55
public selfishness 18
Pythagoras 110, 113

Q
quantum physics 77

R
reasoning, deductive, vs inductive 83
'reflection-in-action' 198
Reich, Wilhelm, *The Function of the
Orgasm* 18
relationships
    Euler's notation 159
    line and node system 158, 160-2
    see also synergy
'relonics' diagnosis system 155-6, **157**
rights, responsibilities, balance 7, 8, 21
rigour
    definition 70-1
    as metaphor 76-7
    and monastic book production 79
    and power structures 77
    and striving for perfection 80
    vs flow 71
    see also academic rigour
Romantic movement 36
Rorty, Richard 42
Ruskin, John 183
Russell, Bertrand 61

S
scepticism, Cartesian 81-2
Schön, Donald 196
self-awareness 45-6
self-consciousness 37, 39
self-reference, Berkeley on 45
Semon, Richard 136
sewage disposal 26-7
shaman 71, 72
shamanism 55, 99
    definition 64
Shannon, Claude 115
silent reading, and solipsism 34-5
skills, transferability 80

Slow Food movement 109
Smith, Adam 36-7, 143, 181
    The Wealth of Nations 7, 21
social individuation 41
    origins 42
society, and the individual 35
Socrates 3, 34, 45
solipsism
    antidote to 55
    Cartesian 47
    and clocks 110
    and the emotions 37-8
    origins 34
    and silent reading 34-5
    see also eco-solipsism
Spencer-Brown, George 112
Stern Report, climate change 2
structural coupling 195-6
Sun Tzu, *The Art of War* 93
sustainability
    limitations of 192
    meanings 187, 188-9
    vs 'co-sustainment' 192, 195
sustainable development, definition 185
Swift, Jonathan, *Gulliver's Travels* 37
symbiosis 145
synergy
    and complex systems 152
    concept 143-4, 145
    cooking analogy 147
    definition 149-50
    etymology 146
    examples 146-7, 148-9
    four orders of 150-2
    maintenance 152-3
    in nature 147-8
    see also relationships
'synergy-of-synergies' 13, 17, 117, 145
    garden as 149

T
Taylor, Frederick 114
Taylorism 173
tetrahedron
    data management filtering 182
    Euler's theorem 161
    grammar of ethical relations 169-71
    nodes **101**
    uses 92, 102-3, **183**
    values, mapping 103-4

'winners' model **181**
Theory of Everything (TOE) 57, 70, 129
thinking, and categories 60
thought, and language 91-2
time
    Aristotle on 117
    Augustine on 117
    experiential present 197
    fluency of 117
    levels of openness 123
    linearity 117
    perceptions of 1
    and temporal states 196-7
Turner Prize 43

U
uncertainty principle 78, 80
Upanishads 113, 189
Utopia
    design for 139
    idea of 3, 131
    Marxist 3
    More's 1, 2-3
    see also Attainable Utopias; micro-
       utopias

V
van Hinte, Ed 174
Varela, Francisco 112, 194, 195, 196
Veblen, Thorsten 8
villages, utopian 56

W
Weber, Max 140

Weizsäcker, Ernest Ulrich von 177
Westwood, Vivien 44
Whitehead, Alfred North 57, 111
Whiteread, Rachel, *Embankment* 43
Wikipedia 74
Wilbur, Ken 91
Wilde, Oscar, on fashion 33
William of Ockham 61, 85, 111
'win-win' axis **182**
'winners', tetrahedral model **181**
Wittgenstein, Ludwig 52
    on language 119
writing
    academic 85
    alphabetical 11, 52, 53, 54, 57, 58, 59,
       61, 62, 63, 83
       and data dominance 86
    approaches to 94
    axioms 91
    and bureaucracy 59
    and context 96
    evolution 59-60
    model 75
    modes of 84
    objections to 59
    pictographic 53, 54, 58, 62
    and the real world 53-4, 72
    rhetorical tradition 75, 82
    scenario emphasis 85
    standardizing function 6

Z
'Z' paradox 192
Zeno 191, 192